WORLDS APART

ILKA CHASE

Worlds Apart

Photographs by Norton Brown

DOUBLEDAY & COMPANY, INC.
GARDEN CITY, NEW YORK
1972

Library of Congress Catalog Card Number 72–76135

Printed in the United States of America

First Edition

To WANDA JABLONSKI, *who pointed out
that Russia, too, was available*

CONTENTS

WORLDS APART

FOREWORD

When I was sixteen I went to Paris for the first time to go to school. I stayed there for two years and later on I lived for a year in London.

Throughout my maturity, if one excepts prolonged interludes spent in the New York theatre, working in pictures in Hollywood or on the lecture circuit, and allowing time out for wars, I traveled abroad with fair regularity.

In 1949 my husband, Norton Brown, and I took our first trip to Europe together and since then we have been reasonably dedicated to the proposition of seeing as much of the world as possible.

To be sure we sought guidance from travel agencies, usually the American Express Company, but once we set forth it was us on our own. A pair of intrepid little figures against the world.

The year 1971 changed all that. The year of the tours! Looking back on it our motto, apparently, was if we're going to make a change make it big! A trip to South America in February I took without my husband but with a group shepherded by the Theatre Guild.

In June, together, we joined a tour to Russia organized by Thomas Cook. On that one we blended into a group of a mere five thousand souls every one of them, with the exception of ourselves, a passionate devotee of petroleum. It was like joining the church and submerging our own personalities in the commonweal.

In September we surfaced again *almost* as individuals on a marvelous, and, after Russia, microscopic tour, only eight of us, traveling on a game-viewing safari through southern Africa, admirably organized by Lindblad Travel, Inc.

So thoughtful are they that in the literature they send out, germane to the particular tour you are making, they enclose a list of suggested reading matter so you may better appreciate the lands and people you are visiting.

I wish all good travel agencies good business and there is no question that there are many advantages to a well-managed tour. Furthermore, certain parts of the globe are accessible only if one is a member of a tour. This applies particularly to the Lindblad itineraries where they make use of their own ship, the *Lindblad Explorer*.

It also obtains in Russia, a country experienced in handling groups but less flexible when it comes to individuals. And it is funny how quickly one accepts this, comparatively, mass psychology. Reviewing our '71 travels Norton and I looked at each other in real mystification. "How did we use to do it before? Before we joined up with all those people?"

"We did it ourselves, Dopey, far from the madding crowd."

It is true that, whatever the advantages, togetherness is and must be an integral part of organized travel and sometimes, despite the responsibility and plain hard work that are the concomitants of privacy, it can be refreshing to be on one's own. Or, more cosily, two's own.

However, I am such a travel buff that what I say is, "Never mind *how* you do it, just *do* it."

CHAPTER ONE

Central America

I mentioned in the Foreword that on one of the 1971 trips I traveled with the Theatre Guild. There may be those for whom the statement needs a little clarification. "Travel and the Guild? I didn't know about that."

But those who know of the Guild at all undoubtedly know that it established its reputation as one of America's most distinguished theatrical producing organizations because, along with its presentation of domestic talent, it also imported to the United States many of Europe's best plays and playwrights.

However, as to all of us, gradual changes came to the Guild too. One by one the founders retired or died and the road was no longer the dependable source of revenue for touring companies that it once had been.

Looking about them Philip Langner and his mother, Armina Marshall Langner, widow of Lawrence Langner who had been the Guild's brightest and most enduring light, observed a current phenomenon: the prevalence of travel and the status symbol it has become.

Remembering the European talent the organization had been instrumental in bringing to America they decided to follow the footsteps of Mohammed. Instead of importing theatrical mountains across the sea they would go to the mountains.

Thinking of their 125,000 subscribers throughout the country, Philip Langner suggested they form the Garrick Travel Agency, named after the Garrick Theatre in New York where their first early successes had been produced and offer their membership Theatre Guild Abroad.

Their first journeys, almost entirely theatre oriented, proving successful they decided to expand and proudly added Around the World to their masthead. To be sure they still feature theatre wherever possible, with the added attraction of often meeting the artists themselves, but they also book patrons to such spots as Katmandu and the Ngorongoro Crater where the passing show may be wondrous strange and exhilarating but where it is not, one must admit, all that reminiscent of West 45th Street.

Yet the old aura dies hard. Describing a beautiful black-maned lion and his lady that she had watched in the Crater, Armina added, "And dear, I want to tell you, I never saw a love scene better played."

When it developed that Norton could not get away for a trip we had originally intended to take together to Central America in February 1971 he said to me, "If the Guild is organizing that tour to South America you told me about you'd have friends along so why don't you go to Yucatán and Guatemala anyway, as we'd planned, and join up with them in Mexico City?"

It seemed a good idea so I ventured forth. I ventured via the team of Eastern Airlines and Pan American, arriving in the evening in Mérida, the capital of Yucatán, after a brief and tumultuous layover in Miami, surely one of the worst maintained and most poorly staffed airports in the U.S.A. You ask a porter, if you can ever find one, to help with your luggage, he stares at you as though you had insulted his mother.

I had been a little apprehensive about the first leg of the journey since I would be alone, but an old and dear friend, Romney Brent, who lives in Mexico City and who would be our peerless leader in South America had assured me he would alert Willie Calderone, a young English-speaking chauffeur-guide whom he knew, who would meet me at the Mérida airport. On him I could depend as a little child upon a strong wise father.

Had he been there, maybe I could have. As it turned out he was otherwise engaged, but I was not alone. I was met with ruffles and flourishes. His sister was there and his mother was there. Also a travel agent, a newspaper reporter, a photographer and a TV cameraman.

The few passengers with whom I had struck up an acquaintance on the flight were no more astonished than I by the surging entourage. My bafflement was due to the fact that I had reckoned without an influential friend, one Mr. Jack Howard of the Scripps-Howard newspaper and television chain. Having journalistic contacts south of the border, and learning I was going to those parts, Mr. Howard had alerted them and they had rallied.

It was lucky the travel agent was along since he was the only one who could speak both Spanish and English. He interpreted the interview between me and the reporter while the lights flashed, the portable TV camera ground and feeling like a visiting head of state—Mrs. Golda Meir or Prime Minister Indira Gandhi perhaps—I clutched the flowers that had been sent by Romney.

Like all reporters, my man wanted to know how I liked his native city. My knowledge of it being limited to the walk from the plane to the airport lobby where they had descended on me, I was able to say that I admired the handsome brown and white marble paving of the corridor. A few more such pungent comments and I was released.

We drove to the hotel where Willie eventually appeared and it was agreed that he would pick me up at nine the next morning.

The Mérida is a quite nice second-class hotel, the main floor especially so. There are two pretty patios, one with a fountain and swimming pool. During the occasional quiet spells it is extremely pleasant but for the most part, rasping piped-in music assaults the ears destroying all tranquillity and privacy and the clientele is shoddy.

The rooms, if a bit threadbare, are clean and the cashier a bit lighthearted. Scrutinize your bill and—when cashing a traveler's check count your pesos—they were agreeable and prompt about making readjustments but they were understaffed and the hotel was crowded.

The next morning Willie showed up on schedule and we drove around Mérida. The city itself is not enthralling but the climate of Mexico is seductive. The day was hot and dry, the sky a marvelous clear blue and great beautiful trees cast inviting shadows. Mérida was founded by Don Francisco de Montejo the Younger in 1542 and the so-called palace, a large town residence, was built in 1549.

The house is owned and still inhabited by an eccentric old customer named Solariega who is, Willie assured me, a direct descendant of the original Don Francisco. The difference in names, he explained, was because "sometimes no men in a heneration, only wims." Men usually are outnumbered by wims and certainly outlived by them.

One is allowed to visit the house and the proprietor himself, a fairly laborious comedian, acts as guide.

A large hammock is strung between two pillars of an arcade and there, Señor Solariega told us, he sleeps every night. He spread it out to show how wide it was. "I have seven children." I did not know whether they had all been conceived there—doing such work in a hammock would, I should imagine, be quite tricky—or whether possibly they all shared it with him.

Foreigners, the sophisticated and the rich sleep in beds but, at least in that part of Mexico, the great majority of people do sleep in hammocks. In a hot climate they are a good deal more airy than a solid mattress.

The most colorful and interesting sight of the city is the market. It is an enormous two-storied building, not as picturesque as an open market, but probably more hygienic, and the fruits and flowers and vegetables are arranged with skill and artistry. A little farther along in an arcade with many open stall shops, I bought a guayabera for Norton. They are stitched and pleated shirts that have pockets, are designed to be worn without a tie and hang outside the trousers. They are good looking and cool and would be perfect for the clammy sweltering months of summer in many parts of the U.S.A.

In the course of the day Señor Lavin, publisher of the paper whose reporter had interviewed me the night before, had phoned to say his wife was coming to fetch me for dinner.

Unfortunately he was unable to accompany her but the señora, a small woman, was a more than able lieutenant, even on that hot evening very dashing in a see-through blouse, suede skirt and boots, supplementary lashes and a rich auburn wig. What would I like to do, she asked. Since it was now seven-thirty I began to think of food, but I was in a somewhat Spanish land. *Dine* at *seven-thirty?*

She was vague about food although murmuring that of course we would eat, but would I not like to do a little shopping first? Then there was an underground river she thought I would enjoy and after that we were to go to a concert which would begin about half-past nine. I was confused about the underground river, it sounded *very* strange, and if the concert continued until eleven o'clock or longer I doubted that I would be alive to eat, but she was graciously giving up her evening to me and who was I to upset the customs of the country?

She piloted me to a shop, Canul, Calle 59—as in New York the streets are numbered rather than named—496 where, because I was embarrassed not to, I bought a second guayabera for my dear husband which he did not need. Finally we took off for the subterranean waters. To my delight I found they were below a restaurant, a large open air affair called Tulipanes and my hostess said we had time to eat before the performance started. The food was very good. Fresh shrimp and chicken baked in banana leaves. The performance itself was a curious affair.

We descended a steep flight of stone steps into a dark, shadowy grotto, where a concrete platform bordered a large pool of gray water, a *cenote* or reservoir. Banquets were placed against the curving stone walls and there were small tables for the customers and their drinks.

The ancient Mayan, Toltec, and Aztec civilizations believed that the god Yum Chac, a distinctly unpleasant character, inhabited the *cenotes,* and to appease him they frequently tossed in young virgins. Most of them drowned but occasional sturdy survivors were hauled out by ropes. They were then supposed to relay tales of the gods and people of the murky depths. If they had any sense one imagines they must have said, "Great god, he say throw no more virgins. Him much displeased by idea." One would also assume that the brighter members of the female sex would have dispensed with their virginity as quickly as possible.

Be that as it may, the evening's entertainment was a kind of facsimile of the gruesome rite.

The already dim lights were lowered still further and down the stairs to the rhythm of tom-toms pounded by two semi-naked youths, floated two girls in white, the victims. They were escorted by a chap I took to be the high priest with flames sprouting from his high headdress and a kingly figure with plumed crown.

Despite oneself, the dim grotto, the flaring flames, the beating of the tom-toms evoked a kind of awe and tension which unfortunately, from the dramatic point of view, was rudely dissipated by waiters hurrying down the stone staircase and threading their way through the cast to serve whisky and Margaritas to the customers.

Still, one got one's money worth. One of the half-naked lads did a dance which included placing his bare feet in the live flames of a small brazier set on the ground, the king's feathered headdress caught fire and was snuffed out by the bare hands of a quick-thinking waiter, there was the flash of a knife blade, an anguished scream from the victim and from the gray water emerged a weird figure, the god Yum Chac. The lights went out, the show was over.

This pastiche was followed by a more worldly spectacle at the

Teatro Colonial where we were joined by a pretty girl, Alys, one of Señora Lavin's six children. Usually a movie house, tonight the theatre had been turned into a concert hall where a Mexican artist, Pilar Rioja, was giving a performance of Spanish dances.

The first thing to strike me was the lady's girth. She was a buxom one, that Pilar, almost impossibly so for a Spanish dancer. However, she danced with vigor and skill and under circumstances that would have daunted a lesser spirit. The movie screen, though veiled by a gray curtain, was set very near the footlights with the result that the unfortunate woman had to cavort on a stage only about ten feet deep. This doesn't allow much leeway for sweeping choreography. She was accompanied by a pianist who starred on his own while the señorita was changing costumes, of which she had a large selection. When he was resting she did her own accompaniment which demanded considerable agility. Backstage she would set up a record and burst through the curtain right on the button of the correct beat, skirts swinging, castanets chattering. The lady had spunk.

In the course of the evening I remarked to Señora Lavin that I was about to take off for Guatemala. She evinced considerable surprise coupled with alarm.

"All by yourself?"

"That's right. My husband couldn't come on this trip."

"But do you feel safe?"

"Why yes, why not?"

Something stirred dimly in my memory. Had I not read that there *had* been some anti-American feeling? However, that is universal and frequently passive and if I recalled correctly, the newspaper accounts were already several months old.

"But you are a woman," continued my hostess, "and you don't speak Spanish and those mountain roads . . . you have no *idea*. Ooh, I wouldn't do it," and she gave a little shiver.

I don't pretend that she didn't give me food for thought but although she could not have been more friendly or hospitable, I felt that perhaps political assessments should be left to her journalist husband. Still I would seek further advice.

The next morning I called the American consulate. A man answered and since it was Saturday I asked if the consul was in that morning, and if he could tell me his name.

"You're speaking to him," said the voice.

"Oh."

I told him who I was and explained my problem. "Is it all right for Americans to go to Guatemala?"

"We haven't heard anything from the State Department indicating that it isn't all right," he said, adding helpfully, "Of course that doesn't necessarily mean that it *is* all right."

"I see. Well, forget the State Department. What do you hear from Henry Kissinger?"

There was a kind of gargle at the other end of the wire. "I realize I'm not being very helpful," he said, "but you know as much as I do."

On the record there seemed no reason not to pursue my original plan, but first I would visit Chichén Itzá, the site of the great Mayan ruins and the reason a traveler goes to Mérida in the first place.

The drive takes nearly two hours and is reasonably tedious but once one arrives there all is forgiven.

The Mayaland Hotel at Chichén is charming: spacious and airy with a big swimming pool, tropical gardens and pretty private cottages. Price: $26 a day. It is a delightful place for either an overnight stay or, if one has the time, a more protracted one. Too bad the food is poor.

The ruins are conveniently situated, the equivalent of a couple of blocks, down the road from the hotel. There are two sites, and the afternoon of my arrival I chose the one known as New Chichén.

It is strange to think that when European culture was in abeyance an extraordinary civilization existed on the other side of the world. Chichén Itzá flourished between 461 and 623 although in the tenth century the man-god Kulkulcan occupied it as his capital.

Today almost all that remains of its past glory are huge heavy pyramids, public buildings, and intricate carvings of warriors, feathered serpents, and Kulkulcan.

In the dining room of the Mayaland I was both startled and interested to see that one or two of the native waitresses precisely resembled the carvings of the god and assorted dignitaries of antiquity. The same backward-sloping foreheads, the same high abrupt bridge of a long nose. Mayans really did look like that!

Although by no means as bloodthirsty as the Toltecs, whose religious rites involving human sacrifice and cannibalism were of a revolting cruelty, the Mayans were not averse to a *little* human sacrifice. Just now and then. To keep their hand in.

If one has the stamina to climb the steep interior staircase of the great pyramid, El Castillo, he will see a stone jaguar with jade eyes, the altar upon which men and young women met their gory deaths.

As I hesitated at the foot of the staircase thinking I *might* steel myself for the climb, an American came down. "How was it?" I asked. "It's clammy up there," he said. "There *is* a jaguar with little teeny jade eyes. I don't know as you'd find it worth the effort." I chickened out at Chichén Itzá.

In 1904 an American, Edward Thompson, began dredging Chen Ku, the deep sacred well or *cenote* of New Chichén whose perpendicular limestone walls drop seventy-five feet to the water which is about forty feet deep. They found jewelry, coins, knives and human skulls, and in 1961, when the National Geographic Society financed an expedition, they brought up not only human bones, but those of thousands of animals who had also been sacrificed.

Of course, even the bloodthirsty couldn't spend *all* their time sacrificing. As Mr. Lincoln so shrewdly observed "you can't fool all of the people all of the time." Nor could the Toltecs and the Mayans—to some extent Chichén Itzá was a mixture of both cultures —murder all of the people all of the time.

Indeed, there is evidence that they did have other diversions. There are the ruins of a ball court where the great, great grandfather of what is today's soccer was played. It is an enormous and massive affair that could easily hold several thousand people.

The solid rubber balls used in play were a foot in diameter and might not be touched with the hands, but were propelled by knees, hips, and buttocks. The object was to knock them through great stone rings twenty feet above the level of the court.

So difficult was this feat to accomplish, that the winner was allowed to take what clothes and possessions he could snaffle from any spectator. One may imagine the wild scramble of the audience to get away from the pastime it had come so eagerly to watch. Sometimes, if he was in the mood, the victor was permitted to behead the captain of the losing team.

One of the most impressive buildings stands in Old Chichén. It is the observatory, resting on a tremendous base of two huge terraces, the lower one 225 feet long and 150 feet wide. One may fairly say that the Mayans were prolific builders and it is very nearly impossible—one would be too exhausted physically and culturally —to take in all of Chichén Itzá in a day even in the most superficial fashion, so that in a sense the hotel's check-out time has something to do with the visitor's schedule. It is 2 P.M. Most people arrive after lunch, do one side of the road in the afternoon, the other the next morning, have luncheon and depart. It is a good plan. You should husband your energies, for it is very hot in Yucatán. A dry heat and tolerable, but it does take something out of you.

I had arranged with Willie Calderone that he would be at the Mayaland Hotel to pick me up at one-thirty the day after my arrival. However, since he had asked if I could not give him some money in advance I made a bet with myself he would not show up. I won it too, although he did send a replacement, Luis, with a cock and bull story about Willie's car having broken down. Had he failed to get the advance money I suspected that his car would have been working like a dream. Even so I was in luck for Luis's car was air conditioned and much more comfortable.

It was a Sunday and on the return trip to Mérida we passed through a village where a bullfight was in progress. Having seen my first and only bullfight in northern Spain at the age of sixteen where the shock was such that I vomited all over the stands I know that they were not for me. However, Luis was eager and assured me they did not kill the bull.

"Please, please, can we not stop off to see it?"

From the way he spoke I gathered it might be a rather cruel game but that in the end they would release the animal and probably considerable local color would be involved.

I let myself be persuaded to get out of the car and to climb a primitive ladder to reach chairs on a sort of makeshift platform in what had to be the most rickety bull ring of modern times. It appeared to be constructed of wattles and banana leaves and on it, teetering precariously upon broken-down chairs were masses of Mexicans, chiefly women, with masses of children; bawling, nursing, laughing, and hanging over flimsy railings like washing over a clothesline. It was a death trap par excellence and I was grateful it was out of doors. In case of fire one *might* have a fighting chance.

Down in the ring were three or four men on horseback and in the hot sun, tethered to a post was a cadaverous steer, a big red X painted on his sunken flanks.

"Oh," said Luis cheerfully, "on Sunday they always have three. The other two they let go but this one is marked. They'll kill him."

That did it. As though he had pressed a button, tears of rage, pity, and shame for the human race poured down my cheeks.

"Not in front of me they won't. Come on," and I groped my way as hurriedly as I could back through the rows of rickety chairs and along the platform till we reached the ladder. Half the time missing my footing I slid and tumbled down it, bruising my arms and legs, tearing my dress while Luis lowered himself after me imploring me to be careful. *"Señora, señora, despacio, despacio por el amor de dios!"*

My reaction was beyond his comprehension and he kept asking in a bewildered way, "But why? What? What upsets you?"

"It's monstrous," I stammered, "monstrous to slaughter a helpless animal in that brutal way. For sport. For glee! Let's get out of here." I jumped into the car and slammed the door. With a shrug he got into the driver's seat and with a reluctant glance behind him at the bull ring and the missed delights of the kill, he headed for Mérida.

Back at my hotel as I was waiting in the lobby for the elevator the doors opened and out stepped a most elegant young toreador. He was wearing a skin-tight suit of green and gold and with his dark curls and flashing dark eyes was quite beautiful. He smiled at me as he passed. I wished him all the worst.

The next morning Willie picked me up again and when I confronted him with the improbable tale of his car breaking down he shrugged and laughed good humoredly. He had been out with his girl.

Our destination was Uxmal, another pyramid site well worth a visit. It is a later period and not as large as Chichén Itzá, but in some respects it is more rewarding. There is greater variety and finer carving. Uxmal was once a great city, and there is still much to be unearthed, but what there is today is impressive, especially the enormous courtyard of which the governor's palace forms one entire side. It is rich with friezes and chiseled decorations and a truncated column which was originally a ten-foot-high stone phallus stands before it. Today it is of more modest proportions, a mere five feet. Even so . . .

Yucatán's close neighbor Guatemala, to which I flew the next day, is a love of a land. Not so much Guatemala City, the capital, but the small mountainous country itself.

The Biltmore and the Camino Real are probably the best hotels, but they are situated a bit out of town. If time is limited the Palace or the Pan American are more convenient choices, but being in the city on narrow streets, they are noisy!

Even so I cottoned to the Pan American. It had a kind of cloud coo-coo land atmosphere that was beguiling. The night I arrived my room had just been vacated and a very black Jamaican maid with hair literally on end, and a garbled Spanish-English accent and vocabulary dashed in and out crying, "I cannot do it all, I cannot do it all, I am *alone* here." Still, as she seemed willing if distraught, I lent a hand and things fell into some kind of order.

The first thing to catch the visitor's eye is fabric. Guatemalan fabrics have a special character all their own. The beds were covered with blankets of natural colored wool, bordered with a charming design. The rugs and curtains were woven with small decorative figures. The chair seats and backs were of homespun woven cord, again of fine design, and I nearly snitched the bellboys' shirts from their backs. They were sturdy but gay, striped red linen bedecked with rows of small bright flowers. I immediately asked the boy who brought my luggage where they came from. He said the material came from Antigua and they were made up for them in the city. Antigua was on my itinerary. Hurray.

In the morning I walked the short distance from the hotel to La Tinaja (the jar), a shop owned by Señora Elvira Aldana, a friend of Romney Brent.

Her merchandise is tempting: fine fabrics, ornaments, ties, dresses, *bibelots*. I bought a thickly embroidered serape or huipil, a kind of top that slips over the head and, with a little adjusting is an eye popper when worn with slacks. The colors are marvelous; deep purples, blues, and reds.

While I thought the Tinaja prices very fair, I should not say that on the whole life for the traveler is cheap in Guatemala. Their dollar is the quetzal, which means bird, and it is startling how quickly the little things fly away.

I had thought to hire a car and driver as I had in Yucatán but when the Clark Tourist Office told me it would be $40 a day I hastily revised my plans. I was lucky in that a car *was* going to Lake Atitlán, my first goal, and there was an extra place. This could be mine for $10. I grabbed it.

My fellow passengers were a Mrs. Downing from San Francisco en route to Rio de Janeiro to meet her husband and Mr. and Mrs. Rifkin from Chicago. In the course of the journey I learned that Mrs. Downing was a liberal, strong on causes, while Mrs. Rifkin was a dedicated worker for the blind and Mr. Rifkin a retired husband who wished she were not. He wanted to travel more than her work would allow.

We were one in agreeing that the country was extraordinarily beautiful and the narrow winding mountain roads stimulating. Although Señora Lavin in Mérida had obviously had nightmare memories of them, and despite a few villainous curves, I thought them benign compared to the Grand Corniche in France, or some of those roads in Greece.

We passed through a village where all the women wore red blouses, blue beads, and long colorful skirts. They had little round cloth patties on their heads which served as a base for enormous baskets of wood or laundry, or whatever they might be transporting. Nor were they ignorant of their picturesque appearance! You wanted to snap a picture, the price might skyrocket to fifty cents.

There is a high lookout point en route from which one has a superb view of Lake Atitlán far below and gradually the road winds down, although still at an altitude of 5000 feet, to the little village of Panajachel and the Hotel Tzanjuyú with its lovely location on the water's edge.

The rooms and baths are simple but comfortable, and the grounds a pure delight. This is a spot where film flows through the camera like water through a sluice, there is so much to record. The hotel garden is ablaze with flowers and to reach the dining room one crosses a bridge spanning an infinitesimal harbor. Round tables are shaded by tapering umbrellas of dried banana leaves, and on the other side of the lake, twin volcanoes give an unexpected Japanese air to this very different land.

I woke about 3 A.M. and stepped out on the broad balcony to see a sky ablaze with stars, and to revel in the total silence, so blessed after the noisy city.

The stars presaged a brilliant morning, and after breakfast we crossed the lake in a launch to a little Indian village on the other side. These passages are made in the morning as in the afternoon the placid waters may churn with unexpected wrath into a tumultuous caldron of high dashing waves. It is a big lake, 16 miles long, 12 miles wide, and very deep.

In the sixteenth century the lake was the scene of sorrow and tragedy when hundreds of Indians leapt to their deaths, committing suicide out of grief and the shame of having been conquered in 1524 by a handful of Spaniards under the command of Don Pedro Alvarado, Cortes's great lieutenant who overran Guatemala.

Our launch carried about twenty-five people and a cargo of baby pigs. As we docked in the village, the inhabitants came running down a steep path to meet us, but although they were friendly enough, we had to appreciate that as tourists we took second place to the pigs, who to them represented a good, solid IBM investment. They buy them for two or three quetzals when they are small, raise and fatten them, and sell them at a pleasing profit.

Amidst terrific shrieking and squealing, the gunnysacks in which our cargo had been transported were hauled up from the hold, and the outraged piglets released.

The children crowded around us chattering, "Pitch, pitch." It took a few minutes to decipher that this meant "picture, take my picture and give me some money." Indeed we were told of an elderly lady who never had deciphered it and who returned to the hotel indignantly demanding to know why the children had insulted her, calling her a bitch.

One enterprising family had lined up six kids on a stone step, five of them holding puppies in their arms. The sixth simply held out her hand. They were, of course, irresistible and cameras clicked and dimes flew, but it is just the same a pity. True, the people are poor, very poor, but it is a sorry way for children to be brought up.

There are twelve villages dotting the lake shore and they are named for the twelve apostles. Each is noted for its specialty; the costumes of the men or women, hammocks, mats, whatever it may be, and they all have strong appeal.

In ours, the headdress was especially attractive. It is formed by a red tape about an inch wide which is wrapped around the head time after time until it broadens out into a kind of halo. Most becoming.

On sale are the colorful loom-woven fabrics: violet and white
striped smocks and pants, the latter embroidered around the bottom with bright stitching, sashes and yard goods. It is not ad-
vantageous to buy on arrival. Better to wait until you are returning
down the village street to reboard the launch after having visited the
small market in the center of town. Prices drop when customers are
about to leave, but I would not say they are exorbitant in any event:
the pants two-fifty and three dollars, a really handsome smock, six.

After luncheon and a siesta, Lorenzo, our chauffeur-guide
rounded us up and we set off for Chichicastenango, a wonderful
place and a wonderful name.

The great time to be there is during Holy Week or when the
fiesta in honor of Santo Tomás is held on the 21st of December.
They are said to be marvelously colorful occasions with sometimes
as many as ten thousand Indians gathering for dances and religious
ceremonies. We were there in early February, but there is nothing
the matter with Chichicastenango then either. The two great magnets
are the market, held Thursdays and Sundays, and the twenty-nine
room Mayan Inn, the latter built by an American, Alfred Clark, in
1932. It is his son, James, who today heads the Clark Tourist Office.
Mr. Clark senior was a connoisseur and collector of rare wood, and
the carved waxed doors of the rooms, the chests and tables are
among the most beautiful I have ever seen.

The rooms themselves are charming, with open fireplaces, fine
furniture and your own boy comes every evening to light your fire.
Both he and it are welcome, for Chichicastenango lies at 6500 feet,
and the night air is sharp. Your first evening you are also offered a
drink on the house and when you go to bed you fall asleep to the
soft crackle and hiss of the dying flames.

The hotel is actually two buildings separated by a narrow cobbled street, enhanced by patios and gardens. The public rooms are
attractive and cozy, and I understand that as a rule the food is very
good. The night I dined there the cook was off pitch, but a day or
so later when I happened to run into the Rifkins in Antigua, they
said that subsequent meals had been delicious.

The early mornings in Chichin are nippy, but by nine-thirty or ten, one could be swimming were a pool available. Perhaps someday one will be built.

The roofs of the houses lining the village streets are of tile and on them, from tiny pods blown by the wind and lodged there, the small fragile stems of a native plant sprout straight upward, for all the world like fairy TV antennae.

It is a hilly little town, and having an affinity for graveyards, I walked down one steep hill and up another to the cemetery where mausoleums, looking like miniature houses painted bright green or raspberry pink, or blue and white, shelter the dear departed. For myself I prefer cremation but were I keen on the idea of "remains," I would hope to be received into the bright and cheery resting places of the Chichicastenangans.

As I was walking there, I saw coming toward me a small girl holding her two little brothers by the hands. The children formed a picturesque group, so I aimed my camera for a snapshot but the child gathered her smaller brother in her arms and started away in such obvious terror that I at once lowered the infernal machine. Some of the natives are still extremely superstitious about the strange black box.

On my return journey, I saw a vigorous young man approaching along the narrow street and behind him loomed a great mountain of dried corn husks. As we drew closer to each other I thought to myself: It must be an awfully tiny donkey carrying that load, I can't even see him. The young man passed me. What was carrying the mountain was a little girl, I should say about five. A kind of women's lib movement is strong in Guatemala, as it is in Africa, where the females do the work.

A few minutes later I joined up with the Rifkins, Ruth Downing and other travelers, and we went to the market, as always, a brilliant, active, noisy scene where fruits and vegetables, meat, bread, pottery, leather, objects of wood and textiles of blazing colors are sold. There is something wonderfully stimulating about native markets the world around, but always, my heart aches for the poor skinny dogs who are booted from place to place, or totally ignored, left to die of hunger and thirst. Ruth and I bought piles of tortillas for them and struggled to find a bucket to fill from the fountain, but any surcease was limited strictly to our presence. That we knew.

Vivette Rifkin went overboard on brief pretty aprons bright with Guatemalan embroidery. "I can sell them in Chicago for my readings for the blind work. We ought to make two, two-fifty profit on every one."

"Do you have a shop?" I asked.

She laughed, "We have a table four feet by four. We call it our boutique but you'd be surprised. We sell a lot of stuff for our people."

We went into the Cathedral of Santo Tomás at the end of the square by a side entrance—the steps leading up to the front door are reserved for the Indians—and sat down quietly to watch them at their rites. Set at intervals along the floor of the nave were narrow oblong platforms, perhaps six inches high. On them, with a great deal of concentration, men and women on their knees, were arranging flowers, fruit, and candles to please the pagan deities they have worshiped from time immemorial. Some of them had little flasks which I at first thought contained the holy water of the Catholics, but when told what it really was, I thought the native idea much more sensible. The flasks hold rum and they sprinkle it on the altars to make the gods a little tipsy and put them in a good humor so they will more readily grant requests. I dare say anything that remains is consumed by the Indians themselves so everybody's happy.

A tall pole stands in front of the cathedral and during the time of the fiesta, from a rope attached to the top, men whirl through the air around it. The activity is called Palo Volador, the Flying or Spinning Pole and is a version of the Flying Trapeze based on a story in the Popol-Vuh, the Bible of the Quiche Indians. A few days afterward in a park in Mexico City I saw it happening. Two young men and two small boys in bright costumes, their feet tied together, were lowered by a fifth chap sitting high atop the pole who manipulated the mechanism. Down they came head first, swinging wider and wider until, with outstretched hands, they touched the ground. Roustabouts ran to release them whereupon they jumped up and bowed happily to enthusiastic applause.

Later that morning in Chichicastenango I ran by chance into some New York acquaintances, the Dyers—Gurney Dyer is vice-president of the Museum of Natural History—and then met the very pleasant and intelligent woman with whom they were traveling. Her name is Joya Hairs. She has a small travel business of her own and one may reach her through the Mayan Inn. She was taking my friends on a safari up the rivers and through the jungle and coastal plain of Guatemala. A trip I hope some day to make.

In the afternoon Ruth Downing and I drove in a mini bus to Antigua and the hotel of the same name. This one, while very different from the Mayan Inn, nevertheless has a great deal to recommend it.

The Mayan is built on a hillside. The grounds of the Antigua are flat. A big swimming pool is set in the center of a great open garden where handsome parrots perch in the trees and lovely textiles that are for sale glow in the sunshine.

Surrounded by low mountains and once immensely prosperous, with magnificent houses and churches, Antigua was the capital of all Central America and was at one time governed by Pedro de Alvarado and his wife Doña Beatriz, a woman of considerable enterprise.

On his death on July 4 in 1541 in Guadalajara, Mexico, she had herself proclaimed governor general but even before that she had proven herself an executive. She had established what she was pleased to call a nunnery and so it was to the extent that a good many women lived there. According to legend, however, they were more ribald than chaste and although the gentlemen were happy the natives were shocked by such goings on.

When Doña Beatriz perished in the great flood of September 1541, only two months after her husband's death, a lot of people thought she got no more than her just deserts.

Twice again and, as far as one can learn without any provocative high jinks, the city was virtually demolished. Both times by earthquakes. One in 1773 another in 1874.

Today its power has ebbed and it is a quiet provincial town with a delightful tree-shaded central plaza and a yellow cathedral with a handsome rococo portal that was spared in the earthquakes. Its interior is of no particular interest, but there are remnants of a handsome old fountain in the rear courtyard.

Since the bellboys at the hotel in Guatemala City told me that Antigua was the textile center where I could buy the shirt material that had so taken my fancy, I combed every little shop I could find. That particular search was fruitless, but I did have the pleasure of seeing American astronauts, Captain Alan Shepard and Commander Edgar Mitchell land on the moon. What I imagine to be one of the few television sets in Antigua was located in a small shop and the crowd that had gathered to watch spilled out onto the pavement.

When the people saw me they smiled and said, "Ah, Americana" and I bowed and smiled graciously as though I had set up the Houston Space Center. Even this did not elicit any shirt material, but a young man who had heard me asking for *tela typico* advised me to drive to the village of San Antonio Aguas Calientes where he said they wove it and where it would be less expensive.

I negotiated a taxi with a cheerful driver and a little boy who wanted to come for the ride. We left town and followed a shady road running through a coffee plantation. The thought occurred to me that if the dire prognostications of Señora Lavin in Mérida were valid this was the perfect place to do away with an unpopular Yankee. No human soul on earth knew where I was.

Sometime after I had returned home from the trip, a friend showed me an article in the *London Sunday Times* awash with abductions, murders, and foreigners held for ransom which, it claimed, were virtually the daily way of life in Guatemala. I can only say that to me and to the other tourists I encountered during my visit, Guatemalans showed nothing but courtesy and friendship.

To be sure, in none of the establishments we stopped at in San

Antonio Aguas Calientes did I find the material of my dreams and the bellboys' shirts, but I do not put that down to anti-American sentiments.

There was no car available to take me back to Guatemala City, but I had been told that the buses ran every hour and it was only a forty-five minute ride. The seats were hard, uncompromising, upright Puritans, but I was next to the window, a boon I was soon to appreciate.

A young mother with a fat two- or three-year-old child got in and sat down beside me and as we bumped along hauled from a bulging carryall a bottle of lumpy gruel which she held to its mouth as her offspring guzzled. I watched the procedure with distaste. In a hot jolting bus the outcome was a foregone conclusion. Alas for pre-science. Ten minutes after having swallowed the mess the infant opened its mouth and without retch or gag or struggle, a niagara of curdled milk poured forth. It missed me by a hairbreadth, but the mother was inundated.

With, I thought, admirable self-control (I myself would have strangled the tot), she proceeded with such mopping up operations as were possible under the circumstances and which were not effective. However, we settled back to comparative peace when five minutes later the wee one bumped its head against the iron upright supporting the seat in front of us and let out a howl. This lasted for another ten minutes when, to my infinite relief, it subsided into a kind of drunken stupor. At the stop before the bus terminal mother and child disembarked, leaving in their wake a puddle of vomit on the bus floor.

I derived more entertainment from a bus ride in Guatemala City, the following morning when a woman came aboard bearing on her head an enormous basket of green bananas. A neat feat, negotiating the bus step with the load of bananas, and she was followed by a woman with a fat live hen. She held it by its feet until she herself was well-ensconced in her seat, then she placed it on her lap where it sat contentedly clucking and I watched hopefully for an egg to drop.

My Guatemala evening proved more sophisticated. Elvira Aldana and her sister Alicia picked me up and we drove to James Clark's house. He was entertaining a large group, the Boston Museum of Fine Arts tour, and presently departed with them but not before urging us to finish our drinks at our leisure. *"Mi casa es su casa,"* he said. The gracious phrase is a fact.

A little later my friends drove me to La Puerta, a steak restaurant across the road from the Hotel Biltmore. It was small and cozy and the steaks were large and delicious but there were two to a person and that was too much.

We drank beer as an accompaniment. While, as I have said, the food of that part of the world is not, as a rule, very good, the true let down is the lack of wine. The little they do produce does not have much to recommend it and imported brands are exorbitantly expensive and usually not of first quality in any event. One accepts the fact and makes do.

The next day I flew to Mexico City to join Romney Brent and the Guild tour.

My friendship with Romney dates back a long time to when we were both active in the theatre. He wrote, directed, and acted. He was a very good actor and one of his most successful roles was in *The Warrior's Husband* in which he played Sapiens the spouse of Antiope the queen of the Amazons: Miss Katharine Hepburn.

His small physique fitted the part perfectly and with his curls and elegant tunic he made a dainty, well-cared-for husband. Yet the appealing and amusing aspect of the performance was that one never doubted his virility. When complimented on this achievement he would say, "But I simply play it straight. After all, women don't go mincing and swishing around. They behave like women. I only want to act like a male who, historically, was cast in the domestic role usually allotted to women."

Romney's mother, although of American parentage, was born in Mexico and his father had at one time been the Mexican Ambassador to Paris where the six Larralde children spent several years of their childhood. The name Romney Brent was something the only male picked out for himself when he decided to go on the stage.

Señor Brent speaks perfect English, perfect French and perfect Spanish. This last is very desirable when one is traveling about South America.

Our group consisted of twenty-three persons and, as is inevitable in this sort of venture, we soon settled into little cliques and groups. I was one of a quartet. Romney, Ruth Anderson, Lois Bond, and myself.

Mrs. Anderson has a house not too far from ours in the country but as is so often the case we had not known one another until introduced by Romney who spent a weekend with his old friend and brought us together.

Ruth Anderson is an amusing woman and was, for several years, a frenetic producer of radio scripts. I use the phrase advisedly. Those not born yesterday, and to whom the words Soap Opera have a nostalgic ring, may be startled to learn that the following was the output of one and the same woman, our Mrs. A.

Ready, radio fans? Away we go! *The Romance of Helen Trent, Backstage Wife, Our Gal Sunday, Valiant Lady, Aunt Jennie's True Life Stories, Big Sister, John's Other Wife, Second Husband, Amanda of Honeymoon Hill.* Having set that mill-grinding record she drew a deep breath, dusted off her hands and took on *Pepper Young's Family.*

The creative fires burned brightest when Mrs. Anderson was at work in a reconditioned chicken house seated at her typewriter under a hand-stitched sampler with the heartwarming motto: "Send the money."

She was the precursor of the computer only more capable than some of the machines I have had truck with, notably those used by department stores, which have cornered the market on errors in billing.

While Mrs. Anderson obviously did not write every word of every script she was the Creator and Editor. The Mind who did the plotting and outlining. Much of the actual writing was done by apprentices and assistants. The beehive functioned at fever pitch and my imagination was fired. One day we were reminiscing about ye olden times.

"Of course," I cried, "I can see it all. Like the school of Peter Paul Rubens!"

"Not exactly," my friend said drily, and then a bemused look came into her eyes. "Funny, I don't know why but in those days time used to fly by."

Why indeed! It's hard to imagine. I too used to work in radio although never as a writer and we knew many of the same people in the world of advertising, entertainment and magazines, and enjoyed gossiping about them.

Funnily enough, as Lois Bennett, Lois Bond had also been a radio star. In the theatre she sang in the Winthrop Ames productions of Gilbert and Sullivan and later her lovely voice soared over the airwaves to the delight of several million ardent fans. Lois is gently cushioned, with a sturdy air and she was the only one on the tour who wore a hat.

Most of us didn't own a hat but Lois owned a hat, she liked her hat and the stiff-brimmed sailor, set straight upon her bright red hair became, like a banner in battle, the ralling point for our group.

The day after my arrival in Mexico City was a Sunday and at 9:30 in the morning we went to the Palacio de Bellas Artes to see the highly entertaining Ballet Folklorico. There is one delightful thing about Latin countries. The devout usually go to Mass but after that the day is for *living,* very different from the philosophy of Bible belt communities.

The Folklorico was founded by Amalia Hernandez and today her daughter is the director. It is lighthearted, warm, comical and charming, achieving, in the Deer Dance, the hunting dance of the Yaqui Indians, remarkable vigor and drama. There is music and singing and while the dancing is perhaps not top rank, it is spirited and fun with such pleasant diversions as a young groom trotting to his wedding astride a straw horse.

We later lunched, and very well, at Les Ambassadeurs on the Reforma, Mexico City's magnificent broad boulevard along which bowl *los collectivos*. *Los collectivos* are communal taxis holding five besides the driver. If there is a vacant seat you may hail one and get in, and although they go only in one direction, if you are going that way you ride for miles for one peso, eight cents.

At that time I had not seen the subways of Russia but those of Mexico were impressive. They were new and they were grand with marble platforms and mosaic walls. There was a policeman at every station, a little custom that bemugged and bedeviled New York City would do well to follow, and there were no advertisements. Instead, an occasional large photo mural or perhaps an artifact discovered during excavation. The trains were orange on the outside, white and soft blue within, and they were quiet as they rolled on thick rubber tires. Cost of splendor, four cents the ride.

A good destination, either by taxi or subway, is the Museo Archeologico. Its pre-Columbian exhibits are unique and the building itself is probably the most beautiful museum in the world. I am not forgetting the Louvre but I refer to buildings designed specifically as museums.

Another of the city's great attractions is Teotihuacán, the site of the pyramids, which is about thirty-two miles outside of Mexico City proper. The two greatest pyramids are those of the Moon and the Sun and the fable connected with them is not without appeal.

It appears they were erected by the gods when neither men nor the sun existed. In both buildings sick and humble gods named Nanahuatzin and Tecuciztecatl did penance. Finally they threw themselves into a sacred fire from whence one emerged as the sun, the other the moon. Originally they were of the same brilliance but another set of gods—perhaps they were jealous—threw a rabbit into the face of one of them and whereas we speak of the man in the moon the Mexicans think of him as a rabbit and claim to see a silhouette with large pointed ears whenever the moon is full.

A rabbit in the puss understandably dimmed the brilliance of the hapless planet which is why the pyramids, where the original gods did penance, are known as those of the Sun and the Moon.

One can see from the existing layout that Teotihuacán must have been enormous with an extensive residential zone as well as the religious and ceremonial center and, unless the climate has greatly changed in the last few hundred years, it was cold. The thing to do is to go in the late afternoon while it is still light enough to look around and then stay for the evening performance of Sound and Light. When we were there the voices were excellent, the play of light interesting, the music less so.

The audience is seated on hard benches on a hillside and the chill wind blows. We had been warned so were well bundled up and blankets are available for a rental of forty cents.

After the performance one or two of us drove to the Hacienda des Los Morales, an old remodeled plantation house that was supposed to be very grand. It *was* attractive and there, for once, the wine was good, but the food was down to the usual Central American standard.

A small and unpretentious restaurant where one fares far better and where the prices are reasonable is the Chalet Suizo. One might go there for refueling after a visit to the Zocolo, Mexico's great square, dominated by the cathedral whose history is haphazard to say the least.

In 1521 Cortes had the Aztec pyramids that stood there demolished and between 1524 and 1526 built a Catholic church on the same spot. After a hundred years it was torn down and they started again with plans that had been authorized by Spain in 1536. At a later date Philip III ordered changes and it wasn't 'til 1813 that the building was finally completed only to be seriously damaged by an earthquake in 1894. Repairs were started in 1905 and they got around to finishing it in 1941.

It is a huge and ornate affair and the day we visited it nearly two thousand people were milling about, shuffling in long slow files, their infants in their arms, their small children, who were waiting to be confirmed by the bishop, trailing behind them.

Under ground, looking for all the world like bank vaults, metal lockers and drawers serve as depositories for bones. One can clearly see the sharp slant of the building's foundation due to the fact that

Mexico City is built on swampy land and filled-in lakes and enormously large buildings tend to sink.

Immediately adjoining the cathedral the parish church with its intricately adorned rococo façade delights the eye and at right angles to the religious complex stretches the eternal length of the National Palace, with its forceful murals by the famous Mexican artist, Diego Rivera. They are impressive but the smaller scenes of daily life painted along the balcony surrounding the courtyard are more engaging.

Across the square an even more secular monument, the city's famous pawn shop. We went in and browsed but were able to resist the rings, bracelets and thousands of pairs of earrings left there for sale.

Another large church that the tourist usually visits is the shrine of the Virgin of Guadalupe, like the cathedral slightly tipped.

We looked at the façade and watched the great numbers of people, men and women, crawling painfully on their knees across the enormous paved plaza to the church steps. Religious faith is a curious sort of reasoning. What kind of a God must those poor souls have believed in to be convinced that he would be pleased by their self-inflicted torment?

A short and delightful excursion outside the city is a trip to Toluca, passing on the way an old Carmelite monastery called Disierto de los Leones, because around the sixteenth century it was the home of a family named Leones and was so remote from the capital that it was considered a desert. A few of the older sections of the building still stand but the real charm is the tranquil garden abloom with pansies and calendulas and sweet with bird song.

Friday is Toluca's big day for that is market day with little mountains of beautiful fresh produce heaped on the ground, shaded by rigged-up canvas awnings. Unlike the super-emporiums at home where size is everything and flavor ignored, the vegetables and fruits of Mexico are mostly sold young and tender: baby artichokes, zucchinis, carrots, and potatoes. Fruit is in abundance including succulent little strawberries selling at sixty-four cents for four pounds. At home forty-nine cents to $1.59 a pint.

The narrow street was jammed with shoppers and sellers and live chickens and turkeys huddled in heaps clucking disconsolately. I fear they knew their fate, poor dears.

There is another good market in Toluca beside that for produce. This one is indoors, Manuel J. Solis prop., and it specializes in native crafts; textiles, clothes, handsome rush furniture, baskets, my fatal weakness, and Mexican silver: cuff links, key chains, all kinds of pleasant practical souvenirs. Also there is a quite decent restaurant called San Carlos, where one may lunch.

Another excursion which almost every one sensibly makes is to Cuernavaca, about an hour and a half from the capital. Conveniently situated on the way is another superb Mexican building, almost as much of a Must as the Archaeological Museum, the library of the City University. It is a great block, twelve stories high entirely faced, as though richly embroidered, with mosaic designs of natural colored stones. There are astrological signs, animals, figures, lettering. The building and ornamentation is the quite extraordinary achievement of Juan Orgorman. It is interesting inside too, but it is the exterior that rivets the attention.

The climate of Cuernavaca is delicious and there is a large, firmly rooted and ardent American colony, some Canadians too, most of whom have houses ranging from cozy to magnificent. On the cook's day off they go to lunch or dine at Las Mañanitas, a star of a restaurant with an American manager, Robert Krause. The prices, alas, are also American but one gets a lot for the money. There is a swimming pool for resident guests and a lovely garden where flamingos, their heads buried in their plumage, sleep standing on one stick-like leg and where a white peacock may preen and majestically unfurl his great tail. With the sun striking through it, it is like a design of shimmering snowflakes. The food is justly famous and there are eleven rooms for guests. I have heard enthusiastic comments from those who have stayed there, but there is always a big crowd at lunchtime and not a great deal of privacy.

The advantage of Las Mañanitas, for a brief stay, is that it is right in town, whereas at Las Jacarandas, a delightful inn with cottages, gardens and a swimming pool, one must have a car or taxi to get back and forth.

The chief reason our group went to Cuernavaca was because Helen Hayes has a house there.

Most of the tour, shepherded by Romney, were spending the day in Taxco, returning to Cuernavaca for the cocktail party which, thanks to old associations and long-time friendship with the Guild, Helen was generously giving that afternoon.

I did not go to Taxco because Norton and I had been there the year before when we made a brief trip by ourselves to Mexico. I strongly recommend it, however.

It is an easy drive from Cuernavaca, and by making a slight detour, it is possible to see a fascinating pyramid; Xochicalco. The carvings, at least those around the base, are in an excellent state of preservation and the color still lingers. It is a fairly steep climb up to the pyramid and the view sweeps over undulating hills and across great plains to the horizon.

Taxco itself is picturesque and when you arrive there and a pleasant young man from the tourist bureau offers you his services, it is wise to accept. Part of the picturesqueness includes what appears to be absolutely perpendicular, extremely narrow, cobbled streets. Looking at them I thought to myself, holy cow! You have to be a human fly.

Taxco is the silver capital of Mexico. Some of the merchandise is beautiful and very expensive, but a good deal is attractive and quite reasonable. Pinada is a top-notch shop. Castillo next door is still good, and not quite so steep in price.

When Norton and I were there we browsed and snooped and made a few modest purchases and went to lunch at the Hotel Victoria from which there is a fine view of the little town rambling up and down the hillsides.

When Ruth and Lois and the others joined us later they said they had done pretty much the same thing.

Instead of going to Taxco, Elsa Larralde, Romney's sister, and I had driven down to Cuernavaca to lunch with Helen Hayes before the cocktail party. She has an attractive house situated, appropriately enough, in the Calle Victoria.

I remembered her telling me once that sometimes, during the long run of *Victoria Regina* she would get confused, forgetting whether she was married to Alfred or Albert, on which occasions she would call him Al. She realized it wasn't very Victorian but it was the best she could do at the time.

Staying with her that day were her son James MacArthur and his pretty bride and an old friend from the English musical comedy stage, Dorothy Dickson.

Sparing her cook's energies for the cocktail party Helen took us to Las Mañanitas for lunch and afterward the young couple and I drove out of town to see the atelier of Mary Brooks Cadwallader. Some years ago she and her husband had a place in New York where they designed, made and sold original and exquisite scarves. To the universal woe of their clientele they migrated to Mexico where, I am happy to say, they are still involved with lovely fabrics. It was pleasant to see Mrs. Cadwallader again and to rekindle, even briefly, an old and pleasant relationship.

At the Hayes cocktail party I met for the first time the entire group with whom I would be traveling for the next two weeks. Needless to say the only names I remembered were those of the people I already knew.

We returned en mass to the city and the next night took off for South America.

CHAPTER TWO

South America

A glance at an atlas discloses information that is scarcely top secret. South America is *large*. Great sections of it must be fascinating and if one has the time and money to travel through Peru, to explore the Amazon, to visit the pampas of the Argentine and to venture down to Tierra del Fuego it would seem foolish not to do so but time is the operative word.

For a variety of reasons our own trip was, to some extent, choppy yet even so there were highlights I would not have missed.

One of our most enjoyable interludes was in Buenos Aires where we arrived after a couple of days in Santiago de Chile. Almost everyone on the tour was looking forward to Buenos Aires, Romney and I especially, because our ambassador there was John Lodge and we had known him and his beautiful wife Francesca since their show biz days.

Unhappily, John himself would not be there. He was cruising with the Argentine Navy off Tierra del Fuego and, with any luck, meeting I hoped, many splendid penguins. Mrs. Lodge, however, was holding the fort and giving a lunch for the tour.

In Buenos Aires our hotel was the Plaza, situated on a lovely park. The parks and gardens of that city are a joy, luxuriant with huge old trees and flowering shrubs.

The day of our arrival I had been in my room about five minutes when the phone rang and a man's voice said, "Miss Chase? My name is Turner, I'm from the American Embassy. May I see you at once?" "Come up," I said. Mystified, I thought to myself, now what? Maybe war has been declared and I am to be the first to know!

Within moments Mr. Turner was at my door. As I opened it he stepped in and looked around. "Where is Mrs. Lodge?" It was a small room and the most cursory glance revealed there was nobody there but us chickens. My mystification deepened.

"I don't know," I said. "Isn't she at home?"

"No, no she's not. She went to the airport to meet you people."

"How kind of her. But we didn't see her."

"I know, I know. There was a switch in planes."

That was true. Our original flight from Santiago had been canceled and we had flown Braniff instead but as no one had known about Francesca's intention of meeting us she, of course, had not been notified.

Mr. Turner continued. "Mrs. Lodge was ignorant of the change and she was most insistent I get her a car to drive to the airport. There was a good deal of trouble about it and now I don't know *where* she is." He looked at me accusingly as though I might be hiding her in a closet.

The car business baffled me. "But surely," I said as delicately as I could, "I know things are tough all over and our taxes are grim but surely the American Ambassador to the Argentine has a car?"

He looked surprised. "Naturally. A black Cadillac." I breathed a sigh of relief. The banner still waved.

The next day we gathered at our bus at ten-thirty and met the nicest guide we would have on the whole trip. Her name was Raquel Bengolea. She was a vigorous, intelligent, well-bred young woman and a pleasure to be with.

We were on our way to an *asado,* a barbecue de luxe and driving out of town passed several large and inviting public swimming pools and shady parks with fine old trees.

In about an hour we arrived at our destination, a sort of ranch, Piñars Azuls (Blue Pines). Beside the pine trees there were lawns, a small souvenir shop and a big paddock with horses for people to ride with what I took to be authentic gauchos in attendance. Our group was only one of many and I should say we were about two or three hundred in all.

There was a shed with a very long counter grill on which six or seven men were preparing the sausages, liver and kidneys that were the opening notes of the great meat symphony that would be our luncheon. They were to be followed by huge sides of beef that other gauchos were roasting on upright grills in a neighboring shed. Raquel told us they estimated that every Argentine averages about 170 pounds of meat a year. George Bernard Shaw must be writhing in his grave.

While waiting for Gargantua's feast, we watched some dancers in reasonably picturesque costumes cavorting on a small wooden floor laid on the grass, and at about one-thirty sat down to test our mettle. We started with *empanada,* pastry wrapped around minced meat. This was followed by the sausages, two kinds, then small squares of liver (over done) and the kidneys. *Then* slices of rare steak. Where to put them? However, I did manage the excellent green salad, homemade bread and a native red wine that was very pleasing.

When dessert arrived I could only look the other way although for the record I took one infinitesimal taste. It was milk jam, a cloyingly sweet concoction of caramelized sugar and boiled milk, and it is popular in the Argentine. Were they to export it to Arab countries which have few cattle but adore sweets, they would make a fortune.

By now it was four o'clock and the hard wooden backless benches on which we sat seemed riveted to our bones, and I was much relieved when Raquel gave the signal to board the bus.

Things have since changed but at that time the president of Argentina was Señor Levingston. When I asked Raquel his first name she looked vague and turned to the bus driver. He looked vague too, but after a brief conference they came up, tentatively, with Roberto. I suppose even a sobriquet like Tricky Dicky has its uses.

Their press, they feel, is free and the universities very definitely are. There are no campuses and no resident students and when we asked if the system didn't make for excessive taxation the somewhat rueful reply was "No, because the professors are so poorly paid."

That evening we drove in our bus to an open-air theatre and the bus was the scene of a small but highly satisfying episode. We had one couple, there is always one, either a couple or an individual, who is a note of discord in what, the traveler hopes, is going to be a tour of sweet harmony.

Our couple I will call Mr. and Mrs. Casten. She was a large and solid woman, he wasn't too frail either, and invariably they got into the bus first and invariably they sat in the two front seats, naturally the best since they provided an unimpeded view.

I'm for everybody having a whack at the front seats but it's a case where turn and turn about is certainly indicated. It was not indicated to the Castens. She, as a rule, was there first and would call out in stentorian tones, "Maurice, I'm in the bus." Maurice could count on that.

So noticeable was their tenure that jokingly I had asked Romney if they had paid extra to the Guild for the privilege. He said, "No, of course not. That's just the way they are."

Having put up with it driving around Santiago and now in Buenos Aires, I got an idea. A nice young girl named Esther was traveling with us. She had dark hair and big brown eyes and was gentle and unassuming. "Hey, Esther," I said, "how about this evening you and I go down early and get those front seats?"

Esther giggled. "Don't you think they'll be mad?"

"It is my fondest hope," I said.

We were triumphant in our little scheme and when the Castens hove themselves aboard and saw that their squatters rights had been pre-empted the expression of stunned incredulity on their faces provided one of the finer moments of the journey.

Lois Bond had a run in with them, too, one I was sorry to have missed but I was not on the bus at the time. Apparently they had been picking on Raquel, excoriating her because a concert or something of the sort that they had been expecting to attend had been canceled.

It was certainly not poor Raquel's fault but she was their whipping boy. The atmosphere of the bus was one of tension and deep embarrassment but nobody said anything until Lois suddenly spoke up.

"Stop it," she said, "stop that this minute." Her words rapped like a metal ruler and the sailor hat trembled with indignation. "You are not to say another *word* to Raquel. Not another *word*. I forbid it, do you understand?"

The Castens were shocked into silence for the rest of the afternoon.

Driving around Buenos Aires one gets the impression that the city is large, accurate enough since it ranks, I believe, fifth among the cities of the world, that the parks are large and lovely, and the streets wide and clean. A marvelous sight was a 150-year-old magnolia tree in full flower.

The day we lunched with Francesca Lodge we found the Residency of the American Embassy to be a handsome building that was once the private house of an immensely rich Argentine family. There was a great staircase at the top of which Mrs. Lodge had banked flags of all nations, and there were galleries, a ballroom, suites of salons . . . in short, Display!

Our hostess was looking very pretty in a pink dress, a pink bandeau around her head and glittering sandals on her bare feet. We had our pictures taken with her and lunched in upper class style.

Among the guests, besides the Guild group, were a few members of the Embassy staff including Yale Newman who used to work with John Daly at ABC. I gathered he preferred TV to embassy life in Buenos Aires. A vital and entertaining member of the party was a woman who runs a popular radio and television show. Her name is Paloma Efron, but she is known as La Blackie despite her reasonably blond hair.

There was also a dazzling young man, Duilio Marzio, an Argentine actor, who was going on tour through thirty universities in the United States.

Francesca seemed a little vague about it for she said to the table at large, "He's going to the States but I don't know what he will do there."

I said, "We'll take care of what he does, just give us his address." The young man blushed and everyone laughed. He was *very* good looking.

After lunch, coffee cups in hand, we strolled through the garden. It is a nice garden and they have a swimming pool, the only hitch being that the property is surrounded by high rises, whose tenants may peer down upon the abassadorial ablutions much as New Yorkers peer down into the grounds of Gracie Mansion, the mayor's house.

The next day we went for a cruise on El Tigre River, our launch winding its way through some of the 7000 islands, give or take a few, of La Plata River delta. It is a very brown river and a picturesque world has sprung up along its banks. Small houses, on small acreage, each with its own dock. They are rakish and gay in design and the large and sophisticated city seems far away. Apparently people can get fresh water from shallow wells and big provision boats—floating supermarkets—daily ply the channels.

Unfortunately it was a cloudy morning because the rainy season was on the verge of breaking. We enjoyed ourselves nonetheless and returned to town in time for Romney and me to appear on La Blackie's radio program. She had invited us the day before at the Embassy luncheon.

When I got back to the hotel I found a message to call Mrs. Lodge. "Where have you been?" she demanded, "I've been trying to get you all day." I explained my activities in the *tan bella ciudad* and she said, "Why don't you come over for tea?"

I hopped a cab and arrived at the Embassy to find about fifteen or twenty American women there, the wives of some sort of economic congress then meeting in Buenos Aires. They left shortly after

1. Chichén Itzá. El Castillo,
the Great Pyramid.
The beady-eyed jaguar
lives high up inside.

2. Old Chichén.
The observatory. Four
doors in the tower face
the cardinal points of
the compass.

3. Temple at Chichén Itzá.

4. Guatemala.
Lake Atitlán. View
from my window in
Hotel Tzanjuyu at
Panajachel.

5. Guatemala. Children in Indian village across the lake. "Pitch, pitch. Take pitch, give money."

6. Guatemala.
Three Graces. Dazzling
smiles, brilliant clothes
"Look, Ma, almost no hands."

7. In the museum grounds. No one to meet
on a dark night. The head of basalt, carved
without metal tools, weighs eighteen tons
and dates from between 1150 and 900 B.C.
It is probably that of an Olmac king
and was displayed in New York's Metropolitan Museum in the Before Cortes exhibition
in the autumn of 1970. Football helmets
were the big chic of the time. They
were worn on the ball court in Chichén Itzá.

8. University City, Mexico. The magnificent twelve-story block of the library designed and richly ornamented by Juan Orgorman.

9. Show off. The white peacock in the garden of Las Mananitas, Cuernavaca.

10. Francesca Lodge and handsome guest at the Residency luncheon in Buenos Aires.

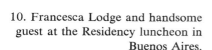

11. Teresopolis, Brazil.
Front row: Ilka, Lois Bond and hat.
Center: Billie de Araujo.
Back row: Ruth Anderson and Romney Brent.

12. Leningrad. The Winter Palace which
is the Hermitage Museum.

13. Ilka and Larissa Dukelskaya, assistant
to the director of the Hermitage. She is
more attractive than this, she was
caught at a bad angle.

14. Moscow, St. Basil's,
the Kremlin wall, and
the Spasskaya Tower.

15. Hotel Rossiya, Moscow.
And there are four of these
façades, don't forget!
If you have to walk it the
circumference is roughly
5977 miles.

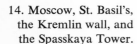

my arrival and Francesca said, "Stick around for a while, it's been such ages since we've seen each other."

We fell to chatting about her family, the colorful Braggiotti clan. When I said something about our nice luncheon the day before she laughed. "Food's not my forte really. It's Gloria and Mario who are the cooks in the family."

Her sister Gloria travels and writes and her brother Mario, was half of the well-known piano team of Fray and Braggiotti. Jacques Fray is dead but Mario, she said, was soon to begin a concert tour through the Argentine and was turning over a percentage of the take to help in the rehabilitation of Venice.

When she asked if I wouldn't like to see the house I jumped at the chance. As I have said, it is a palatial affair with suites for visiting VIPs, and huge bathrooms and a spacious apartment for the Ambassador's family. It occurred to me that the housekeeping arrangements must be complicated and time consuming, but the Lodges were also posted in Madrid and by now Francesca had worked out a system for marshaling her troops promptly and efficiently.

She had a plan for each floor and the various rooms and apartments each had their own color. The members of the staff responsible for those areas had the same color beside their names so she could tell at a glance who was responsible for what. Pentagon take note.

She had her own office and the Ambassador, of course, had his. I felt reassured to see that, in his absence, affairs of state were in the capable paws of two dachshunds lolling on the couch amid the documents.

John, she said, had called her the night before from Antarctica. He was enjoying himself among the penguins, but he confided that they did smell pretty high.

Her own problems had something of an ecological aspect too if ecology is synonymous with one's surroundings. The bleat of all ambassadors and their wives is the same: the expense of running an embassy.

Since a large part of the time of American politicians is taken up with prideful Tarzan-like breast-thumping about how we are the richest and most powerful nation on earth it is exasperating, not to mention disillusioning, to the women whose husbands represent all this grandeur on foreign soil, to realize how much they are supposed to entertain, how imposing a front they must keep up, on the paltry allowance meted out by Congress to the embassies.

In the brief time we were in Buenos Aires there had been approximately thirty for our luncheon the day before, and I believe another party that same evening. This afternoon there was the tea party. There were to be fifty for dinner Saturday night, and two admirals and their wives were arriving to spend a few days in the house. Even with the Ambassador away the entertainment rarely slackens. Nor does the cost!

Francesca was funny about the entertaining though, claiming that when John was home everyone enjoyed themselves immensely. "He has them laughing and singing and chattering away in no time. When it's just me every one hems and haws and clears their throats and tries to think of something to say."

I doubted the statement. Mrs. Lodge has an outgoing personality, years of experience in the social whirl and I had not noticed any tension or undue formality either at the luncheon she had given for us or at the tea party for the congress wives. However it was obvious that embassy problems weighed on her. She said, "I cannot wait for John to get out of political life" and the words came out like little trip hammers.

"I am going to write a book and call it *No Logic*. The government wants everything, but try to get the money to pay for it! Look at this, just look at it."

We were standing at the window of one of the luxurious suites at the time and she picked up a curtain. I looked. The material hung in shreds. "I don't know how many times I've written to Washington for money to replace them. It requires an act of Congress for God's sake!"

"Well, dear," I said, "what can you expect? Thirty billion a year for our constructive work of killing and defoliating in Southeast Asia,

and slaughtering little babies. Communists after all, we've got to
protect ourselves. You don't seem to understand our vital interests."

Most Presidents, of course, favor rich ambassadors. Maybe they
will pay for the yard goods out of their own pockets. But, naturally,
some ambassadors are not rich, merely able, and even the rich ones
balk at large disbursements for a temporary residence. Supposing
they are replaced? Supposing the President drops dead? Supposing
he is not re-elected and all diplomatic resignations are automatically
handed in? Hence the pleas to Washington and the resultant ulcers
in the innards of Embassy wives.

Not wanting to outstay my welcome, I left to allow my hostess time
to rest before attending the night's festivities at another embassy,
and later joined the Guild group when we all went to dine in an
eerie, sepulchral, underground restaurant. I like steak within reason, but to the Argentines it is a way of life. They have restaurants
called *churrascorias* (grills) where only beef is served, but there are
places where you can get *feijoada*, a native dish made chiefly of beans
and spices, although it too is not devoid of meat. After a while a mess
of white bait begins to look pretty appetizing.

From Buenos Aires we flew to São Paulo in Brazil. From the air
its most notable feature is the many high rises that stick up like
tombstones or big teeth. New York's skyscrapers don't look like that
but I think placement must have something to do with it. São Paulo
doesn't have that many and those that are there stand isolated from
their brothers.

From the moment of our arrival our movements were conditioned
by Carnival. The Brazilian Carnival is an outgrowth of the old Por-
tuguese Shrove Tuesday when they released their high spirits by toss-
ing about sacks of flour and bags of water. Mammy and Pappy
would scarcely recognize it now.

Depending on one's mood or stamina, it begins the Friday or
Saturday night preceding Ash Wednesday, which extinguishes it. In
the days when religious influence was stronger, the idea was to live it
up before the Lenten death, but change is in the air.

Religion is important, but so is money, and the trouble is that Carnival coincides too closely with the rainy season. If they get rained out, then what? Hundreds of thousands of dollars down the drain, that's what. There is talk of possibly switching the great jamboree to the winter season, sometime between mid-April and November. From the tourist's point of view, it would make sense for at that season South America comes alive. Winter is benign, but it *is* winter and activities—art, sports, business, restaurants, everything flourishes. One thinks of Rio as the heart of the Carnival, but in fact, all Brazil chimes in.

São Paulo, the great industrial center of the country is far larger than Rio or Brasilia, the capital. We did not go to Brasilia, nor did we see President Emilio Medici who in 1964 took over the government in a military coup. He seems to be ensconced for as long as he wants to stay, unless another coup unhorses him. He may not be voted for or against, but people can vote for senators and deputies who conceivably may influence him. Many feel he is good for the country since taxes are now collected and schools, hospitals, and roads are being built. The rate of illiteracy is still 40 percent, but night schools have been opened and everyone is urged to attend them.

And certainly Brazil is a vigorous land. In 1955 the population of São Paulo was two million, today it is six million; the tremendous spurt attributable to the automobile industry.

The first night we were there when, around 3 A.M., I heard a great racket in the street, aware of the season, I assumed they were starting to set up grandstands for their own Carnival celebration, but looking out my window of the Othon Palace Hotel, I saw they were merely emptying garbage cans. *Muy norteamericano.*

A day or two later, on arriving at the airport for our flight to Rio de Janeiro, we found it to be a cacophonous madhouse of beating drums, waving flags, showers of confetti and crowds of screaming youth. Not, as we at first thought, a revolution, merely a greeting to their soccer team that had just won a big game away from home. Two young black heroes were borne across the enormous waiting

room, on the shoulders of their exuberant fans. Soccer, to the Brazilians, is what baseball is to us, and the Maracanã Stadium in Rio,
seating 150,000 spectators, is the largest in the world.

The flight to Rio was forty-five minutes, and there was a good
deal of commotion at the Hotel Trocadero in assigning rooms. Not
inefficiency on the part of the management, simply the crush of
Carnival time.

We were finally pigeonholed, and were lucky in that most of the
rooms overlooked the Avenida Atlantica and the famous Copacabana Beach. Unfortunately, at that time, the road was pretty well
torn up, but the unsightliness was temporary; they were adding another lane for traffic. I thought they were digging sewers.

One of the most pleasant interludes of our stay in the city occurred the afternoon we were received by a delightful woman,
Barbara Eleadora, a Brazilian art and drama critic. From what we
saw or could learn of the theatre in Rio she must have a good deal
of time on her hands. However, she has a charming house in which
to pass it.

It is a tall, thin house situated in a lovely old cobbled courtyard
where many Rio de Janeirans yearn to live but it is difficult of access
and one must have connections such as a great grandfather who
built the house you now live in as was the case with our hostess.

Like her house she was tall and thin with dark eyes, blond hair
and a voice, compared to which, the late Miss Tallulah Bankhead's
was a falsetto.

The walls were lined with books and vibrant modern pictures,
several of the most notable having been painted by her daughter,
a young lady of genuine talent. There were other guests as well as
our Guild pals, one of whom wore her hair in long black shining
braids and looked like a glorified Pocahontas. Her beau was no
slouch either but he looked more like Paul Newman than an Indian.

There were the usual drinks but I sampled a native one, batida,
made from distilled sugar cane to which is added lemon, soda, and
ice. Very good.

We were lucky in our contacts, the next day driving to Teresópolis, a mountain resort where Billie and Olivar de Araujo, old patients of Norton's and friends of us both, have a country house set in spacious and lovely grounds.

It is one of those curious houses that look quite small from the outside and are unexpectedly roomy within. We swam in the pool trying to dodge the three small grandsons, enchanting kids who flipped about like dolphins.

As we were having a pre-luncheon drink we mentioned the batida we had so enjoyed and Olivar said it was popular because in Rio, depending on quality, a bottle of whisky *can* cost $40. I felt quite faint and thanked my stars I can't stand scotch.

Our host was enthusiastic over new discoveries of minerals in his country and spoke lightheartedly of strip mining. Ruth Anderson and I who have seen the bitter results of the system in the U.S.A. spoke against it but Olivar's enthusiasm did not dim.

He shrugged and laughed and, with an expansive gesture, observed that "Brazil is so big, so big."

"And so vulnerable," we said, "and so swiftly destroyed."

It is true that the country is making rapid strides and the more superhighways they build, the more they rape the land and cover it with concrete, the happier they are. Temporarily. Plant and animal life are being annihilated at an alarming rate, ugliness is manufactured by the hour, a great deal of money is made and the results bruise the heart.

If one wishes to go to South America the time is now, before progress has destroyed it all.

It must be admitted that a potent diversion from these dark thoughts was Carnival. However, the day of the Samba dancing, the peak of the festival was gloomy: gray, drizzling, and overcast. Ruth, Lois, and I went to the zoo which, we assumed would be a good one. The birds and aquatic animals were relatively well off. The great cats were in wretched cages, and two shabby elephants were penned together on a little mound where they couldn't even get on a level footing. A keeper said their quarters were being fixed. It was still inexcusable.

The rain increased until, late in the afternoon, it was falling in sheets. We were fearful that the Samba dancing, would be called off, but at the last minute, in an unaccustomed mood of cooperation, the skies cleared. The festivities would go on as scheduled.

Although we had been fragmented during the day, this time our entire tour of twenty-three drove together in our bus to the Avenida Presidente Vargas, down which the parade would pass.

Think of the greatest crowd you have ever been in. A mass demonstration, a sports stadium, Woodstock, refugees pouring across a border, wherever it was, it was a sylvan retreat compared to the crowds thronging the Avenida. A million and a half people, they said, were in the streets and I would consider the estimate conservative.

Before we got out of the bus, Jorge, our guide urged us to "shake hands please, and form a shane. Do not untake your hands." It was sound advice, but it didn't work. We descended from the bus hanging on to each other's hands or belts or skirts, but the pressure of humanity was so great we were forced apart. Fortunately, we each clutched our own ticket with the gate, row and seat number printed on it and tried hard, by dint of pushing and shoving, to regroup as best we could.

Brazilians have been producing their Carnival for, I believe, something like one hundred years, so I presume they know what they are about, but the grandstands looked to me to be flimsy affairs for the crush of humanity they were accommodating.

The crowd was in high good humor which was reassuring, and I just hoped that no ill-advised jibe, no sudden squall of temper would shift the wind. As it was, we were trampled on and knocked about but in a mood of cheerful enthusiasm.

The grandstand seats were backless wooden benches and the walk ways between no more than planks eight or ten inches wide. Trying to pass those illegally standing there, as you shoved and inched toward your allotted place was no easy task, but the real trouble came when you found Brazilians, who had arrived early, seated in your seat refusing to budge. You showed them your numbered ticket to prove that spot belonged to you, that it had been bought and paid for. You cajoled, you pleaded, you shouted, you spit vitriol, they looked the other way. I tried to imagine the reaction to such behavior in the Yankee Stadium or the Rose Bowl.

Most of our group did manage to pry themselves into place, I did not. There didn't seem to be any ushers or attendants about and when we leaned down over the barrier to appeal to the police on the ground they shrugged and hurried away. Some went to gather up those who had fainted or had been hurt in the crush and who were being placed in a small white ambulance that continued its busy runs throughout the evening, in no way dampening the crowd's enthusiasm.

There was one brief moment of glory provided by, of all people, Dolly Casten. She and Maurice had got into their own places when someone kicked him in the back. Her reaction was automatic and instantaneous. In one unbroken curve she swept her heavy white handbag from her lap landing it square in the middle of the offender's stomach, knocking the wind out of him. We all cheered.

But Lois, Romney, and I were still out of luck. Our inability to dislodge Brazilians from our rightful places obliged us either to sit on their laps, which wasn't altogether practical, or to stand directly in front of them, their bent knees pushed into the back of ours. We had the satisfaction of blocking their view but our discomfort was such that it was not rewarding. Where were you, oh Jorge, when we needed you most? Perhaps he would have had no better luck unseating the usurpers than we had, but he could at least have sworn at them in their own tongue.

The parade, procession, dance, performance . . . it is hard to classify it, was underway when we arrived. It starts about eight at night and goes on until five, six, or seven the next morning. I understand that many people stick it out. We were not among them, nevertheless it is a fantastic affair and a once in a lifetime experience.

Throughout the year the Cariocas, the people of Rio de Janeiro, plan their great spectacle. They rehearse the dances and routine the processions. They write the songs, which may be satirical and political, they may be lamentations or treat of love or recall history, and they are sung by everyone. The samba schools, the dancing groups composed of about two hundred people each, come prancing down the great avenue to the never-ending beat of the bands, their fabulous costumes glittering in the sparkling colored lights of the enormous electrical displays. The illuminations and the costumes are unimaginably brilliant, and the color of the bodies they adorn rich and varied.

About 60 percent of the Brazilian population is white, the other 40 percent a mixture of Negro, white, Indian, and Asian. Dazzling jewels on dark-hued bodies glitter and flash in the light. Crimson and gold and silver and great splashes of blinding white, leaves of green and purple and tangerine, curling plumes, spikey feathers, frosted stag antlers, swirl by the bedazzled spectator. For sheer vitality, there cannot be anything on earth to match it.

Along with the dancing throngs fantastic animals (of cloth, wood, jewels and papier-mâché) cavort gaily down the center of the wide aisle formed by the packed grandstands to the cacophony of drums and fiddles, pipes, guitars, and tambourines. This is too much splendor and excitement to be rained out, so I hope the Brazilians will change the date of their unique festival from February to a more stable season of the year.

There are apartment houses lining the Avenida Presidente Vargas and I would suggest to anybody contemplating Rio at Carnival time that he move heaven and earth to get a seat in somebody's window where he can watch in comfort, and for a little while, the unparalleled outpouring of energy, high spirits, rhythmic noise and exuberant imagination.

CHAPTER THREE

Russia

There are three things the prospective traveler to Russia does well to bear in mind. One: It is their country. Two: Most foreigners are profoundly relieved that this is so. Three: You don't *have* to go.

I do not want to sound ungracious and number three does not apply to diplomats and businessmen but I do think the casual tourist should weigh his prejudices and preconceived notions and decide whether he is willing to risk a few surprises, pleasant and unpleasant. If he is he will see a vast land and have a curious and memorable experience.

In our own case Wanda Jablonski, the friend who had been instrumental in getting us to Saudi Arabia in 1969,* was again the catalyst. Wanda is the publisher and editor of a trade paper, *Petroleum Intelligence Weekly,* widely respected in its field. For business reasons she was going to Russia when the World Petroleum Congress met there for its eighth session in June of 1971.

We are neighbors in the country and lunching one day with my husband and me she observed that she didn't see why she should

---

* See *Around the World and Other Places.*

have to go off all by herself to join the 5000 delegates who were expected to gather in Moscow from all parts of the world. Since Norton and I were such travel buffs why didn't we come along too?

"Dear," I said, "travel, yes. Oil, no. I mean we're ignorant." My husband concurred. "What we know about oil you could put under your little fingernail."

Wanda chose to regard this as a non sequitur. "Nonsense. I feel the need of a temporary new director on my staff. Norton, I appoint you to the job." My husband accepted the position with a deprecatory little gesture and I seemed to see oil rigs sprouting from his shoulders.

"What about me?" I demanded, "What will I be?" My friend looked at me coldly. "You," she said, "will be the director's wife."

"Oh."

"You don't sound madly enthusiastic."

"No, no I'm delighted. I *am* a wife after all."

"That's right." Miss Jablonski and Dr. Brown spoke in unison.

"Have you any objections?" my husband added.

"Darling, don't be ridiculous. Of course not. Being your wife is my pride and happiness. I was just wondering though . . ."

"What?"

"Well, couldn't I maybe have a title too? Just a little one, Wanda? Nothing pretentious."

The publisher gracefully tossed me a fish. "You can be a secretary," she said, "a recording secretary. You can take minutes. That'll make it legitimate."

We could always have gone to Russia on our own but Wanda tempted us. "The Russians have been wanting the Petroleum Congress for a long time," she said. "I suspect we will get some really red carpet treatment."

That appealed to our greed and snobbism. Accordingly, in our official capacities of staff members of P.I.W., we joined Cook's Tour A 8014, leaving New York June 5th. It was flying delegates to the Moscow Congress proper and then taking a splinter group of thirty-four across Russia returning to New York via Tokyo and San Francisco.

The pleasant entrée to the substantial main course was a three day stopover in London. We shopped, we enjoyed the numerous parks of the city, we went twice to the theatre and on Sunday we drove into Surrey to dine with Bill Travers and his beautiful wife, Virginia McKenna. We had first met them in Africa in 1964 when they were there filming *Born Free* and had become extremely fond of them.

Their house is set in the deep country that Great Britain, despite her population of over 55,000,000 crowded into 94,000 square miles, preserves with such tenacity and wisdom.

On the way down we passed great walls of rhododendrons and rambler roses spilling over cottage fences and drove through green tunnels of trees arching over the narrow winding roads. Lovely.

Although I consider my husband a combination of compass and homing pigeon when it comes to ferreting out obscure locations, in this instance a rented car and native driver seemed the better part of prudence.

Our man was named Charlie and we gathered he worked week days driving his employer's Rolls-Royce but weekends he was on his own time. He was impressed when we told him our destination—the Traverses were well-known theatre and movie stars long before *Born Free*—and he was quite overcome when, on his return from the village where we had sent him to get his supper, our hostess invited him into the kitchen and gave him a piece of cake. On the way back to London, he said, "When I tell my 'govenor' Virginia McKenna gave me a piece of chocolate cake with her *own hands* he won't believe me."

The Traverses, their four children and assorted animals, spend as much time as possible in Surrey when they are not working on a new African venture.

We had seen the three older children in Africa when they were much smaller. The newcomer, Daniel, aged four, was in bed, so regretfully we did not meet him. Ginny said that when they show him pictures of themselves and the other kids in Africa he keeps demanding, "But where am I, where am I?" It is difficult to explain nonexistence to a four-year-old.

At dinner we discovered that Mrs. Travers had recently become a vegetarian although there was a roast chicken for Bill and us. Mr. Travers seemed not altogether enchanted by his wife's new religion and I should think it must be confusing to the children. But Ginny feels strongly on the subject.

At that time she was troubled because she was still wearing shoes and carrying a handbag of leather. However she told us that a compassionate and understanding friend, a vegetarian of longer standing, had said to her that one does these things gradually. I imagine it is like embracing Catholicism or Mormonism or Buddhism. One cannot go whole hog at one fell swoop and God is tolerant of novitiates.

After their picture, *Born Free,* was released Bill followed it with a documentary, *The Lions Are Free,* which he produced himself. It shows George Adamson rehabilitating the lions who had been used in the movie so they could learn to fend for themselves in the bush. This film, presented on television in Great Britain and the United States won considerable acclaim.

The Traverses were leaving within a few days to return to Africa to finish another documentary, *The Lion at World's End.* This one would be about Christian, the affectionate young cub Bill had discovered in an antique shop in a section of London called World's End.

He had gone in originally in search of a desk. The two young men who ran the place were short on the particular kind of desk he was looking for but they did say, "Come on down to the cellar. We've got something there that will interest you." Supposing that they meant to show him a fine piece of furniture Bill accompanied them.

It is probably an understatement to say that when he saw a playful six-month-old lion, he was astonished. That, however, is what the young men had saddled themselves with, although, to be sure he had been only six weeks old when they had purchased him in Harrods, London's famed department store.

Their problem was all too obvious. It's not easy to bring up a growing lion in a London antique shop. Mr. Travers dropping in that way was obviously the hand of Providence at work.

Bill offered to give the beguiling beast temporary sanctuary in Surrey and a few days later Christian departed his lair of signed pieces and rare *bibelots* in a gypsy caravan trailer hitched on behind the Traverses car.

Sometime after that Bill took the two boys and his boarder to Africa and George Adamson's camp in the bush, Christian's future home.

The Traverses had some wonderfully funny stills from the early takes of *The Lion at World's End.* Two especially won our hearts. The first was where Christian, recognizing one of his owners who had been away in Kenya for a few days, leaps into his arms nearly bowling him over with the ardor of his greeting and the other showed the Traverses seated on a bench with the lion's great head nuzzling into Bill's neck. That one they asked us to take to a Russian friend of theirs when he and Ginny heard we were en route to Moscow.

Before Moscow, however, we had to stop at Helsinki, regretfully only the airport, and then fly to Leningrad. In Helsinki we were to change from the Finnair plane from London to the Aeroflot that would fly us to Peter the Great's Window on the West.

Since we had a couple of hours to wait I visited the buffet. Knowing that it would be late by the time we got to our hotel I thought to cache away a little sustenance just in case and after buying sausage, cheese, and good brown bread felt fortified and secure.

About 7 P.M. we left for the forty-minute flight to Leningrad. We took off in the bright daylight of a northern summer night, a daylight which though somewhat subdued by the weather still glimmered through the chill rain which, after the first day, was to be our lot in Leningrad.

The plane was uncomfortable and the refreshments consisted of an apple, a piece of candy, orange juice, and a small glass of warm champagne. Well, you can't do an awful lot in forty minutes.

We touched down and seventy-one naïve Americans struggled from their cramped seats expecting the steps to be rolled forward and

the doors to be opened. It was a *long* time before that happened.
First a blond young man came aboard and gathered up our passports, then, when we were allowed out we learned the tourist's first
harsh lesson. This is the People's State and none of the people are
porters. We each kicked and shoved our own luggage along into the
indescribable confusion of the customs shed. We were packed together writhing and muttering like a gigantic can of loquacious
worms.

Finally a large tough blond woman barked at me to come forward.
Norton had been swallowed up in the density some way back, so I
hoisted my luggage onto the counter as best I could. When she waved
me forward after the most desultory search of only my briefcase I
pulled the bags down again. That part hadn't been bad at all and I
breathed a sigh of relief. Too soon as it turned out. I thought to
shove my way through the chaos into the open air when another
female official stopped me and said, "Any food?" Surprised by the
question I told the truth.

"Yes," I said.

"Give," she said.

"But it isn't fruit or seeds or anything like that."

"Give." I gave. And kicked myself. Her question had been automatic. She hadn't even seen the small plastic bag held behind my
capacious handbag. I could easily have retained it. She snatched it,
however, and departed. I do not doubt she had a very nutritious supper that night.

On the bus driving to the hotel we met our first Intourist guide,
Anna. She spoke good English and was, I thought, not unattractive.
Dr. Brown thought differently. "Face of washed granite," he said.

The Hotel Leningrad, large and Hilton-like, rises on the banks of
the Neva. Anchored under our windows was the cruiser *Aurora*
whose guns on October 7, 1917, fired that other shot heard round
the world, starting a revolution that had very little to do with life,
liberty, or the pursuit of happiness. Yet it would be frivolous to deny
that there was not ample provocation for a demand for change.

Our room and bath were small but adequate and the bath water, while café au lait in color, was hot, soft, and abundant. We had been warned so we came prepared. There are no stoppers in the washbasins of Russia. Most of the tubs do have them but never the basins and the ones on the tubs are firmly anchored by an iron chain so they cannot be pressed into double duty. At this point it occurs to the visitor that if you are going to have a dictatorship it is better to have dictators with a little sophistication. Perhaps those who can understand that hand towels three yards long and bath towels of extremely small squares of thin rough cloth are not necessary or adequate. Also that bath mats are a nice idea. Nor would there be any real harm in placing the towels, such as they are, in the bathrooms. We were baffled at first. Where to find them? Of course! Hanging over the headboards of the beds. Where else would they be?

On our first night in Leningrad it was nearly 1 A.M. when we got to the dining room and although the food by that time was naturally dried out they were still serving it. It was sufficient and we were grateful. One entire wall of the restaurant was taken up by a great bay window overlooking the Neva. It sounds dramatic but unfortunately the view was distorted because the glass was flawed.

The next morning a tour had been planned for the wives of the petroleum group but Norton and I took off by ourselves for Leningrad's famous Hermitage Museum. The Winter Palace, where it is housed, is a vast building and elegant. Leningrad itself is an elegant city. The terrain on which it is built is flat and the city is without a skyline. I must say I prefer cities with silhouettes. Prague, Edinburgh, Istanbul, the domes and spires and chimney pots of Paris, or New York which is nothing *but* skyline. Yet with its broad avenues and network of rivers and canals Leningrad has a character of its own. Founded in 1703 by Peter I (Peter the Great), it was called Saint Petersburg until 1914 when it became Petrograd—Petersburg being thought to sound too Germanic. Ten years later, on the death of their hero, the Russians changed the name to Leningrad.

It was Catherine the Great who started the Hermitage collection when in 1764 she bought 225 pictures in one fell swoop, from a Prussian merchant, Gotzkowsky. In so doing she was following the custom of the eighteenth century when indiscriminate en bloc buying was the passion of the art world. Catherine wrote proudly to Voltaire that none but herself and the mice could look at her pictures. There's status for you! Perhaps she felt that lesser eyes than her own would bore holes through the canvas.

Gradually, of course, others, probably to begin with only the upper crust, began to gain access to the treasures and by the end of the eighteenth century the Hermitage ranked as one of the great galleries of Europe.

After the October or November revolution of 1917, it depends on whose calendar you use, what the Soviet Government euphemistically refers to as the "nationalization" took place. That is to say the museum was further enriched by the famous private collections confiscated from the Yusupovs, the Shuvalovs, and others.

Catherine's original "hermits dwelling" at last became so chockablock full of masterpieces that the entire vast stretch of the Winter Palace was put at the disposal of its directors for housing what is today estimated to be 2,500,000 exhibits.

One of the most dazzling rooms, although no pictures hang there, is room 204 in the Pavilion Hall on the first floor. It is two stories high with an upper gallery, moldings, columns, arches, tall french windows and glittering chandeliers. The building was designed by Bartolomeo Rastrelli, an architect born in Paris of Italian parents. The façade is the soft green of a fresh almond shell and it is broken by flat white columns—coloring and design we discovered to be typical of Russian palaces. They may be blue, green or, as in the case of the Kremlin, yellow. All with white columns.

The Winter Palace that one sees today is actually not Rastrelli's work as the building was gutted by fire in 1837 and rebuilt in the 1840s by two of the leading architects of the period, Stasov and Bryulov, although the façade is still as Rastrelli designed it.

Norton and I were extremely lucky for Thomas Hoving, director of New York's Metropolitan Museum, had given us letters of introduction to Mr. Boris Petrovsky, the director of the Hermitage, and to an assistant of his, the charming and erudite Miss Larissa Dukel-skaya.

On the morning of our first visit we tried to find them. It was then we learned that trying to make contact with Russians is a process so formidable that the strongest spirit quails. In fairness it must be said that this is not because the O.G.P.U., the dreaded secret police of the Stalin era, are standing over the citizens preventing them from fraternizing with foreigners—although even today too much fraterniz-ing is not considered the healthiest of pastimes—rather it is the language barrier that is the hurdle. The language and the Cyrillic alphabet.

Even if unversed in European tongues a vague, tenuous, commu-nication is sometimes possible because, given the spelling, one may guess at the meaning. Not so with Russian.

This truth burst upon us when we first saw the letters which because of their location, on a public building, obviously had to be U.S.S.R. The way the Russians write them is C.C.C.P. P is R and C's are S and the Russian word for Union begins with our S. The word we came to know best was Pectopah and the Pectopah was the place we most frequently gravitated to because that is a restaurant.

Our trouble the first morning, when we were trying to get in touch with Mr. Petrovsky, was twofold. To begin with we had not the faintest idea of where, in all those acres of building, his office might be located nor, of course, did we know how to ask for him.

In the end, however, our perseverance paid off. Having walked through miles of galleries up and down endless staircases, there are 117 (our legs began to feel as though we had navigated them all), having approached countless elderly female guardians of the mu-seum's treasures and presented the carbon of Mr. Hoving's letter pointing out Mr. Petrovsky's name on it—the name, written in the Roman alphabet, was not much help to them—we finally sensed that the hunt was narrowing down. Sure enough, eventually we were led to the door of an office where there were several people who spoke French and English. Falling upon them like desert wayfarers upon the water hole we made known our hope that we might have the pleasure of meeting the boss. Our wish was fulfilled. Mr. Petrovsky finally emerged from his sanctum and was most courteous. There too, however, we had something of a communication problem since his English was scanty and, although his German was fluent, ours was not.

After about five minutes of badinage he skillfully, and very intelligently, extricated himself from our company and sent out to us the friendly and cooperative Larissa Dukelskaya with brown eyes, soft brown hair, and a sympathetic manner. English might have been her native tongue.

What, she inquired, would we especially like to see?

"The Treasury."

"Come, let us go. But please, now I will take your coat."

That first day in Leningrad was our only day of sunshine but it was brisk and the museum was chilly. I should have much preferred to keep my coat on but something in her manner warned me that she took it not so much out of courtesy but because she was required to.

It was our first encounter with that old Russian custom which as much as any other goes a long way to divide what we think of as the free world from that of the dictators. Keeping your coat on indoors in Russia, no matter how public the place, is far worse than keeping your hat on as the flag goes by. It is worse than going into a Catholic church in Spain with your upper arms bare. It is worse than telling a mother her baby bores you. *It simply isn't done.* Try hanging onto your coat in a restaurant or in the theatre! Were it a question of a tip for the coat-room attendant it would be understandable but that isn't the reason. The attendants don't get tips. It's custom. "It is," as the Russians say rather grandly, "our culure."

Also, it was later explained to us that in winter when the weather is bitter cold a lot of people bundled up in heavy coats simply take up too much room in a theatre seat. There, one may concede, they do have a point but why not a tailored coat in a chilly museum? Perhaps they fear you might rip a Rembrandt from its frame, roll it up and walk out. It's unlikely but they are taking no chances. And of course many of the Treasury items are small and theoretically filchable although securely housed in heavy glass cases. Before entering Norton had to give up his camera, although it was allowed in all other parts of the museum. I surrendered my handbag, abstracting my wallet as unobtrusively as possible although one gets the impression that a theft in the Soviet Union would be a newsworthy event.

The Treasury consists of gold Greek jewelry and extraordinarily fine Scythian sculptures of golden animals found in burial mounds in the Ukraine and dating from 700 to 300 B.C. There are shield ornaments and a superb woman's comb topped with a delicate sculpture of tiny golden warriors in battle. There are necklaces and diadems and earrings of subtle workmanship.

In Greece I have seen pieces that are as fine and, to my way of thinking, some that are finer but it would be a sorry oversight to go to the Hermitage and not see the Treasury. The collection is open to the public but one does not view it automatically. It is best to arrange beforehand, either through your hotel or Intourist if you want to visit it. There are also some charming small trees made of jewels. Jeweled dresses and waistcoats were at one time the fashion and when the mode changed the aristocracy thriftily salvaged the gems and made them into sparkling bibelots.

An especially fascinating exhibit in another part of the museum was unearthed in the burial mounds of the Altai Mountains on the Mongolian border and bears striking witness to the longevity of the deep freeze.

The construction of the mounds apparently was such that the permafrost penetrated the mountain graves and in one of them was found an extraordinary treasure, preserved by the cold, dating back to the fifth or fourth century B.C.

It was a funeral chamber of logs, a coffin with the mummified corpse of a chieftain, a wooden cart made without a single nail, horse masks and harnesses. But even more extraordinary than those objects was a cut woolen hanging or carpet of about 80 square feet. The woven design of abstract figures, horses, stags and seated goddesses in their original colors, beige, red and black were still intact. The tapestry had formed three sides of a funeral tent. They also had uncovered the wooden poles that supported it and the carved bird finials that topped them.

This particular exhibit is unique but the Hermitage examples from more numerous and more familiar sources also rank high. They have a beguiling canvas by the elder Cranach—*Madonna and Child Under an Apple Tree*—El Greco's *The Apostles Peter and Paul*, Rembrandt's *Return of the Prodigal* and another enchanting Rembrandt, a portrait of the wife of his frame maker with a humorous and winsome face.

That afternoon we piled into the first of the buses that were to become so familiar for a tour of the city. As I have said most of the avenues are broad and some 120 bridges crisscross the Neva and narrow canals.

Anna spoke of the terrible siege of Leningrad during World War II when, early in September 1941, the city was surrounded by the Germans. They had forty-three divisions including seven tank divisions and November 7 was the day Hitler planned to hold a victory banquet in the Hotel Astoria.

The civilian population joined the Russian Army in one of the most dramatic and heroic holding actions of human history. They built roads across the frozen rivers so trucks could bring in supplies yet even so toward the end their daily rations consisted of 150 grams of a mixture of sawdust and oil. It was 1944 before the siege was lifted.

In the course of the afternoon we visited St. Isaac's Cathedral, the third largest church in the world after St. Peter's Basilica in Rome and St. Paul's in London. It too has a great dome and flat pilasters of green malachite and lapis lazuli. The wall paintings looked new and shiny and I myself did not think them particularly interesting.

St. Isaac's does have a curious phenomenon that draws a fascinated crowd of spectators and that is a lead weight suspended from the top of the dome on an enormously long piano wire. It clears the floor of the cathedral by only a few inches and without any mechanical assistance it changes position as the earth rotates on its axis. The device may not have much to do with religion but few Russian churches go in for that. They have Lenin instead.

The morning tour, undertaken by some of the others while Norton and I were at the Hermitage, had included the fortress of Peter and Paul where both Gorki and Dostoevski were at one time imprisoned. It was the first edifice to be erected in Peter's new city and it is the burial place of nearly all the Russian Czars, Nicholas II being a notable exception.

According to many authorities his body was hacked to pieces and burned, the remains tossed into an abandoned mine shaft along with those of the Empress Alexandra, their five children, their doctor, and three servants after their murder at Ekaterinburg in July 1918.

Another notable monument is an equestrian statue of Peter the Great with his name carved on the base. Catherine's name is also engraved on it. She had it done for no particular reason, one gathers, just to get into the act too.

There is also a statue of Czar Nicholas I. He was bad news but they leave him there because the statue is unique in equestrian sculpture, the entire weight of rearing horse and rider being supported on the horse's hind legs. Peter's mount rears too but his tail rests on a serpent, so that's cheating a little.

Our bus drove along Nevsky Prospect where there are shops but we weren't allowed to stop and mosey about. Being hungry after so much sight-seeing, thinking wistfully of the pretty and oh so succulent coffee houses of Vienna, or the cafes of almost any European city, of even a New York Schrafft's, I asked Anna, our guide, if there wasn't someplace we could stop for tea.

"No" she said, "in our country everything is very difficult," and she was obviously annoyed with me for making it more so. Wanda agreed with her and said I hadn't caught the spirit of the tour. "Wanting to shop and have tea! How could they keep track of us all?" She was right. In Russia keeping track of foreigners is extremely important.

We were allowed to stop at the Hotel Astoria to ask for mail as that was where we had been told we would be staying but Intourist is capricious and the traveler goes whither it listeth.

The Astoria was in the center of town and on a smaller and more human scale than the Leningrad which while enormous was isolated and a good place for the Russians to stash foreigners whom they don't want wandering about on their own. Basically they are in a bind on that because they are coming to be seduced more and more by the monetary value of the tourist. They yearn more and more for that glorious hard currency he brings into the country.

There was an interesting feature on the Soviet Union published in a June 1971 issue of the *London Financial Times* which explained how the Russians have established a tourist research center in the Siberian town of Akademgorodok.

Once the researchers have learned to pronounce that name they devote their time and effort to studying the value of the globe-trotter and to plotting how best to lure him.

To quote the *Financial Times:* "No straight figures are given out, but, on the average, the profit from one tourist is equal to the export of nine tons of coal, fifteen tons of oil or two tons of grain. If Lake Baikal were fully exploited as a tourist center it could earn twice as much hard currency as the total export of oil. However, this is still far in the future and the Soviet Union is barely able to cope with the present volume of tourists."

As a tourist it makes one feel rich and important and, of course, everything in the country *is* in the making. Not only tourism.

Leningrad is large, Moscow is large, Russia is vast and yet their housing shortage is still serious. Despite the number of hideous barracks-like apartment houses going up all over the country a young married couple with an apartment of their own is enough of a rarity to set tongues wagging. An individual living alone is virtually unheard of. The norm is for two or three or more families to share an apartment with the kitchen and bathroom a communal affair.

When I observed to Margaret Gussow, the wife of one of the Petroleum Congress delegates from California, that I thought the apartments looked distressingly drab from the outside and what must they be like within she replied, "Listen, I agree with you, they're horrible. But I was here twelve years ago. Then people were living in shacks made of flattened tin cans. The barracks are better." They are. And one must admit that American developments such as Lefrak City on the Long Island Expressway are grim manifestations of man's greed and lack of taste.

I doubt that in Russia the gimcrack housing is due to personal greed on the part of government officials. They sincerely want improvement in the lives of the people but the humanities must wait upon giganticism.

First they want the strongest army, navy, and air force in the world. They want the biggest tractors and dams and hydro-electric plants. At long last, *they* want to be top banana. If they could afford to do all that and provide amenities at the same time they would do it. As matters stand now they can't. Therefore decent consumer goods, labor-saving devices, household equipment, appliances that go far to make for practical and convenient living in America and many other countries too, are still ignored. I think the Soviet Government has the *good* of its people at heart, always supposing that good coincides with the government's viewpoint, but I think it cares not a whit for people's happiness or pleasure and any sense of individual freedom is sternly suppressed.

There is one aspect of their way of life, however, that is admirable. Their streets are spotless. I have never seen such clean cities in my life. The fairies who perform this miracle are women; many are old but many are youngish to middle-aged. In the winter it is the women who shovel snow. In summer they use brooms and they use their fingers, bending to pick up cigarette butts and wrappings from any chewing gum children may have been able to wheedle from visitors. The children adore gum and zero in on any passing Americans murmuring and supplicating. Since I dislike chewing gum they found me poor prey but hope in a young breast dies hard and every American was fair game.

Apropos of the street cleaners I don't know how the women are recruited for these jobs. Are they forced into them? Is the pay good? Do they volunteer out of patriotism or is street cleaning the threshold to a better world?

The Russian Government has one tenet that dispensers of indiscriminate American welfare might bear in mind. "He who does not work, neither shall he eat." Obviously no one is speaking of the old or infirm but the attitude of "why shouldn't I give birth to any number of children and why shouldn't we all relax on Welfare?" is unheard of in the Soviet Union.

The Russians are determined educationalists. Eight years of compulsory education are universal but in practice they now usually work out to ten, children attending school from the age of seven to seventeen, with five years of university to follow for those who can pass the exams. As far as we understood, there is none of this open enrollment business because everybody is just as good as everybody else and never mind if you don't get high grades for entrance requirements are too stiff anyway.

Russia is Animal Farm. "All animals are equal but some animals are more equal than others." It is only the more equal ones who get a whack at higher education.

Booklets, pamphlets, brochures in many languages are there for the taking at every airport and in every hotel and I picked up an informative little paperback called *Soviet Union Today*. Some of it may be unintentionally candid but it is instructive and part of what follows is gleaned from its pages. Parenthetically I may say also that it is more readable than most of the propaganda. Wishing to learn how the other sixth lives—Russia covers one sixth of the earth's surface—I had a go at several of the free handouts but the prose is so turgid, sanctimonious, and tendentious that the mind gets mired as in a papyrus swamp and I gave up after a few paragraphs.

A vast emission of hot air is common to bureaucracy the world over, vide among others the U. S. Government and the Pentagon, but the foreigner certainly gets the impression that the Soviet capacity for boring everyone within eye and earshot into insensibility is unparalleled.

It is true, however, as they state, that in all the Russian institutions of learning tuition is free and there is much to be said for the system. Also to be said is that when the state gives you everything the state, not unnaturally, feels that you owe it everything and when you have graduated it sends you where it wants you to go.

Graduate medical students from big cities, for example, are usually sent to practice in remote villages where there may be a genuine need for medical care, but where the individual young doctor may be wretched. At the end of two or three years he has the right to say where he wants to settle down to practice but he cannot choose Moscow unless he was born there. The capital is a separate country and one must have a passport to get in.

This system, while ideal for preventing the population from getting out of hand, leads to irksome labor shortages and one imagines the state must occasionally have to give a little to get a little.

We had heard, and it is true, that women work beside men in road building and in construction. They also man, or woman, the railroad crossings and physically they look fully capable of so doing. I imagine the life of a combat soldier would suit many of them to a T.

We met an American member of the Petroleum Congress who, riding Moscow's famed subway, stood up, poor dolt, to give his seat to an elderly woman. She turned upon him in a rage, berating him in a furious stream of Russian for having dared to assume she was not his physical equal. Women's Lib over there is a fait accompli and makes our leaders of the movement look like fragile Victorian belles.

In Leningrad they go in for buses and tram cars running with what we consider to be the old-fashioned overhead power lines.

They go at a good clip too and you'd best be nimble because they are in no mood to slow for pedestrians. There are few private cars and those there are belong almost exclusively to government officials, government taxi companies or Intourist. A small number of cars are also doled out to artists. Ballet dancers, singers and actors fare reasonably well in that department.

We were told that at one time during his administration Nikita Khrushchev had the idea of introducing hire cars. He felt that since people didn't use a car twenty-four hours a day it would be practical to introduce a method whereby they could rent them when needed. On the face of it it was a good idea but it hit two snags.

Since in the beginning there weren't many of them the hire car immediately became a status symbol. Who was important enough to have first call? A class society was being introduced! That, however, could have been ironed out in time. The real hitch was the fact that they didn't know how to work an insurance system. There was, it appears, a cause célebre which brought about the downfall of Mr. Khrushchev's brain child.

A man rented a car and after driving a few miles got into a collision. No one was injured but his fender was badly bent. Since there are few spare parts in Russia the garage told him it would be a long time, maybe six months, before they could repair it and for every day of those six months he would be obliged to pay rent on the car.

The man understandably let out a howl that echoed through the walls of the Kremlin. The Commissars looked at each other, shrugged, said, "The hell with it" and abolished the system. After all, what did *they* care? They *had their* cars.

While on the subject of automobiles members of the A.P.I. (American Petroleum Industry) noted with sadness that in Leningrad, a city of 4,000,000 people there were four service stations. No point in building what you don't need.

Still, things are loosening up a little. Foreigners may now rent cars and drive themselves around the country but this privilege can hardly be called a jaunty freewheeling vacation. There are road blocks every few miles, papers are checked and a limit is set on the length of time the motorist may take to get from one point to another. The reason for this is to make sure that he hasn't strayed from the designated route into forbidden territory.

We got hold of a map from the American Embassy with the forbidden parts shaded. From a foreigner's point of view much of Russia is very dusky. However it would be foolish to pretend that there isn't visibility over large areas, not only geographic but artistic: museums, theatres, ballets *and* the circus.

I don't go to circuses because I can't bear what they do to wild animals but the Russian circus is so famous that on one of our Leningrad nights we decided we would go. The junket actually was organized by young Ken George of Midland, Texas. Ken was tall, blond, handsome, and the baby of the party. He had his twenty-third birthday in Alma-Ata. He was traveling with his father, Clem George, and I have rarely seen a more affectionate, kidding, happy relationship between father and son.

A member of the tour told me that when she told him I was a writer and planned to do a piece about our trip he said in his slow Texas drawl, "Ah sho hope she isn't plannin' to do little character sketches of us all."

Darling Ken. Looking at him there was deep poignancy in the thought that "Golden lads and girls all must, as chimney sweepers come to dust." He was a golden one.

Not only was he beautiful and courteous, he was extremely bright and a real operator in the nicest way. It was he who reserved a block of seats and advanced money for the circus tickets so we wouldn't have to fuss about them individually.

The circus was under canvas, the big tent set up in what we took to be fairgrounds halfway between the city and the airport. There was a large crowd and for the first time we saw children.

The trapeze work was extraordinarily good, especially a girl who, hoisted to the top of the tent, swung out and round and round from a metal ring holding on to a tab by her teeth. A great brown bird, an eagle I imagine, was perched in the ring, wings outspread. I do not know if he was merely decorative or if he had a function. Maybe his wings gave a certain balance to the aerial circling. I prefer to think he was of some use. Why imprison a free creature simply for effect?

Dogs and horses in circuses do not upset me. If well treated they can have a reasonably decent life and there was a brief comical act with four dogs that was enjoyable. A man held out a stick at shoulder height and one after another three borzois dashed out, leapt over the stick and ran off. Then out rushed a Scotty who, going hell for leather, darted between the man's legs and vanished. Big laugh. Big applause.

There were funny clowns with an infinite variety of hats, some brilliant trampolin acrobats and a magician with six pretty girl assistants and bowls of water which kept appearing and disappearing in magical fashion.

We were nearing the end of the performance and I was beginning to think we would get away scot-free without having to see any wild animals but mine was a fool's paradise. The last act of course was the Spectacle. A huge coarse mesh cage was dexterously suspended by ropes from the top of the tent. Eight beautiful tigers were herded into it through a metal grill work tunnel.

We then had the usual business of the tigers sitting on stools, a trainer goading them to show how courageous he was and by way of finale forced leaps through burning hoops.

Trying to soothe my agitation Norton said that the tigers looked sleek and well cared for and so they did, but it is scarcely a life for a wild animal.

The next morning our entire tour group went again to the Hermitage. The day before when I had told Larissa Dukelskaya that we would be returning she gave me two or three phone numbers where I could reach her in the museum. "Call me when you are here," she said, "and I will come out to meet you."

I spoke to Wanda. "You haven't seen the Rembrandts so I tell you what. Let's go through with the group; then you and I will slip away and get in touch with Larissa."

Wanda warmed to the idea and slipping away was no trick. It is keeping together that requires not only determination but glue since the Hermitage, indeed all the museums we visited, are crowded with Russians admiring their treasures.

To a lesser extent we experienced the difficulties of the day before in cornering our quarry but by pointing to the numbers on the post card Larissa had given me and uttering her name I was able to get one of the ancient guardians to let me use a telephone. It was when Larissa asked me where we were that I was stymied. "Well now let me see. We're in a rather small hall where there are some big vases and . . ."

"Let me speak to the woman," Larissa said. I handed over the phone. The guardian may not have been an Intellect but she knew where she was and within minutes our friend appeared.

The museum's collection of Western European art is, of course, world famous and one would require many, many days to see and savor it all. To mention only the French; paintings from the fifteenth to the twentieth century occupy over forty rooms. They have some of the finest examples of the Impressionists that exist anywhere, Gauguin, Picasso, Renoir, Van Gogh, Monet, Cézanne . . . the only one of the great names not represented by his most outstanding work is perhaps Matisse. When I told Larissa that the previous summer I had seen the Matisse exhibition at the Grand Palais in Paris she looked a little wistful. "You have seen the best," she said. She then gave Wanda and me an unexpected treat.

The Kröller-Müller Museum of Otterlo in the Netherlands had sent the Hermitage a large number of early Van Goghs for a loan exhibition. It was not yet hung but Larissa led us into a big room where there was no one but ourselves and there, propped up against the walls, were some of the most wonderful Van Goghs I have ever seen: sketches, water colors, and oils.

We also looked at the museum's two small and beautiful da

Vincis. That is to say we ducked and peered as best we could over the shoulders and under the arms of thronging Russians.

The going was a little easier in the long hall known as the Gallery of the Patriotic War of 1812 (the Russians always make sure you understand that every war is patriotic) where hang portraits of the three hundred and thirty-two generals who opposed Napoleon. Many were painted from life or from miniatures but when they came to a chap whom none of the three artists, an Englishman and two Russians, had seen and when they could find no surviving likeness, they tastefully upholstered an empty frame in dark green silk, engraved the name and rank on a small plaque and hung it anyway.

For some reason it reminded me of the story of the tourist in Israel gazing at the grave of the Unknown Soldier. "So that's the tomb of the Unknown Soldier," he said reverently.

His companion, a native Israeli, said, "Yes that's the tomb of Abie Finklestein."

"What do you mean?" asked the traveler indignantly, "It's the unknown soldier."

The other man shrugged. "As a soldier he was unknown, as a tailor he was famous."

At twelve-thirty we had regretfully to leave our attractive and knowledgeable guide but that was the precise time we had been instructed to return to the bus parked in the magnificent Palace Square. We hurried away for taxis are sparse and take forever to come and the walk back to the hotel is a hike no one would wish to make under any conditions, let alone after a couple of hours of traipsing around the enormous museum.

A tour had been planned for Peterhof or Petrodvorets in the afternoon, the idea being to go by hydrofoil and return by bus, but the weather was so rainy and miserable it had been decided to make the round trip by bus.

Also Larissa had suggested to Norton and me that instead of Petrodvorets we visit Pushkin, the old summer palace, Czarskoye Selo, or Czars Village. "I think," she said, "you will find it more interesting."

Nicholas II and Alexandra had lived there and there they had been imprisoned by the Bolsheviks. We decided to go and thus encountered one of the mysteries of Russian transportation. A private car would have come to over $60 and that we decided was too steep but we could rent an Intourist car for $11. We didn't understand it but we took it.

Driving out of the city we passed the circus tent, wet and sorrowful under the rain, and I thought of the poor sad beasts and the great bird immured there. The crushing boredom of captive animals is heartbreaking.

In my imagination I had pictured Czarskoye Selo as being small. Well, small in the sense that the Petit Trianon is small. How wrong I was! The Summer Palace of the erstwhile Czars is gigantic. Very nearly the size of the Winter Palace. Those lads went rustic in spades.

It too was built by Rastrelli as well as, piquantly enough, a Scotsman named Cameron.

Like the town house its columns also are white but its color is a deep brilliant blue.

Pushkin, as it is now called, was bombed and terribly mutilated by the Germans during the war. It was looted as well by the Nazi generals who occupied it. There was an extraordinary salon paneled entirely with sheets of amber. One of the generals stripped this from the walls and carried it away, doubtless with an eye to installing it in his own house.

He was later captured by the Russians and said he would tell them where he had hidden the panels but he died—whether he was killed or not the guide does not say—before he could divulge the secret. The panels have never been found. The Russians think they may have been transported to the Gulf of Finland and hidden near there or, that in all probability, they burned as amber is highly flammable.

Later on, in Moscow, we met a German oil man who observed that a friend of his had got to Czarskoye Selo during the war. "He didn't do it any good," I said.

"Of course," added the German hastily, "that's as far as he did go. From there he went home."

"He was wise."

The Russians are naturally bitter over the havoc wrought by the enemy but it was no worse than that created by the Russian troops who marched into Austria. It was no worse than what the Americans did to Hiroshima nor than what we have been doing to Vietnam for a good many years. "War," as General Sherman succinctly observed, "is hell."

In the palace there are a great many photographs of it as it looked before the siege and of how it looked when bombs had destroyed whole sections of the central wing. The work now going on is that of restoration. It is a formidable task but they are pushing ahead.

There are enchanting rooms with mirrors and delicate plaster carvings, handsome mantelpieces and slender bamboo-like columns. Much of the interior loveliness is due to Mr. Cameron. There are superb tiled stoves, walls stretched with patterned silk—the patterns copied from the original, and beautifully proportioned furniture including a fanciful white chest of drawers carved from the ivory tusks of walrus.

The great central hall with its quadruple staircase rises three stories high. The balustrades, the elaborate carvings of wood and plaster are painted dead white and crimson silk curtains hang at the windows. It was magnificent the day we were there and with sunlight pouring in it must be breathtaking.

Of all the splendor, however, the inlaid marquetry floors are probably the most notable feature. The floors are exquisite and the caretakers rightly insist that visitors wear felt slippers over their own shoes.

It is true today that the pride of any country is its past. In France the châteaux of the Loire, Carcassonne, the Cathedrals of Chartres and Notre Dame. In England the Tower and the Stately Homes and Stonehenge. In Italy the churches, the palazzi, the frescoes. Reverence for and recognition of what has been is universal throughout Europe and Asia. The temple complex of Angkor Wat, the fabulous carvings and palaces of India, the art and architecture of ancient China and Japan, these are jealously guarded treasures.

Russia is no different. The only thing about the Russian attitude that makes the visitor smile a little is that their ancient wonders were created by men and women now held in scathing disrepute. It is unfortunate that the Exploiters, the grinder downers of the working class had so much taste, imagination and money. And seeing the enormous amount of skill and labor, not to mention rubles, going into the restoration of Pushkin, a beautiful but empty shell where nobody dwells, one wonders what those who are obliged to live crowded together in cheaply constructed apartments think about it.

After spending a couple of hours at the palace we returned to Leningrad, where Wanda joined us for a hurried dinner and then she and I took off for the ballet.

The interior of the opera house is pure delight: pale blue, gold and crystal. Perhaps not quite as beautiful as that gem, La Fenice, in Venice nor as cosy and amusing as the tiny theatre in the castle of Gripsholm Slott, outside of Stockholm, which is one of the oldest theatres in Europe but a lovely affair nonetheless.

The first act was vocal. A male and female choir massed against a gigantic hammer and sickle and over to one side a hefty tenor, all of them singing their lungs out. Russians have good voices but the first act would have been more enjoyable were there less of it. They are a patient people who like to get their money's worth but Wanda and I felt it was overly long. I was just as glad Norton wasn't with us. My dear husband hates the theatre and it is almost impossible to get him to go to one in New York where he understands the language. He was not very fertile soil for any Russian pastiche.

After intermission came *La Sylphide,* with fresh and pretty costumes and good dancers but I ceased long ago to be galvanized by that particular ballet.

In the second intermission we raided the bar for vodka and

open-faced garlic sausage sandwiches. Very good and they sustained us for the third act, a Shostakovich ballet in three parts composed during the Nazi occupation. The three segments were Serene Happiness, Invasion, Requiem. The titles evoke the mood and perhaps for Russians the remembered emotional impact makes it dramatic and interesting but as a work of art standing on its own Wanda and I found it rather dull. We are neither of us Clive Barnes, however, and our judgment may be wrong.

Early the next morning we engaged in the first of what were to be countless hassles over luggage but in fairness I must say that wherever else they may have fallen down the Russians were extremely efficient in handling the mountains of bags that inevitably accompany a large tour. In very nearly a full month's traveling over that huge land they never lost a piece and our bags were picked up and delivered to our rooms with commendable speed.

Indeed it was the pick-up part that induced ulcers. As any woman knows, toilet articles and make-up are the last items to be packed but they had to be ready on the nose with one's other bags. We all carried a couple of pieces of hand luggage but the pots and the bottles and the jars from which facial camouflage emerges are the heavy items and no husband wants to lug them. Also, in good Dr. Brown's case, he was already laden like a Sicilian donkey with thousands of films and every known make of camera.

He had been much concerned before we left home having been told that each traveler was limited to one camera and ten rolls of film. There is not a word of truth in this. Take all you want, the Russians don't turn a hair.

We had first learned we need have no worries on that score from a friend who returned from the U.S.S.R. two or three days before we were leaving. I pumped her for every scrap of information she could give me and when I asked about cameras and film she said, "Don't worry. There was one fellow in our party, he isn't going to know where he's been until his film is developed. He never looked at anything. He was buried in his camera the entire time."

Norton doesn't go that far, he uses his own eyes too but he is a camera buff and I am the buffee. There is only one kind of handbag I can possibly travel with and that is the open tote bag. My own props—compact, lipstick, comb, etc.—are held to a minimum since I am the depository for the master's various lenses which he changes with frequency and speed to accommodate light and subject.

The morning of our departure from Leningrad we took off from the hotel at ten-thirty in the pouring rain. Poor Anna, who was not of a particularly ebullient temperament in any case, was distraught. Not that she cared about us personally one way or the other but I suppose humanly she wanted travelers to be charmed by her native city, which, to a great extent, we were.

I know that Irving R. Levine in his book, *Travel Guide to Russia,* published in 1960 and written after he had spent a great deal of time there, recommends winter as the ideal time to visit the country. He finds it more romantic under snow. I imagine there is a good deal to be said for that point of view but I can't think Leningrad would be an ideal location. In summer it is light all the time and in winter it is dark. That was another of Anna's woes. She told us she earned 150 rubles a month for which she worked seven days a week. Intourist guides are given two months' paid vacation but in the case of the Leningraders this period is given in the winter. It is dark for virtually the whole twenty-four hours of the day and they have no place to go.

En route to the airport we stopped for lunch at a restaurant called the Rossiya where we fought, and lost, the battle of the coats, despite the fact that a good draft swept through the dining room. The soup was good, the rest of the food negligible.

Our plane was large and filled with Russians and before take-off one of them was playing a guitar and singing softly. It was charming, much more enjoyable than that canned stuff which assaults the ears in our dear homeland.

As the motors revved, he put away the guitar and the charm ended. Their equipment is old, the toilets filthy and the food laughable. If you don't happen to be hungry. If you are you stay that way since you really can't digest what they give you.

At home we have been tutored to bring our seats to an upright position for landings and take-offs. In Russia they don't care. You may be upright or you may be reclining and you may stay that way throughout the flight due to the fact that many of the seats don't work. Service is virtually nil and, in summertime, the heat inside the plane intense since the pilots control the air conditioning and don't turn it on until they have reached a certain altitude and cruising speed. As we were to learn, the Trans Siberian Railway has three classes: hard, first and de luxe. Passenger ships, at least the one we were on, two: cabin and first. Domestic airplanes one: terrible.

Still, in spite of the crates they fly the pilots seem to know their job in that they get you up, carry you over and bring you down without mishap. That fundamentally is the function of a plane but although the affluent society may bring about the downfall of human and spiritual values, for the little time left us, the living is sweet. Dear Pan Am and Qantas. Dear Alitalia, dear Air France, Varig, BOAC, TWA, American, all the rest. You are nice, nice planes.

There was only one time when the pilot seemed a bit hysterical. The wheels hit the runway at I should think roughly three hundred miles an hour. After he had got his breath back and we were taxiing to the terminal dear Dr. Brown said mildly, "Well, I certainly thought we were going to ground loop."

The flight from Leningrad to Moscow takes about an hour and we set down in hot sunny weather, a welcome change from the cold, rainy city of the north.

There was a wild churning for luggage, with the men of our party mostly unloading the bags themselves, so we could attach tags with our room number at the Hotel Rossiya which had already been given to us by John Gessner, the Cook's tour manager. Happily, as the flight was domestic we had no customs problem.

On the way into the city everyone peered eagerly from the windows of the bus at the rows of big modern apartment houses which were being built. Also I noticed for the first time that strange anachronism: the Russians don't cut the grass. This is understandable in the country where I believe they use it for fodder but in city parks and along the streets it is mostly scraggly and gone to seed, making the whole place look bedraggled. Because of this and the many cottonwood trees the city of Moscow is full of what appears to be dandelion fluff. It floats through the air and great drifts pile along the gutters. It is soon gathered up by the ubiquitous female street cleaners but it can't be good for those prone to hay fever or asthma for it lodges in the ears and tickles the nostrils of one and all.

Along the road were a good many blue and white banners proclaiming a welcome to the Eighth World Petroleum Conference and Norton and I nudged each other saying "That's us" and Wanda beamed approvingly. "What did I tell you? Red carpet."

Nor were banners the only decoration. Russians do not have billboards desecrating the countryside and that is an eminently civilized idea but they do have posters and statues of Lenin in such profusion on every road, in every street and square, that you get the impression he must be running for office.

We were making quips about this when, glancing out the windows as we neared the hotel, there it was! Red Square! I should be less than honest if I did not say my heart beat faster. One has heard of it for so long, seen so many pictures, witnessed on television so many parades and suddenly, here we were! Of the places I have seen I think perhaps my favorite urban site in all the world is the Piazza Navona in Rome but Red Square is very beautiful and marvelously dramatic.

We passed St. Basil's Cathedral, that enchanting conglomeration of colorful towers and onion domes which, built by Czar Ivan the Terrible to commemorate the freeing of the city of Kazan from the Tartars, seems, to many foreigners, to epitomize Russia. I have just stated the Soviet version of why it was built. The Columbia Encyclopedia, which may be considered a more objective source says of Ivan's adventure, "He conquered Kazan (1552)."

We had a quick look up Red Square, from the long Kremlin wall stretching on our left to the austere Historical Museum at the upper end and then drove on to the Rossiya.

The Russians claim, and they must be right, that the Rossiya is the largest hotel in Europe. There are 3000 rooms and most of them are double. I myself felt that some of the hotels we had stayed in in India were larger but Norton said that though they might be in the amount of ground covered, the Rossiya, with its four twelve-storied wings and one tower rising twenty-one stories has *got* to be bigger. It encloses an enormous rectangle, the southern façade facing the Moscow River and the western the Kremlin.

There was a period of chaos as we were checking in. Our guide had peremptorily gathered up our passports as we entered the lobby but we immediately had to retrieve them when the desk clerks demanded them before they would assign any rooms.

Foreigners sometimes have trouble with American customs and immigration but once that rigmarole is behind him the traveler is a free man. Not a hotel in the country gives a damn whether he has a passport or not. It's a lovely, lovely way of life.

Our room was on the fifth floor and my advice is never to go higher in a Russian hotel since the chances are you'll have to use the stairs. The elevators don't work. One cannot say they *never* work but they are not dependable. You press the button and sometimes, after a long, long wait a car will appear. Sometimes it won't. Maybe you will be lucky and it will go up or down uneventfully but often it will stick between floors. Norton was in one once when that happened and an Englishwoman fainted.

They did, however, have a system that was rather good. If too many people piled in a buzzer sounded and last comers had to get off one by one until it stopped. Don't get your hopes up though. For even when the buzzer does stop it doesn't necessarily mean that the elevator will move. Eventually some of us learned to jump up and down and bang on the door and that usually started it.

Once when I was alone in a car with an American delegate the buzzer sounded. "Oh dear," I said, *"now* what does it want?" My companion laughed. "I think it's whimpering because there are only two of us. It feels we don't appreciate its capacity."

I must say that when the elevator did stop and you started to yell, a female voice would shout instructions in Russian through an intercom as to what buttons you should push. She was mission control and she was always at the ready so you knew they anticipated breakdowns. Of course we couldn't understand what she said but fortunately the first time a stoppage occurred there were a couple of Russians in the car too and we watched what buttons they pushed.

The twenty-one story tower was in our wing, the north, but the elevator numbers only went to seventeen then skipped to twenty-one. We were convinced that was where all the monitoring and bugging systems were installed and that that was where the oracle, who issued instructions about the elevator, had her lair. We decided buttons must light up to show her where the trouble was.

Nobody doubted that the rooms were bugged. Probably not every room in the vast hotel, they would have had to have interpreters by the thousands, versed in every language, to listen to what would be 98 percent innocuous palaver, but they undoubtedly placed high-ranking men in the petroleum industry in rooms they could monitor.

Indeed we heard that one of the delegates deliberately made a misleading statement in a conversation he was having with some colleagues. The statement had an authentic ring, however, and the next day at one of the conferences a Russian oil man quoted it saying something to the effect that "as is well known in America" using almost the very words that had been cleverly planted.

On our first afternoon in Moscow, after we had settled in a bit, we went to register at the conference, blazing the trail we came to know so well.

As I recall, that time one of the elevators in our bank of ten actually worked and we reached the ground floor without mishap.

We then had to round the corner of the building, proceed through a huge garden courtyard formed by the four wings, turn again into a broad avenue with a view of St. Basil's at one end and the high skyscraper University of Moscow at the other. A few steps brought us to a reception bureau where the delegates registered and where they had set up a service called the Ladies Center.

I was at sea about the registering but Norton said it was just like registering for a medical convention and he was enjoying himself. Remembering my appointment to *Petroleum Intelligence Weekly* I asked if I should do anything in my secretarial capacity but my husband said no, this was a time I was to be a wife.

I accordingly betook myself to the Ladies Center and was glad to have done so. This was a service they had obviously worked hard on for well over a year, and it was for the most part admirably planned. It had been organized by a group of women with Madam L. F. Shashina as chairman and the ladies deserve a hearty hand. I believe that Madam Shashina was the wife of the director of Intourist but I was not able to verify it.

The Center was well staffed and even so they could have used more guides, informants, and clerks than they had. Since the full influx of delegates and their wives had not yet arrived we first comers were lucky but after that life was one long cue after another.

The Center passed out free booklets admirably printed on coated paper with colored illustrations of places and exhibits we could visit and with brief explanations of what we would be seeing.

The most popular choices were The Armory of the Kremlin, A Moscow Stud Farm, A kindergarten, The Arkhangelskoye Estate Museum, The U.S.S.R. Economic Achievements, The Tretyakov State Picture gallery and the U.S.S.R. Diamonds Fund in the Kremlin.

There were other diversions too, The National Fashions House of the U.S.S.R., the Ancient Russian Art Museum and several more including a three-hour tour of Moscow's famed subway system called, what else?, the Lenin Metro.

I marked us down for four or five excursions but the Metro I passed up. I should not have been averse to seeing a couple of their stations but as one who loathes the New York subway I had no intention of spending three hours of my life underground in Moscow even if the walls had been painted by Leonardo da Vinci.

All of the above-mentioned junkets were free. They handed us tickets and we had only to present ourselves at the bus at the appointed time on the appointed day.

For somewhat more distant trips there was a modest charge. We signed up to go to Zagorsk, a town renowned for its ancient churches but to our infinite regret we learned too late of a possible trip to Tolstoi's house in Yasnaya Polyana. This requires a full day but two or three of our friends who did it said it was well worth the effort. His town house in Moscow is also open to visitors.

There is another excursion which I cannot speak of at first hand either but it certainly sounded as though it should be investigated. Mary Sulzer, the friend who had returned from Russia just as we were leaving New York, told us that her party spent two nights at Vladimir and Suzdal. These are ancient Russian cities of the twelfth and thirteen centuries still intact. Mary said it was an extraordinary experience, her only complaint being that she wasn't there long enough. In her opinion there is so much to see one could easily stay three nights.

There are numerous cafes and snack bars in the Hotel Rossiya and five or six restaurants. Our first night there we dined in the wrong one. I had ordered roast chicken, envisaging a plump succulent bird tarragon permeated. What was served was one shriveled drumstick, a slice of pickle and masses of semi-fried potatoes. We did have a scallion and unripe tomato salad and ice cream for dessert. There was always ice cream for dessert and it was always vanilla and always good. They never have cakes or pies or fruit and aside from scallions and cucumbers and occasionally tomatoes, never any green vegetables, except cabbage, if that may be considered green.

I don't know whether they are antagonistic to the idea of planting peas and beans and asparagus, artichokes, broccoli and zucchini; whether, like no coats indoors and uncut grass, it is part of their culture or whether their climate is not conducive to green vegetables.

In view of their vast territory, embracing every zone except the really tropical, this last seems unlikely. Perhaps they have not yet learned to preserve and transport produce or maybe they don't care about it.

We did have an occasional carrot and frequently canned peas. They simply opened the can and poured them on the plate without cooking or flavoring of any kind. We had potatoes, boiled or vaguely fried, twice a day, and there was meat but it was indistinguishable. Pork, beef, lamb, one couldn't tell.

The brown bread and butter are very good and the way to survive is to eat the bread, butter and ice cream and drink the smooth, forty degree vodka. I believe that forty degree corresponds to eighty proof but it is very smooth and we seemed able to tuck away a fair amount without much reaction.

What the meals lacked in variety and flavor they made up for in sufficiency and the space food, those sticks they give the astronauts, that a couple of members of the group had prudently brought along, or the powdered soup that we ourselves had laid in were unnecessary. It might be added that I took along a cup and an electric element for boiling water and whereas the adapter did not work in London it worked very well on Russian current.

It was the next morning when we were breakfasting in one of the hotel cafeterias—there are telephones in every room but there is no room service—that we learned from Reid Brazell, a member of our tour and a director of the American branch of the French Total Petroleum Company that there was a quite good restaurant on the twenty-first floor where he and his wife and some of the others had dined the night before.

I don't know why the message had not percolated to Norton and me because, sure enough, right beside the elevators was a sign reading RESTAURANT, 21TH FLOOR. We rather liked the Russian twist of the twenty-unth floor which of course, immediately became known as "21" or, to the old loyal customers, Jack and Charlie's.

I do not ask the reader to accompany me step by step on the mileage covered in the Hotel Rossiya but one morning's hike may give an idea of what was virtually a daily work-out and accounts for the fact that, despite the almost pure starch diet, one does not put on much weight.

After breakfast I followed the long route to the Ladies Center to pick up our tickets for Zagorsk. I didn't have enough rubles to cover the cost but I had dollars. However, as the girl had already made out a ruble receipt she asked me please to change the dollars into rubles. "At the bank counter down the staircase in that corner."

I started off in the direction toward which she had pointed. The only staircase I could find was a stalled escalator. This seemed a little odd but with a shrug I started down. Maybe it was Russian. The escalator led to a basement where a couple of caretakers behind locked glass doors looked at me strangely. I went back up, wandered about and saw another staircase, this time a real one, quite grand, white marble and red carpet. Went down and found self in large lavatory area. Went back up found girl. Explained problem. "Oh," she said, "so sorry."

She got up from behind desk and led me to the three shallow steps of the central hall where everyone was milling about and which I had already traversed twice and pointed to the bank counter.

We nodded and smiled at each other and I joined the long line where there were at least seventeen people before me. Then I realized I did not have my money paper, which was stamped when we entered the country and which, we had been admonished, we must never be without.

Long trek back to room to get it, walking the five flights both ways, long trek back to Center. Line still interminable but having been subsidized by Norton I now had sufficient rubles to pay for the tickets. Return to girl who hands them to me with the receipt. Ordeal ended. Distance traveled: five miles. Pounds lost: two.

While on the subject of money, the prudent traveler, for once, will cut down on available funds in coin of the realm. Cling to your traveler's checks by all means but if traveling across Russia, as we did, don't stock up on rubles. The reason being that everything will have been paid for in advance. Transportation, rooms and food.

This is always true to some extent when traveling with a tour but usually there are extras one wants to be prepared for. In Russia they are rare. You'll probably have an occasional bar bill but the temptation to buy anything is virtually nil. The best stuff is in the hard-currency shops in any event. Once out of Leningrad and Moscow there are few restaurants where you are likely to dine independently. Tipping is a sometimes yes, sometimes no, affair and dollars can serve.

It is not true, as we had heard, that you cannot change rubles back into dollars at the border. When we arrived at the port of Nakhodka we handed in our Russian money and they gave us back the full amount in American.

I would gladly tell what we paid for our rooms if I knew but that is difficult to break down on a tour. According to the July 1971 issue of a travel letter called *Visa:* "Deluxe hotels everywhere charge $34.45 single for bed and breakfast. $38.90 for room and *all* meals. Double rooms are $23.35 per person for bed and breakfast: $27.80 each for room and all meals. *Take the bed and breakfast arrangement.* For one thing Intourist will not refund money for meals you don't eat. For another there are good restaurants in Moscow and Leningrad. *Deluxe accommodations entitle you to the services of a guide six hours a day, a car and chauffeur for three*—but you have to ask for them."

That Sunday morning, having finally settled our own financial affairs, at least for the time being, we started out for our first real exploration of Red Square. As even those who have never been there know from television it is an enormous area, rectangular in shape, paved with cobblestones, bounded on one end by the adorable fairy tale St. Basil's Cathedral and on the other by the somewhat grim and spired Historical Museum. This has an archway through which one passes to leave or enter the Square on a cobbled ramp sloping down to a large main thoroughfare.

GUM, a huge department store stretches the entire length of one long side of the rectangle. Like the Rossiya Hotel it too has to be the largest in Europe. The bazaar in Istanbul may be larger but it is in a different category and Turkey is more or less in Asia.

The crenelated Kremlin wall faces it across the Square. Above the wall rises the green dome of the Senate Building. The main entrance to the Kremlin enclosure is the tall Spasskaya Tower with its huge clock marking the hours. It is now crowned by a red star that lights up at night but in the days of the Czars, imperial eagles perched there. There are five towers in all, each with its star, the Senate Tower rising directly behind Lenin's tomb which is of red granite, black banded, square, sturdy, and sot in its ways.

I expect I missed my opportunity but I did not go in. I was not particularly interested in gazing at dead Mr. Lenin nor did I wish to spend an hour or more standing in the never-ending line that snakes its way up the hill, through the Historical Museum archway and down Red Square to the mausoleum. I believe, however, that if a foreigner shows his passport to one of the policemen on duty the line is usually held up, the Russians patiently making way for the visitor to pass ahead of them.

Rain or shine the line moves on. At 7 A.M. on a gray drizzling morning we looked out our window and saw them there. Hundreds and hundreds of people moving in slow single file. At night when the tomb is closed the people stand staring at the closed doors and the two immobile guards ever on duty. Their tour of duty varies with the weather. A shorter spell in the bitter cold winter, longer in summer. Either way their boredom must be exquisite.

By the Kremlin wall and adjacent to Lenin's tomb is a grave rarely mentioned or noticed. It is that of Inessa Armand. She was a stanch revolutionist and is said to have been Lenin's one true love. His affection for Krupskaya, his wife, seems to have been genuine but was probably platonic. Whether or not Inessa was ever, in actual fact, his mistress is open to speculation but that she meant more to him than any other woman is, according to Louis Fischer, who wrote *The Life of Lenin,* well established by their letters and his remarks about her to other people. Nor was his devotion to her any secret from Krupskaya.

She died in the Caucasus in 1920 and when Lenin walked in her funeral procession those nearby said he was so overwhelmed by grief as to be unrecognizable. Indeed, they thought he would fall. Again, to quote Mr. Fischer, Alexandra Kollontai, a prominent Bolshevik whom Lenin had appointed as People's Commissar of State Charity and who later became Soviet Minister to Norway said, that in her opinion, Lenin could not survive without Inessa and that it was her death that precipitated his own fatal illness.

Possibly. Madame Kollontai had to know more than most of us ever can but it is hard to envisage Vladimir Ilich Ulyanov (Lenin was a pen name) in the role of lovelorn suitor. He had a brilliant, probing, all encompassing intellect, demoniac energy, a boundless capacity for self-discipline and study, and a will of solid granite. I suppose those attributes and a capacity for love are not necessarily mutually exclusive but given the life he led, the boundless responsibility he insisted on assuming, fighting tooth and nail to keep anybody else from getting that power, he really didn't have much time to brood over the departed, no matter how dear.

But to revert to his tomb, I heard an American, who obviously felt as I did about standing in line, ask if it couldn't be arranged for him to see the tomb early the next morning. "No," said the little Intourist guide to whom he had addressed himself, "Friday it has the day off."

As is common knowledge, Stalin used to lie beside Lenin but he has been removed. I quote briefly from Irving R. Levine's *Travel Guide to Russia,* written at the time when the Soviets were still touting Stalin as only a slightly lesser god.

"Seldom has civilized man conceived a more macabre monument. Here, deep in an underground chamber, air conditioned, dramatically lighted, lie the embalmed bodies of V. I. Lenin and Joseph Stalin in glass sarcophagi. It is a shrine of Communism. It is a testimony, too, to a highly developed Soviet science of preservation. Their eyes shut, their waxen faces wearing benign expressions,

16. Wanda Jablonski at the Service Center of the Eighth World Petroleum Congress.

17. GUM department store. Red Square, Moscow. On and on and on it goes. On and on and on.

18. Lenin, holy Lenin. The statue is within the Kremlin walls and the evergreen trees are a species of Colorado, U.S.A. spruce. So much for the Iron Curtain.

19. One of the lobbys of the Palace of Congresses.

20. Opening ceremonies of the
Eighth World Petroleum Congress.

21. Ilka at the buffet luncheon,
opening day of the Congress.
Soulful expression induced by
much fine fare.

22. Great thoroughfare leading into Red Square. The rush hour. Most of the time it is not so crowded.

23. Troika at the stud farm. We thought of them as Brezhnev, Kosygin, and Podgorny, only handsomer.

24. Gur-Emir Mausoleum, tomb of the Emperor Timur.

25. Old man with his little grand-daughter looking at a Polaroid picture of himself given him by Watson Wise. Quite probably it was the first likeness of him-self he had ever seen.

26. Kalyan Minaret, or Tower of Death, dating from 1127. Bukhara.

27. Women at machines in the embroidery factory. My benefactress is hidden by the standing group at the left.

28. Ken George and the hat that got embroidered.

29. Miss Hot Pants of the Lola Day Nursery, Tashkent.

Lenin and Stalin are on display for thousands of reverent or simply curious people to see each week."

Mr. Levine also remarks that irreverent non-Communists referred to the bodies as "the gruesome twosome" and "the cold cuts." Apparently the Egyptians had nothing on the Russians when it came to embalming techniques. Skeptical tourists have been known to spread mischievous rumors that the mummified corpse has been replaced by a wax effigy. Whether or not this is so I cannot say.

Louis Fischer tells us that in the 1930s the Soviets, irked by persistent rumors that the corpse was, in fact, a wax figure, invited members of the foreign press to visit the tomb with an embalming chemist. It was the chemist's opinion that the body could last a century. He opened the hermetically sealed glass case, tweaked the gentleman's nose and turned his head to the left and right. "It was Lenin," says Mr. Fischer. "The iconoclast is now a modern Russian icon." In the dead of night does the icon's mouth perhaps twist in a sardonic grin?

It will soon be fifty years since Lenin's death—he died in 1924—and the cult still flourishes. Just as in other countries a belief in Jesus or Buddha, Confucius or Mohammed is absorbed from earliest childhood so the Russians absorb Lenin.

The Communists separated church and state vigorously and effectively, declaring religion to be the opium of the people. They then substituted Lenin for God but they see no contradiction in the procedure. Rather, since Lenin *is* the state, it was a doubling up of the state's power. Materialism and spirituality are one.

Should the day ever come when the Soviet Government changes its mind and decides to denigrate him as it did Stalin the process, one would imagine, would be both prolonged and painful but given enough time and enough brainwashing they could probably succeed.

We keep returning to Mr. George Orwell. When a nation is isolated from the rest of the world and literature and the press are controlled and manipulated it is not too great a trick to impose Newspeak and Newthink at will.

After all, the Soviets built Lenin up. Should it suit their purpose in the future they may tear him down although such a proposition at the moment is unthinkable heresy.

As Louis Fischer observes: "The Kremlin encourages Lenin-worship. It projects a carefully shaped image of Lenin on the Soviet mind." That the image does not always jibe with the facts does not disturb them.

After strolling around Red Square for a while Norton and I passed through a small entrance in the wall next to Spasskaya Tower into the Kremlin proper.

As a rule when foreigners speak of the Kremlin they are thinking of the building that houses the government just as Americans think of the Capitol or the Hill but the word means fortress and is an entire area enclosing gardens, churches, and palaces.

Almost the first thing one sees is a large statue of a seated Lenin leaning slightly forward, his elbows on his knees, on a high pedestal. The pedestal is set on a square foundation of polished black marble brightened by a bed of fibrous scarlet begonias.

We looked at him for a while and took each other's pictures standing at the foot of the monument and then went on to view a huge bell with a great hole in its side that has never rung and a large ornate cannon that has never fired a shot but which is a favorite background for Russian snapshots.

By degrees we made our way to the Palace of Congresses where the opening of the Eighth World Petroleum Congress was to be held.

The Palace of Congresses is plain splendid. It is, in effect, an enormous theatre with an auditorium, stage, balconies, boxes, and several immense airy lobbies. There is a great deal of crimson tweed upholstery and gold ornamentation. The seats are roomy and comfortable and in one arm of every seat is a small head set for listening to simultaneous translations of the speeches of various speakers. The capacity of the house is, I believe, about 4200 and I was interested to learn that it was designed by a woman architect.

I have always felt that architecture is a field more women should enter but I have thought of them designing houses and apartments.

It is they who, for the most part, spend their lives in them and they ought to be very good at the job. However the Palace of Congresses is certainly a bright red star in the crown of its female designer.

Strolling about in the lobby, waiting for the ceremonies to begin, I thought to buy a bar of chocolate at a small stand nestling against a pillar. When I looked at the price on a piece of cardboard I thought not to. One ruble, fifty kopecks, or $1.66. That was our first run in with the price of Russian consumer goods. From there on the prices rose.

A man's suit looking as though it were cut from cardboard costs about $80 or $90. A television set can run between $800 and $1000. Rents on the other hand are nothing. $1.50, $5, $7 a month. All education is free as are all hospitals and medical care.

Since they can't have everything at once one has to admit that Russian priorities make sense.

Being early we had our choice of seats and finally settled for the center of the front row of the mezzanine from which we had an excellent view of the entire house as well as the floral arrangements flanking the podium on the stage where members of the Russian Government and the petroleum industry sat. Placed at intervals were alternating brightly colored bouquets, a high one, then a low one, a high and a low. That was to the left of the speaker's stand. To the right a less skillful hand had taken over or maybe by that time the florist was just tired. Those bouquets were set down higgledy-piggledy any which way and I said to Norton, "That's how they run the elevators. Kind of laissez-faire." There's a human quality about it which is not unendearing, unless you happen to be stuck between floors.

The house gradually filled with delegates until it was better than three quarters full although it never did develop into standing room only. At high noon a high-ranking member of the Russian Petroleum team declared the Congress open and made a high-sounding speech of welcome to the delegates from around the world.

He was followed by an American, Mr. Frederick Rossini, presi-

dent of the World Petroleum Congress, who said how glad everybody was to be there. There were a few other speakers too and
they all explained how great oil was and how much it contributed to
the well-being of mankind and how without it we would sink back
into barbarism and we should all be very grateful to the noble spirits
all over the earth who made this blessing possible. There was a moment of silence while everybody felt grateful.

Lenin, who in 1916 was writing gleefully about the imminent "ex-
haustion of the American oil fields," would have been depressed.
He would have been even more depressed could he have known
of the statistics bandied about by several of the petroleum connois-
seurs with whom we became friends.

Near Samarkand in Russia there is a field containing some 35 to
40 trillion cubic feet of natural gas. In 1966 one was discovered in
Siberia with a capacity of 60 trillion cubic feet. The Groningen in
Holland has 60 as has one in the Texas panhandle.

As Louis Fischer writes, Lenin revealed "a low opinion of man's ingenuity and of the earth's resources" and Mr. Fischer goes on to mention "the unfathomable lakes of oil" that have been tapped all over
the world and of the eternal sources of energy that will be utilized
if petroleum reserves ever are exhausted.

Everything that was said at the Congress about the glories of oil
was true and were I unable to heat my house or run my car I'm
afraid my cries of rage and frustration would ring out with the
loudest. However, all the time they were talking I couldn't help
thinking of the sea birds strangling and dying in great waves of oil
washing ashore from spills and of the beaches polluted and dese-
crated when tankers rip open or run aground. I thought of the
fragile permafrost of Alaska and of the fate of the wolves and
caribou if and when a pipeline is laid from the north slope.

I also remembered that before we left home Wanda and I had
had a slight contretemps on the subject when I said that talk of the
pipeline made me very uneasy.

My friend looked at me with the flat expression of one who
really doesn't know what the *hell* the other person is talking about.

"Do you want to be warm or do you want to save wolves?" she demanded. "Both," I said.

I still think that with forethought, planning, and *caring* both are possible. It has never seemed to me an either-or proposition.

Apparently in Siberia, Russians have only to poke a stick in the ground and oil bubbles up although they did say something about their own permafrost problems and in fairness two or three of the oil kings themselves acknowledged that tragedies do happen and they are, they said, working hard to prevent their reoccurrence and are making progress.

On this note of optimism we broke for lunch. We were the guests of the Russian Government and as we streamed out of the hall announcements in French and English informed us that buses were waiting to take people to the restaurant. Seeing ranks of buses move forward, fill up and move off, Norton and I hopped aboard one. We drove a few blocks to a large restaurant where everybody got out.

As we were slowly surging through the lobby I noticed that the man beside me was holding a brown ticket with gold engraving on it whereas ours was white.

"Do you suppose that means we're on different floors?" I asked.

"No, no," he said, "you're in the wrong place. You're supposed to be back at the Palace of Congresses."

"Oh."

Sure enough the invitation did say that but sheep-like we had followed the crowd. About eight or ten other people had too. How to get back? There were only a couple of taxis and they had red lights on top and obviously belonged to the People's Police. A lot of buses were parked about but all we got from every driver we approached was a strong *"Nyet." Nyet* as the whole world knows means No and the word is very big in Russia. It is to Russians what *Verboten* is to Germans and a pain in the neck to visitors.

Finally, to our great relief, a cop came along, banged on the hood of the bus and shouted to the driver what was obviously the equivalent of "Don't be such an old pig, take these people back." With ill humor the driver opened the door, we piled in and returned to the palace. Luncheon had still not been announced so we hadn't missed anything.

With time on my hands I decided to explore the lavatories. I went down a broad shallow flight of steps into what has to be the Supreme Soviet of the toilet world. The previous summer Norton and I had spent a week in Iceland and there we saw toilets that sparkled like diamonds. It was a pleasure to open a bathroom door just to look at them but, like the country, the scale was small. Here they sparkled too but they were proportionate to the land. Arranged in a vast marble area they gleamed and twinkled in what seemed to be hundreds. They were discreetly screened by shining white swing panels and they were gratis. None of that infuriating fishing about for an invisible and usually nonexistent dime. In Russia you pee free. We were two or three women together and we were overcome by the splendor but Camelot, alas, was limited.

Having made an all out, gargantuan effort in the Palace, the Ministry of Toilets collapsed everywhere else back into tradition. That of Genghis Khan. Across the land of Russia, in airplanes in the sky, the public toilets are for the most part unspeakable. I will spare the reader the revolting details and simply say that it is hard to see why a country that in the last fifty years has made technological strides before which the whole world bows cannot seem to organize its sanitary arrangements. If the government has some warped idea that maybe a cholera epidemic will combat the population explosion and should be encouraged it's on the right track. On the other hand, since the populace has been coping with the system for so long, the chances are it has become immunized.

In any event, having seen that communism can contribute something to human welfare, even if on an elementary level, we were in good humor when at two-fifteen a bell rang summoning us to the banquet.

This was held in an enormous hall on the top floor and our hosts had not stinted. Buffet tables a city block long were laden with delicious food. Caviar, sturgeon, smoked salmon, chicken, jellied meats, excellent brown bread and butter, salads, fruit and every few feet, rising like little skyscrapers, islands of bottles: vodka, wine, and beer. It was the best wine we had in Russia. Their beer is called Piva and one is better off without it.

Since there must have been 1500 to 2000 people, seating was out of the question but it is remarkable what balancing skills one can develop when it is a question of gorgeous goodies, especially when they include caviar.

After such a spread it seemed unlikely that we would be eating again for the rest of the week but prudent Dr. Brown reserved a table at "21" after the gala concert that was to be the evening's entertainment.

He went further than that and before we left for the Palace he stopped off at one of the cafeterias and brought back to our room some sausage, bread, and a bottle of vodka. It was not all that large a bottle and I nearly fainted when he told me he had paid over six dollars for it.

I am happy to say that was the last time he did because we soon discovered the Beriozka shops, the hard-currency stores that are to be found in virtually every hotel in Russia. They accept only foreign money and the difference in price is worth while: $1.50 for a bottle of vodka instead of $6.66.

Having returned to the hotel and partaken of this modest snack to stay us against the evening's festivities we mingled again with the crowd wending its way across Red Square. Back inside the Palace we were much impressed by the speed and skill with which they had transformed the great podium of the morning, a cumbersome affair of platforms, benches and tables, speakers stands and banks of micro-phones into a flat, light, and spacious area for the dance.

When we say concert we usually mean music and song. The Rus-sians can mean that too but normally they mean ballet. All kinds were presented to us that evening: classical, folk and the Moiseyev troop who have toured the United States. When the men did those great leaps, legs flung to one side, heels clicking in air the Americans went wild. It was great!

Sometime later when I put all that down I thought to myself, a writer should be more specific than that. The step must have a name, what is it?

I addressed myself to our friend Sally Brayley Bliss. Sally is a dancer, a choreographer and associate director of the ballet company Jeffrey II. She is also a slim and decorative redhead. "What's the name of that Russian caper?" I asked. "You know, the one where they leap up in the air and kick."

"I don't know," she said. "If we want to use it we just say, 'Do the Russian step'" She paused a moment. "I suppose you *could* call it a character cabriole."

"Sally, listen. This is going to be in a *book*. It's got to be accurate. Is it really that—what you may call it?" Sally looked at me, firm and stern. "Who is to say it isn't?"

Well, as I said, when the Russians did the character cabriole the Americans went wild.

The artists were their young, up-coming group of dancers and the numbers and soloists were announced with pomposity. "The People's Artists of the Soviet Union," "The Winner of the Lenin Prize," "The Winner of the International Concourse." When the Russians say International they don't mean it in the global sense but rather a competition between the various Socialist Soviet Republics. Still, when you're as big as they are, that is not exactly parochial.

While we thought everything they did, they did very well, there was little that was novel, original, or innovative, Avant garde they were not. Artistic progress is difficult if not impossible with the heavy suffocating hand of the State ever ready to cut off the first breath of fresh air.

When the performance was over we returned to the hotel and went up to the restaurant to find we had a table by the window. The view over Moscow was good but it was a misty evening and there were not many lights. The view of San Francisco from the top of the Mark or of New York from almost any place is more exhilarating. Understandably enough, with so many to take care of, "21" was reluctant to reserve a table for only two people. Almost everyone therefore took a table for four or six since there would always be someone coming along to share it.

On this occasion two Germans came by and as we had not seen any of our particular cronies we were glad to have them join us. They were both oil men from Hamburg and they spoke excellent English.

One of them told us he came frequently to Moscow. He had been there in October and he said, "You cannot imagine the effort these people have made to get the hotel ready for this Congress. They want to make a good impression and they want things to go well." He also added that he was happy to be a capitalist. I agreed.

"Dictatorships are not good," I said.

"No. We had Hitler."

Maybe he felt that way. Maybe he had secretly admired Hitler. I don't know.

The food at "21" was reasonably good if erratic; better at some times than at others, and one got quite large servings of caviar for $2. Even in Russia however there is something of a shortage and after we left Moscow we saw very little of it.

The opening ceremonies of the Congress were on Sunday. Norton and I had purposely left Monday free of any excursions as we wanted to get in touch with people to whom we had letters.

We quickly discovered that if one does not speak the language it is far simpler to go in person than to try to contact Russians by telephone. To begin with telephone directories, as we know them, do not exist.

At the congressional service center they did have two small books, one with the numbers of foreign embassies, another with those of Moscow institutions such as museums or, one I was interested in, the Soviet Writer's Union. However, I don't know how ordinary travelers, without an affiliation such as ours, are able to manage.

I took down the number of the American Embassy with Ambassador Jacob D. Beam's extension just in case. My contact with the Writer's Union came later.

The day before I had ordered a taxi. With carefree optimism the Intourist people said there was a stand outside the hotel where one could pick up cabs at will. This was not a fact. At rare intervals a taxi *might* appear but he would never take you and there were always ten or fifteen people waiting in line.

The more effective mode of procedure was to order one in advance. When you did however an Intourist girl invariably asked you where you wanted to go. In fairness I think this was probably to find out how long it was likely to take and because some drivers knew certain areas better than others but the end result was that Intourist always knew who would be where when.

On that particular day we had three addresses we wanted to stop at so we mapped a plan of progress.

Our first destination was the friend of the Traverses, to whom they had asked us to take the picture of Christian when we dined with them in Surrey. The second was a doctor, the deputy commissioner of health for the entire U.S.S.R. He was an acquaintance of a doctor friend of Norton's and we had a letter to him. The third was Frieda Lurie, one of the directors of the Soviet Writer's Union whom Mary Hemingway knew quite well.

Ernest Hemingway's writing is popular in Russia and while they do not believe in shipping out royalties, either to foreign authors or their estates, the Russians have no objection if the writer or, as in this case, his widow, wants to come to Russia to spend the money. Mary is a friend of ours. She had written to Madame Lurie about us and asked me if I would take her a small present. I believe it was a scarf.

The people at Intourist were cooperative about writing down the addresses in Russian so as to make it easier for the taxi driver and off we went.

We arrived fairly quickly in what apparently was the neighborhood of our first objective but finding the correct address proved more

complicated. We stopped at a door in a wall that was an entrance
to a courtyard and the driver pointed and gestured obviously hoping that was the right place and that our quarry would be within.

We entered a somewhat dilapidated courtyard carrying our flat
manila envelope with the photograph of Virginia and Bill Travers
and the lion Christian. Bill had also written a letter and that envelope, with the address in Cyrillic script, he had stuck onto the
larger one with Scotch tape. We moseyed about looking for number
14. Presently a grandmotherly type appeared leading a small child
by the hand. Was she the one? We pointed to the name and address. No she was not but at least she knew who was! Motioning
us to follow her she went out into the street, walked along the wall
for a few yards and entered another courtyard.

This one was equally dilapidated but it had a kind of scraggly
charm; uncut grass and a couple of delicate trees. Our guide rang
the bell of a ground floor flat and indicated we had reached our
goal.

"Spaseeba, spaseeba, bloshoi spaseeba," I said. That was thanks
and big thanks.

In a moment a young, notably hefty blond appeared. Her bare
feet were thrust into sandals and she was wearing a not very fresh
housedress but she had a broad pleasant face and bright blue eyes.
Was she Madame So and So, friend of the Traverses? Looking
as though we were apparitions from another planet she replied in
English that she was.

We held out the envelope. "We saw them just the other day in
England," we said, "and we have something for you."

She took the envelope and smiling, struggling to overcome her
bewilderment, she asked us if we wouldn't please come in. We followed her into a tiny hall and then into a living room that would
have been fairly good sized had it not been nearly filled by a large
square table. A narrow sofa ran along one side of the room under
a shelf loaded with photographs and ornaments and a sideboard
took up most of another wall.

A heavy cloth covered the table on which stood a vase of ex-

tremely deceased flowers and strewn about were a great many news-
papers. A woman on the other side of the table began gathering and
folding them up. Our hostess gestured vaguely in her direction, we
nodded to each other but there was no formal introduction.

"Please, please, excuse me a moment," she said, "I am doing my
homework, is why I look this way. I change. One moment please."
We urged her not to bother on our account, we could only stay a
few minutes and were sorry to intrude. "No, no, please. I come
back" and she went off to change her dress.

Norton and I smiled uncertainly at the other woman. Who was
she? A relative, a friend? We had heard that nearly every Moscow
family was obliged to share their apartment with somebody else.
Was she the other tenant? We never did find out.

I will call our lady Charlotte. That is not her name and it is
hard to conceive that a visit such as ours could mean anything at
all to the authorities but a system like the Russians' is not guided
by sweet reason and one takes precautions.

Presently she returned, considerably spruced up, and begged us
to give her news of the Traverses. She had first met them when they
came to Moscow for a film festival and she went to the crowded
shelf over the sofa and took down a copy of Virginia's book, *On
Playing With Lions*. Her pride and interest in it were touching.
She was delighted by the photograph and told us that her husband
was also a movie actor. They were shooting that day which is why
he wasn't home.

We asked where she had learned to speak such good English
and she told us that she had seen quite a lot of the United States
and Canada, touring with a company of Russian ice skaters. This
tidbit came as something of a shock. She looked hefty indeed to be
an ice skater and we concluded that the flashing blades must have
been a few years before.

As we took our leave she apologized for the chaotic condition of
her house saying it was in such disorder because they were soon
moving to a new apartment and she looked distinctly pleased by the
prospect.

She accompanied us out to the curb and as we were crossing the little courtyard pointed out a bright red car somewhat the worse for wear. It was theirs. Her husband it seemed had had a slight accident and they were waiting to get it repaired. When later I asked Norton how long he thought that would take he said, "With the kind of maintenance they have here? Forever." He was thinking of the elevators that stuck and the toilets that didn't flush.

When we told Charlotte our next destination was the Ministry of Health she considerately explained to the driver how to get there.

It was fun to have met her and to have seen the inside of a Soviet household even for so brief a period. I said to Norton, "I'm awfully glad she was home, it's nice to meet a Russian but can you imagine if she had been out and we'd just gone in and left the photo and the Traverses' letter on the table? She'd have spent the rest of her life trying to figure out how they got there."

At the Ministry of Health a sharp disappointment awaited us. We were shown into the office of the doctor to whom our letter was addressed only to learn that he was in Romania and would be there the entire week we were in Moscow. Unfortunately there was no one else who spoke enough English to make a meeting fruitful. Norton was upset by this and so was I. He had hoped to learn something of Russian medicine and of their method of health care in general.

Nor did we fare much better at the Soviet Writer's Union. Madame Lurie would be in about one o'clock, they said, but it was then only eleven and we didn't want to hang around for two hours. I left Mary Hemingway's present and wrote a little note saying I hoped very much we might have the pleasure of meeting the friend of our friend.

Late that afternoon, after trekking through the endless corridors of the hotel and waiting in a long line at the desk of one of the Intourist girls, I was able to get her to put in a telephone call for me. I reached Madame Lurie who invited Norton and me to lunch with her at the Union on Wednesday at two o'clock.

That, I said, would be delightful. I then made the long march back to our room only to discover that Wednesday was our day for driving to Zagorsk and the ancient churches with famous icons. We would not return till late afternoon.

I should have gone back immediately to the Center and the telephone but I was too tired to face the procedure all over again. Instead I wrote a note explaining our predicament and asking Madame Lurie if she would not lunch or dine with us on either Thursday, Friday, or Saturday? Her convenience would be ours.

I do not trust my handwriting. Indeed when I told three or four friends that I would send them postcards from Russia and that I was sorry I couldn't send them in code so the censors wouldn't know what I was saying they laughed in what I considered a rather callous fashion and said, "Don't worry, Cookie, your handwriting *is* a code. The censor isn't born who can crack it."

With these insults from my dear ones echoing in my ears I took my letter to an Intourist girl and asked her please to address it in Cyrillic script. This was Monday evening, my hope being that Madame Lurie would receive it in the morning mail on Wednesday.

I don't know why I hoped that in view of a little conversation I had had with a member of the hotel staff. A day or so previously I had asked her where one went to collect mail.

"Mail?"

"Yes, you know. Mail. Letters."

She looked blank and I suddenly bethought me.

"Post. Where does the post, posta come in?"

Jackpot.

"Ah, posta!"

"Da."

"You are English."

This seemed a non sequitur but I said, "No. American."

"There are no letters for you."

"How do you know? You don't know my name."

"No letters for nobody."

That took care of that and all the time the nearly five thousand foreigners were in Moscow, as far as I know, no one received any mail. The State doesn't believe in it. Whether they attempt to read it all I cannot say and it is true that in late November some of the letters that had been mailed to us in June were returned to the senders.

John Gessner of Cook's told us that all the travel agencies have given up trying to reach their representatives when they are in Russia. If something important comes up and they *have* to get in touch with them they telephone. The long distance phone works pretty well.

Hoping that Madame Lurie would receive my note was wishful thinking but also it seemed possible that domestic mail service might be efficient.

However, hedging against a snafu, the morning we left for Zagorsk I asked an Intourist girl if she would be good enough to telephone the Writer's Union and ask Madame Lurie if she had received a letter from me and if not to please explain why we could not come to lunch. When I returned in the afternoon I asked her if she had delivered my message. She assured me she had. This, I am afraid, was a little white lie because I tried many times to reach the lady by telephone and left many messages but I never heard from her again.

Eventually she did get my note because, when we were back home in New York, Mary Hemingway showed me a letter from her saying she had arranged a luncheon for us with two or three other writers but that we had gone out of town for the day. If she was miffed I cannot blame her.

Zagorsk was unique but I have seen a great many religious edifices in my life and if we couldn't do both I think it would have been far more rewarding to meet and talk with intelligent, educated Russians on home ground than to wander through a few more churches. I regretted my action then and I shall regret it always.

The evening of our abortive day we shared our table at "21" with four Canadians; a young couple and older friends of theirs, a Mr. and Mrs. Joubin. Mr. Joubin had an amusing, prickly, darting mind and he cared nothing at all for the U.S.A. and was a strong apologist of the U.S.S.R. He worked with the United Nations, traveled widely and considered that the Russians had made re-markable progress since his previous visit five years before.

He thought it pretty stupid of the United States to keep putting men on the moon. "The Russians are playing a much cooler game with their sophisticated orbiting machines and a far less expensive one."

He said this with a certain relish which was understandable. It must be rather pleasant for Canadians to see their advanced, power-ful, big brother occasionally put down.

Norton and I sometimes wonder about the wisdom of spending all those billions on the moon when poor old Earth is rocking along in a state of semi-disaster with the threat of everything getting worse but since it was inevitable that man *would* reach the moon we're just as glad Americans did it first.

Astronauts have an enormous glamour quotient and as long as the history of the world is studied those American names must ever rank with the great Firsts of exploration and science.

Mr. Joubin went on to say that in many respects the Russians were far ahead of the United States in scientific achievement. Nor was he alone in thinking so. Mr. Hans Lang, a member of our tour, said they had an extraordinary group of mathematicians, stars of true magnitude, and Mr. Clem George of Texas, father of the ebullient and charming young Ken, acknowledged ruefully that there was much to be said for the Russian oil industry.

"They've got it pretty good," he said. "To begin with they have vast reserves of oil and when the government wants it it goes and gets it. None of this bothering with leases and royalties and rights. No legal problems, no labor problems, just oil and the state."

And one must admit there is a strong case to be made for national resources belonging to the nation in which they are found and co-ordinated with world needs as a whole. To drain a lake, to deflect a river, to level a forest in one country may be grievously damaging to another.

It is shortsighted to say "What do we care about *them?*" or to expound on "enlightened self-interest." The seas wash all shores, the air moves round the globe. That which affects one affects all.

I am no economist. (I can hear the Harumphers harumphing, "That, my good woman, is crystal clear.") But I do not believe in plundering the planet. And while I think that in any endeavor, the greater one's ability the greater one's profits should be, it seems to me that air, water, oil, minerals, forests, and wild life should not be the private domain of the few but should be administered to the advantage of all.

Were I an economic dictator on the arts and sciences, in the world of sports, I would set no limits on honest financial gain because the resources of the individuals who practice them are their own brains and bodies. Let them reap rewards commensurate with their skills or with what the public is willing to pay for the pleasure of seeing them or owning or participating in their performance.

Nor is there any use in pretending that however keen one may be on one's job reward isn't a strong motivation. And that much human convenience, pleasure and happiness do not stem from the ability to retain and enjoy the fruits of one's own labor.

While still at the dinner table I said something of the sort to Mr. Joubin and, thinking primarily of convenience, I added, "We take so many things for granted. Cars, for instance. Here they have these enormous squares and boulevards virtually empty of traffic—which is not bad of course, lovely freedom from carbon monoxide—but that is not the reason they don't have them. With all the Russian ability and know-how why shouldn't they have more private cars?"

"Because the government considers them fripperies," said Mr. Joubin. "They're totally unimportant. What's important is Russia's heavy industry, her progress in manufacturing and in agriculture. What they're doing is enormous. First things first. Give them time, you'll see. These people are dedicated. They'll be the foremost nation in the world."

I'm not sure this isn't true but one gets a little weary of the repeated theme "Give them time."

"How much time do they need?" I asked pettishly. "The revolution took place in 1917. That's fifty-four years ago. So all right, there was time out after that. Their civil war lasted until 1921 and left the nation a shambles. Then the famine, in part due to nature but exacerbated by the pigheadedness of Lenin and company forcing the peasants to do everything *their* way. That lasted what? Two years? Then along came World War Two. Say another six years out there, that makes thirteen. They've still had forty-one years in a century of rapid communication where world knowledge, the experience of others is disseminated instantaneously, often simultaneously. Take the moon landings as an example. What we know—what the astronauts know the whole world knows."

Mr. Joubin laughed. "Forty or fifty years. What is that in the life of a nation? Nothing, nothing at all."

"It's a hell of a lot in the life of an individual," I said, "and what else are nations composed of?"

We neither of us changed the other's mind but it was a reasonably stimulating meal. Later when we were alone Norton said, "You don't make allowance for the Russian background. Some of the oldest Russians alive today and certainly most of their parents were serfs. They've come from way, way behind. I agree with you, this 'Give them time, give them time' gets a bit tedious but you might as well be patient because whether you like it or not patience is what it takes."

My husband is a patient man. It is one reason he is a good doctor. He is willing to wait a bit and give nature a break. He became something of a legend in his hospital—the Roosevelt—the day he said to a young intern who was all for plowing ahead, all for experimenting on a patient with every new bit of technology and equipment at his fingertips. "No, no. Don't do something. Just stand there." The young intern went into shock. The patient recovered.

We had a good deal of gloomy weather in Moscow but one of our rainy days was brightened by a trip to a stud farm. Since I feel an affinity for nearly every animal who breathes I warm to horses too but with me they are not the overweening passion they are for some people.

Norton feels the same way but we decided that was an excursion we would like to make for a couple of reasons. One was that the farm was a short drive out of Moscow so we would see something of the countryside and the other was that we imagined fine shining animals frolicking in paddocks and they would be a good subject for pictures.

We drove out of the city along Kalenia Boulevard, a ten-lane highway. Even though they have few cars at present, the Russians must know something we don't. Their plans for future automotive production have got to be impressive!

What they do have at present, as one reaches the outskirts of the city, is an enormous statue of a male and female worker, their clasped hands upraised in a vigorous, healthful salute. They are obviously well stuffed with potatoes and yogurt, they are full of verve and thrust and they are very funny. The Communists love them. We saw the same kind of thing when we were in Romania and Bulgaria in 1965* and were amused then by the chest-thumping self-adulation, the People's Heroes.

This particular pair stand at the entrance to the park or fairgrounds where the buildings housing the Soviet Industrial Achievements are located. Norton and I did not visit it, but some members of our tour did and one of them, John Downing, from Calgary, Alberta, said the exhibition was noteworthy. "It's the religion that makes all this bearable."

He was referring to the drabness of their lives, the relentless supervision, the paucity of consumer goods and conveniences. Religion is frequently the source of unhappiness and an industrial religion, where all is steel and iron and blast furnaces, where every amenity of human life must be sacrificed to it, is somehow reminiscent of the terrible god Moloch worshiped by the Carthaginians. They constructed an idol in the city, and into his arms infants were placed and dropped into a blazing furnace below.

The Russians obviously don't do that but a good deal of the sweetness of life is sacrificed for future annihilating nuclear warfare. And one must add in honesty, it isn't only their government

*Fresh from the Laundry.

that, by the expenditure of billions, distorts what could be sanity and tranquillity, education and health, gaiety and happiness into ugliness and death.

As I write this the United States of America is raining down millions of tons of bombs, destroying an innocent land and a people who never attempted to invade us and who have never threatened us.

However, on the way to the stud farm, we entertained such dark thoughts only superficially as we crossed railroad tracks guarded by fat elderly females, their heads wrapped in babushkas, drove through a small birch forest, the white trunks gleaming in the glancing rain and thought how lovely it must be in sunlight. We drove past the ubiquitous posters of Lenin and, looking at the dark fertile soil, wondered why they did not plant vegetables.

To a foreign eye a curious phenomenon in the Russian landscape is the lack of houses. It seems very strange to drive through the country and see no farms. At intervals, along the road, there might be clusters of small houses, all with tin roofs, outdoor plumbing and small fenced yards but the fences were broken down and weeds choked the yards. Everything needed a coat of paint and nothing looked neat and prosperous. Despite their ramshackle appearance we assumed their great virtue was that they were inhabited by only one family and that if the family did grow vegetables it could keep and eat them.

I asked one of our guides if this was the case and she said, "Of course." She was probably right but I think that "of course" is the first phrase a Russian learns when being taught English. A tourist asking an embarrassing or too personal question, "Are you allowed to keep what you grow?" "Are you free to travel?" "If you don't want to send them to the day centers can you keep your children at home?" "Of course."

We finally arrived at the horse farm and piled out of our buses but to our disappointment the frisky creatures were not cavorting free in the paddocks. We were shown into a large building where there was a great ring or rather oblong chamber with an earth floor. Three sides were of glass, the fourth wall was banked with rows of wooden benches for spectators. The size and shape of the enclosure were reminiscent of the riding academy in Vienna where the magnificent Lipizzaner horses perform.

It had nothing like the elegance of that great hall with its balconies and columns and glorious crystal chandeliers, built by the Emperor Charles VI in the first half of the eighteenth century, but in it they showed some splendid horses. The first two to come out were a deep burnished gold, two of the most beautiful animals I have ever seen.

There were representatives of a breed that many years ago traveled over 4000 kilometers in eighty-four days. There was a Cossack type chap in a square-shouldered black wool cape and gray fur cap who dashed around the ring on a black beauty and a Russian cavalry officer guided an elegant creature through a little dance. The horses had names like Dixon and Transvaal, Crimea and, unexpectedly, Liquor.

The director of the academy stood in the center of the ring with a mike and told us about the horses and about one in particular, a venerable old party of twenty-four who had sired six hundred offspring. The director also described the auctions that are held in May and October and that are attended by dealers from all over the world. The horses usually sell anywhere from $1000 to $20,000.

The performance was interesting but the tempo was a little slow although it picked up when four horses abreast came trotting out pulling a surrey with tinkling harness bells. They were followed by two tiny black ponies drawing a go-cart. There was also a troika, three fine gray fellows with the arched harness piece rising above their heads and the director said with pride that in 1910 a troika team had won the Paris Grand Prix.

On the return journey to Moscow, for reasons unknown to us, the procession of buses moved at a snail's pace and it took us over an hour to do about ten miles.

As we entered the stud farm building I had noticed a spacious kind of cafeteria area and had hoped they might be serving sandwiches or something after the performance. That had not happened and with our slow progress home by the time we got to a restaurant and finished lunch it was well after four.

However, as a pleasant change, we were able to identify the meat we were eating. It was goose and it was good but it caused a mishap. Biting down on a small bone, I felt a flash of searing pain in a lower tooth on the left side of my jaw. "Oh, George," I cried. I called on George rather than God as George Lindig is our dentist and I felt that under the circumstances he could do me more good.

Unhappily he was in New York but Norton tried to comfort me, saying it was probably only a bad bruise and would go away. It was a nice try and I hoped he knew what he was talking about. Also, since the pain which shot me right up into the air only came when I chewed on something, I was able to forget it between meals.

Besides I was diverted by *the* grand gala of the Eighth World Petroleum Congress scheduled for that evening. It was to begin at seven and we had learned that the Russians were usually very prompt. Our friend Wanda looked at us as though we were crazy when I told her Norton and I planned to get over to the Palace by six.

"For God's sake, why?" she asked.

"Because," I said, "I have a shrewd suspicion that even those who didn't show up for the opening meeting or that first ballet are going to pile in tonight and we want to get good seats. I'll take a book and read to pass the time."

That I didn't get in much reading was due not to lack of concentration on my part but to the fact that we barely got into the Kremlin.

We crossed the broad avenue into Red Square and remembering the ease with which we had previously gone through the comparatively small gate next to the big Spasskaya Tower arch we headed toward it. We were stopped by the shrill blast of a police whistle and a police baton pointing away from the wall and toward the GUM department store side. Since there was a big cordoned-off area in front of the tower we assumed he meant to go around that.

"Oh, come on," Norton said impatiently to the cop. We were only feet away from our goal.

"I know," I said. "It doesn't seem to make much sense." Still I had read too much about the O.G.P.U. and the N.K.V.D. and the K.G.B. the current Russian Secret Police to want to argue with any of their representatives. We accordingly made a big U then headed back toward the entrance. Another shrill blast, another threatening stick pointing us away from the gate.

"What the hell's the matter with them?" snapped the doctor.

"I don't know, dear," I said, "but we obviously don't appeal to the man."

The nasty suspicion that popped into my mind proved true. We didn't only have to go around the roped off part, we had to go all around Red Square itself. All the way up the long side, all the way down to the Alexander Park and all the way up the steep ramp entering through the arch of the Museum building. And that's how it was from then on. The nice convenient little gate had been an opening day indulgence only.

I had been prescient about wanting to arrive on time. Despite our lengthy detour we were still early but there were already a great many people ahead of us. Our little scheme of percolating inconspicuously to a preferred location however had been nipped in the bud by the authorities. They had locked the auditorium doors and nobody could get in. We were obliged to go down to a lower level to check our coats but the building was comfortably ventilated and this time one could have no complaint. We went back upstairs and, trying to pretend we weren't trying to cop the best seats, promenaded casually back and forth in front of the center double doors. However the pressure of oncoming culture lovers behind us practically squashed us right up against them. We literally had to brace ourselves with our hands and push with our behinds.

On the dot of seven a whistle blew. Other doors were opened but our fat female usher had moved from her post. Norton and I hesitated a moment.

"For God's sake let's go!" cried a voice. We were thrust through the doors and went catapulting down the aisle. It was the opening of the Oklahoma Territory to the homesteaders all over again. Peo-

ple poured into the seats like flood waters. Breathlessly Norton and
I scrambled for two in the last row of the first block. They were very
good seats too since the floor was raked and we had a fine view and
ample leg room.

We still had a considerable wait before the performance began
and I noticed with interest that the Russian beside me was reading
an English language newspaper. I couldn't see what it was since he
was on the bottom half of the front page, the title folded down. He
also had a copy of *Pravda* and when he had finished he carefully
folded the English paper inside it, leaving both on the seat when he
got up to stretch his legs.

I was hoping eagerly it might be the New York *Times* or the
London *Daily Mail* but I doubt it. The next day, Monday, we saw
two or three English language papers on the hotel newsstands but
they were all printed by the Communist press.

The original intention of those who planned the entertainment
for the Petroleum Congress had been to have two gala evenings
of ballet at the Bolshoi Theatre, since they knew the house itself
was as great an attraction as the performance, but even an au-
thoritarian state must bend to art. They were told that because of
schedules and conflicts it would be impossible for their top artists
to appear in an identical program twice in the same week. They
therefore decided, and quite wisely, to hold one performance on the
enormous stage of the Palace of Congresses.

It was *Don Quixote,* a full-length ballet in three acts, and the
sets, costumes and lighting were as notable as were the dancers;
lovely, strong and limber creatures, obviously some of their very top
stars. I wish I could give their names but once again I was stymied
by the Cyrillic script of the program. This kind of ignorance is
maddening, it isn't all that hard to learn Russian lettering, and I
strongly recommend doing it. I recommend it to myself too in the
event I am ever allowed back, but if the Russians read this book I
fancy my chances of a return visit are slim.

Norton and I left the Palace shortly before the end of the performance and walked across Red Square to the Rossiya Hotel. It

was not very late, perhaps a little after ten and the Square was deserted. Not a car broke the sweep of the spacious thoroughfare. The lighted red stars shone down on emptiness with the exception of the two guards and a token knot of people staring at Lenin's tomb.

At the hotel Norton suggested stopping off at our room first and a sound suggestion it was but I was starving and said, "No, let's go on up to the restaurant."

"But you can leave your coat."

"What does it matter? I'll check it at '21.'"

I will, eh? In the doorway of the restaurant loomed a giant whose mission in life was to keep people away. There were two or three groups ahead of us and as we approached he cried out like the guests at the Mad Hatter's tea party: "No room, no room!"

"But we have reservations."

"No room."

"We will see the administrator."

Administrator, we had learned, was the password. Whether he was a spy for the Kremlin I can't say but even the waiters, and they were a recalcitrant bunch who went their own way and took their own time, gave ground a fraction when the administrator spoke.

Even that magic word however was not potent enough to get me through with my coat on.

"I'll check it inside."

"*Nyet.* Downstairs, second floor you check."

In other capitals of the world headwaiters can seem antagonistic too but they rarely apply physical violence which our chap seemed on the verge of doing, such was his zeal to get my coat off me.

"Oh God," muttered my husband. "What did I tell you? We should have stopped."

"Yes, darling, you are quite right, we should have. Now please be an angel and go to our room as you wanted to and take my coat. I'll order a double carafe of vodka."

Having carried the day the gorilla let me in and I sat at our table where, sooner than I had dared hope—this time the elevator had not jammed—Norton joined me. His luck in having made the trip without mishap had restored his good humor.

That first evening we had shared our table with the two men from Hamburg. Our companions this time were two German women, buxom and bold.

Champagne was already cooling on the table when we got there and double portions of caviar awaited them. When they arrived the one who seemed to be the hostess told us her name was Krazna. The other one remained a mystery.

They drank the champagne in great gulps, gobbled the caviar and ordered more. "Keep bringing it, keep bringing it," cried Frau Krazna, "and lemon, lots of lemon." She slipped a wad of rubles into the waiter's pocket. She was a relentlessly vulgar creature and I kept thinking to myself what her kind must have been like when they got to Paris.

That night for the first time the meat was really delicious, a tender filet but its sole accompaniment was the everlasting potato. This grandeur the petroleum potentates missed out on for they were at the American Embassy being entertained by Ambassador Beam. I am sure they had caviar but they would probably have given an oil well for a head of lettuce or an artichoke.

The next day we were off to Zagorsk a short drive from the capital. Today it is an industrial center with a population of about 600,000 but its claim to fame and its attraction for tourists are the ancient monasteries which still flourish modestly.

Boris Godunov is buried there and his daughter survived a siege there in the fifteenth century but the oldest monastery, Troitsko-Sergiyevskaya-Lavra, dates from 1340. Sergiyevskaya was a monk, a shrewd politician and a friend of Czars who did himself no harm.

The oldest church is also the loveliest with marvelous icons. Perhaps others believe, as I used to, that icons have to be religious figures, usually dark, with the heads and shoulders framed in silver or gold. Frequently they are but they may also be frescoes on wooden screens or plaster walls, so long as they represent saints or the

Virgin and Child. The paintings in the most ancient chapel have something of the quality of Italian frescoes.

Another chapel has blue, star-sprinkled onion domes and there is a handsome soft blue and white bell tower. This structure is more recent, dating—so the guide said—from the eighteenth century, but the other monasteries or churches were built between the fourteenth and sixteenth centuries.

There is a large ornate and richly carved building with the date 1903 embedded in its threshold. While it has an altar it is in effect a refectory and meeting hall.

A Russian Orthodox priest with a high black hat, a black robe, a pale face, and a black beard showed us around and allowed me to take his picture.

In the last two or three years an important bishop of the Orthodox Church was invested at Zagorsk and many people, chiefly the old, worship there.

As we understood it, the state pays the monks a pittance and the rest of their income derives from gifts of the faithful. Religion is not totally banned. The Soviet Government found that impractical for, as one of their politicians said, "Religion is like a nail. The harder you hit it on the head the deeper it becomes imbedded in the wood."

The only thing is that if the state feels that a person is getting a little too regular in his attendance at religious services he is likely to find that in some mysterious way he is not getting the advancements or perquisites or increase of income he might normally expect.

There is an amusing toy museum at Zagorsk and a museum of applied arts which is dull. By the time we had finished our sightseeing it was well past the lunch hour. Every one was hungry but the only facility was a wretched little cafeteria where they served tasteless Russian beer and some papier-mâché sandwiches. This kind of thing is exasperating. Zagorsk is an enormous tourist center. People come by the thousands, they pay entrance fees and there is no reason why there shouldn't be decent restaurants.

Driving back to Moscow we saw a curious sight, a funeral in a truck. There was a coffin, a big wreath and mourning family and friends clustered around. They were, I suppose, on their way to the cemetery.

Had we passed them a bit later we would have been tempted to hail them for a lift as two of our six buses broke down and we all had to be reallocated with some of the group sitting on the bottom of the bus or the arms of seats. Back at the hotel the elevator stuck between the fourth and fifth floors.

There are times when the visitor wonders why Russians don't exert on the home front some of the chilling efficiency they brought to bear in overrunning Hungary and Czechoslovakia.

Our appetites not assuaged by the food of Zagorsk we went to one of the cafeterias to find that the day's menu consisted of brown bread and butter, as always very good, hard-boiled eggs and cucumbers. "Cucumbers are rich in all kinds of vitamins," said the doctor. Hooray.

He further practiced his profession by peering into my mouth to check up on the tooth which was causing me a fair amount of anguish every time I chewed anything.

Unable to spot any trouble there he went off to minister to Mr. William Tavoulareas, the president of Mobil Oil, who had come a cropper with a bad back. I gathered that the laying on of hands did the trick, so on his return we started on our big adventure, a visit to the Bolshoi Theatre.

One of the oil men had assured us it was not far from the hotel. "Go to the end of Red Square and it's off beyond that."

The rumor that taxis were available at one of the entrances to the Hotel Rossiya having proved a canard we set off on foot. We walked the length of Red Square and looked about us. Later we learned that had we swiveled our heads slightly more to the right we would have seen our goal but that evening we didn't.

We asked several Russians the way to the Bolshoi Theatre. We felt that was reasonably understandable and so it was but assorted citizens had their own ideas of its location. Finally, a pretty blond girl overhearing us gestured to us to follow her.

She plunged at once into the bowels of the earth with us scurrying after her like Alice's White Rabbit. There are many pedestrian underpasses in Moscow, for the boulevards are wide and the squares enormous and even though the traffic is not heavy there is enough of it to make navigation risky.

We hurried along for some time and then, to our surprise, our guide plunged ever deeper. This time down a steep flight of stairs into the real subway, complete with turnstiles devouring kopecks. Norton and I looked at each other. This *couldn't* be right. "No matter what she says or does, let's don't get in a train," Norton said. I agreed with him. "That oil man said it was an easy walk. This is crazy." Still there we were in an authentic Moscow subway station. Having heard so much about their splendor I looked about me with disillusion.

True the platform was clean, which was a nice change from New York, but the walls were ordinary old tile and trains pulled in and out and crowds of people hurried by just as they did at home. Where was all the vaunted splendor? Later we were to learn that only *some* of the stations are grandiose, many of them are common or garden and this, alas, was such a one.

Still our guide kept going ahead of us. Desperate I caught up with her, took her arm and burst into a snatch of song in what I fondly fancied to be a rich contralto. I also executed a couple of agile dance steps. This caper, of course, was intended to symbolize theatre, the entertainment world, and were we headed toward same?

She laughed and nodded. *"Da, da"* and getting into the spirit of the thing sketched a slight tarantella.

"She says yes we're right," I said to Norton. The doctor doesn't like to be made conspicuous, still he grinned. "You could have gotten the meaning over to her just as well by showing her our tickets," he said but it had been a long time since I had acted and I was enjoying myself. Besides, although there were a great many people about they were too preoccupied by their own affairs, too eager to get home, to pay any attention to us. There was no question, however, that the girl herself was beginning to look puzzled.

At last, to our infinite relief she took us up a flight of stairs. Although not yet at street level we had left the trains and tunnels and a minute or two later we climbed another flight and came out in the open and there, across a broad intersection was the Bolshoi. We thanked our indefatigable little friend and hurried to the theatre.

For reasons I cannot explain I always thought it would look like the Paris Opera House. Smaller but that kind of architecture. Not at all. The Bolshoi looks like a Greek temple. Macabre note: It is situated on Sverdlov Square. According to Robert K. Massie the author of *Nicholas and Alexandra,* Jacob Sverdlov was an intimate of Lenin who occupied the key administrative post of President of the Central Executive Committee of the All Russian Congress of Soviets.

With Lenin's full knowledge it was he who ordered the massacre of the royal family at Ekaterinburg in 1918. The name of the town was subsequently changed to Sverdlovsk in his dishonor.

By the time we got to the theatre, after our tour of the subway, the curtain was already up. We were shunted upstairs and shoved into a box. As our eyes became accustomed to the dark we realized that it was crowded and there was only one seat left. Norton pushed me into it and leaned against the wall for the rest of the act.

The performance that night was a Rimsky-Korsakov opera, *The Invisible City of Kitezh.* When the curtain fell we vented our annoyance on the old woman who had pushed us in saying, "We have paid for two seats why do we have only one?" She snatched our tickets from us, looked at them and yelled at us, *"Parterre, parterre."* We should have been in the orchestra.

We thought we might stop off at the cafe but there was such a mob milling about the counter we gave up and went on downstairs where after a bit of searching we found an usher who showed us to our rightful places and I had a chance to look around.

The Bolshoi is a thoroughly satisfactory theatre. The Leningrad Theatre, in soft blue and gold, had been lovely but probably the authentic theatre colors are crimson and gold. The Bolshoi has five tiers or balconies and an enormous golden chandelier suspended from a painted ceiling.

Here, too, as in Leningrad, the orchestra seats were armchairs with the exception of the last two rows which were crimson banquettes with upholstered backs and arms set at intervals. They looked very comfortable.

The Invisible City of Kitezh is perhaps not its composer's masterpiece although Rimsky-Korsakov is good and noisy; lots of brass and trumpets and drums, always enjoyable, and if the principals were not first rank the chorus was powerful and the scenic effects fantastic.

I mean to say when you have surging crowds, burning wooden villages devoured in flame and smoke, a huge tableau of a charging army and great palaces reflected in lakes what more do you want? It was Theatre with a capital T and it was dazzling.

To our friend Irving R. Levine and his *Travel Guide to Russia* I am indebted for the information that "the dancers of the Bolshoi number 250. Five hundred people are employed in shops that manufacture wigs, ballet slippers, flowers, swords, costumes and stage effects such as wind, fire, rain, and flood." I can personally vouch for the fact that these magicians are artists.

I would gladly have stayed to the end of the opera but as I have said the theatre is not my loved one's cup of tea so we left after the second act. Also there was a valid enough reason other than a lack of rapport with the entertainment world. It was now after ten and we wanted to reach the National Hotel before it was too late to get a table for dinner.

The headwaitress said we would have to wait ten minutes and although Norton was skeptical she was as good as her word. In the meantime we went to the bar for a drink and discovered to our surprise that they would take only dollars in payment. There is a fine inconsistency in Russian life. They jeer the U.S.A. as a decadent, capitalist, imperialist country but they too thirst for the dollar considering it, even in its present enfeebled condition, highly desirable.

When we went back into the dining room the headwaitress had a table waiting and we shared it with two Italians, oil men, who proved most companionable but who would eat only pasta, lamenting its quality.

The National Hotel is very near the Bolshoi as is the Metropole where one can usually get good blini, those delicious pancakes with caviar and sour cream.

When we had finished dinner we found that it was an easy walk back to the Hotel Rossiya. We were grateful to our well-meaning guide who had led us on the wild-goose chase through the subway but decided that occasionally an intelligent tourist knows more than an ignorant native.

The next morning a good many of the numbered hours of my life were frittered away trying to reserve a taxi to drive us to the restaurant where we were going to dine that night.

A nice Intourist girl in the Concert Hall where the Ladies Center was located wasted fifteen minutes of her time and mine hanging on the telephone and scribbling down information only to surface with the news that she could do nothing. I should try the transportation girl at the Service Bureau on the second floor of the north wing of the hotel.

I made the eternal trek to the Service Bureau and there came upon one of the brightest and best girls I had dealt with. Yet the fact is they were all good. They were intelligent, capable, and pleasant and it couldn't have been easy. Every time they raised their eyes it was to see phalanxes of people lined up before their desks and more hordes pressing in behind.

Next to the Russians themselves, who of course did not require Intourist service, the nation with the most delegates to the Congress was the United States and it seemed as though ninety-nine percent of them were Texans. I went around scooping up those molasses accents with a spoon. However, there *were* others: Iranians, Danes, Italians, Germans, Egyptians, and the girls had to cope with them and their mother tongues. They did it admirably. Nor could they look forward to surcease in the near future. Petroleum was to be followed by Psychiatry. There probably weren't as many psychiatrists as there were oil men but their problems might have been even more complex!

In any event my bright button did arrange for me to have a taxi and I was to call back at 7:45 to get its license number. She asked me for a ruble which I didn't have, my spouse having pocketed the swag. He kept the money papers and our passports—whenever the hotels relinquished them—because he doesn't have confidence in my ability to cope with mundane affairs.

When I confessed my poverty she shrugged and laughed. "It's all right, don't bother." I don't know what she wanted it for. A commission? A deposit on the cab?

Somewhat bemused by the encounter I started off on my own for Red Square. That morning Norton was attending one of the lectures. I went into St. Basil's Cathedral and climbed the towers to the interior of the domes where there is an intricate complex of small, cramped chapels poorly lighted. Even so there is enough visibility to appreciate that every inch is painted with colorful and dramatic icons.

I lost my way several times and in the tiny twisting corridors bumped into a group of gasping giggling girls but it was an enjoyable interlude.

If contrast, too, may be said to be the spice of life, I experienced it that morning, for after the tiny chapels I crossed the square to GUM. GUM is overpowering. Along that entire expanse which runs the length of Red Square there is no door. Show windows but no door. You have to go all the way to the upper end to get in.

The interior is composed of enormous aisles, very wide, very long and roofed with arched glass so that it looks like a European railroad station. There are aerial bridges with goods displayed in the upper arcades and in the center a great fountain. On the air hangs an aroma of unwashed humanity and the merchandise is deplorable. From an American point of view. We were told, however, that Muscovites themselves think little of GUM, considering it a Mecca for unsophisticated Russians from the provinces.

The quality of nearly everything we saw was sleazy and the prices exorbitant. In the United States, if you work at it, you may pay as high as $6 for a pair of panty hose but as a rule a very good quality runs between $2.75 and $3.50. Cheap ones may be found for $.79 and even $.59. In GUM a pair that doesn't compare with our cheapest cost $7.50 to $8. Lipsticks were not so bad, $1.15 to $1.25 and $1.50. Small unattractive scarves cost $9, $10 and $15.

GUM sells everything, including food, with long lines of shoppers waiting to get in to buy cheeses and canned goods. There are ice cream cone stands inside and outside the building and they are highly popular. The Ministry of Cones must be one of the most profitable in the government.

A good deal of camping and beach equipment was on display but it too was expensive and I thought it ironic and not very kind to show it. How many Russians could afford it, where would they go to use it and how would they get it there? If ever one needs a car it is for camping or picnicking.

There is one good thing to be said about GUM though. You save a lot of money through having no desire to buy anything. Indeed that is the tourists complaint; the scarcity of tempting merchandise or souvenirs. In the opinion of the women on our own tour the best buys were Russian phonograph records, art books—I myself bought two or three of them later in the trip—and the folk art boxes. These vary in size from those so small they hold only a pair of earrings or cuff links to ones large enough to contain cigars or even objects of more substantial size.

They are made of a composition material, I believe compressed papier-mâché, heavily lacquered in black and painted with Russian scenes; princes and princesses, St. George and the Dragon or, as on the one I bought, a fairy-tale castle. Happily the People's State does not seem to have infringed on this particular art form but the boxes are not cheap. They start at around $8 and go much higher. Amber is also a commodity they offer in abundance.

In both GUM and the Beriozka shops they sell wooden toys,

specializing in nests of brightly painted peasant figures: Matreoshka dolls. You unscrew your peasant around her middle and within is a smaller one, a smaller one inside that and so on diminishing to the last teeny tiny little doll no bigger than a seed. Unfortunately those protracted series are rare. Mostly you have to settle for a three-peasant family.

Moscow has several glorified pawnshops called Commission Stores where Russians take their belongings if they want to sell them. It might be jewelry, china, silver, ornaments, or *bibelots*. They are professionally appraised and if sold the shop takes a commission and the owner gets the money. We were given the addresses of some of these places but never seemed to find the time to visit any.

Margaret Gussow, it was she who had been to Russia twelve years before, bought a balalaika and Marty Shepherd, committing what I considered an act of loyalty comparable to laying down one's life for a friend, bought, for a friend, a set of china. She and Margaret toted these awkward spoils all the way across Russia to the Sea of Japan, across that sea and across the Pacific Ocean to their respective homes in California and Texas. When you are flying Russian planes and economy class on American jets, lugging looney souvenirs by hand all the way, you are profoundly uncomfortable and truly dedicated. Escaping unscathed from GUM I rejoined Norton and we went on to enjoy two of the pleasantest hours we spent in Russia.

Before leaving New York our friend Nancy Adler, of the New York *Times* Adler family, had suggested we get in touch with Bernard Gwertzman, the paper's representative in Moscow. This we had done and he and his wife invited us to lunch. "I'll come by the hotel and pick you up," he said over the phone, "you'll never make it on your own." How right he was.

He had also told us that his license number was KO 4 and that all cars owned by Americans started with KO. Maybe the People's State Motor Vehicle Department had meant to have it O.K. and got confused.

In any event he picked us up as agreed and drove us to their apartment. It was a nice apartment, by Moscow standards extraordinarily so, but it was in a ghetto. A respectable, reasonably attractive ghetto but still a ghetto in the sense that all foreign correspondents are segregated from the rest of the foreign colony and, of course, from all Russians.

The New York *Times* has had a lease on the apartment for several years and all their people have stayed there. At the time we saw them Bernie and his wife Marie Jeanne had done a stretch of nearly two and a half years and were looking forward to returning to the United States and living in Washington in the autumn.

"Have you liked it?" I asked.

"It has been," said Mr. Gwertzman, "very interesting."

"The apartment's bugged," his wife informed us cheerfully, "but we don't mind. We say anything we want to."

Both the Gwertzmans speak fluent Russian but even so Bernie told us that his job was difficult since the Russians never give out any information. "A lot of my time is spent reading dispatches and Russian papers," he said. How correspondents manage who don't speak Russian, and most of them don't, I can't imagine.

We met another member of the family too: Fitzie the cat. Fitzie was taking out her citizenship papers and when the Gwertzmans left she too was coming to America.

"It's sickening," Marie Jeanne said, "the way diplomats and correspondents have pets and then when they go they simply leave them to fend for themselves."

We agreed that that kind of irresponsibility is heinous. Far better to have an animal put away than to leave it to loneliness, cold, fear, and starvation.

Speaking of animals, I observed that I had been struck by the fact that in Leningrad, a city of nearly 4,000,000 people, we had seen two dogs, not counting those in the circus. In Moscow, a city of over 7,000,000, also two. Although it seemed incredible I assumed it was due to the housing shortage and the fact that two and three families are obliged to share an apartment. There is no room for animals. Also the food, almost exclusively starch, is not good for dogs. It is not good for Russians either, judging from the anatomies populating the streets, but when I expressed this theory to Mrs. Gwertzman she said I was quite wrong.

"You don't see them," she explained, "because they are not in the neighborhoods frequented by tourists. But you come into a residential district, especially at night at the dog-walking hour, and you'll see plenty. Russians love dogs. They share their food with them, they even have vets." And she went on to say that what she found distressing was the fact that they had so many *big* dogs. "Great Danes, Saint Bernards, and it's true they really don't have room in the apartments for them to get any exercise."

When we told the Gwertzmans we had been to the stud farm, Marie Jeanne said eagerly, "Oh, we're going there tomorrow, a little excursion has been arranged."

They had two cars and a chauffeur at their disposal but apparently entering and leaving the city at will is not the way it's done. One must have Permission, it must be Arranged by the Authorities.

If one is an adult this kind of surveillance is tedious. It can't be much fun for teenagers either.

Although born in Washington our hostess was of French parentage and the delicious luncheon we were served by a neatly dressed maid bespoke her ancestry.

Thinking how much they would enjoy such food I asked the Gwertzmans if many of their Russian friends came to see them. "No," they said, "they never come here. Very rarely we go to visit them but usually we meet in restaurants." They made appointments two or three weeks in advance and hoped nothing would happen to prevent their friends from joining them.

While we were at the luncheon table the Los Angeles *Times* telephoned to ask if the New York *Times* would look after its plants while it was out of town on a brief trip. The New York *Times* graciously agreed to do so. Noblesse oblige.

Since I was having trouble with my bad tooth we spoke to the Gwertzmans about dentists. "What do foreigners do if they have to go to one?" Norton asked.

"Usually they fly out to Helsinki," said our host. "They have several very good American-trained dentists there."

"I see," said my husband. "Well, Helsinki isn't really practical for us. We're leaving for Samarkand Saturday and here it is Thursday. I'm a little worried about Ilka though. I think maybe, just as a precaution, she ought to be looked at."

Bernie tried reassurance. "I wouldn't say Russian dentists are bad. They have *some* good ones and some good doctors too. It's just that by our standards they're a little rough."

Since they both spoke such excellent Russian I asked the Gwertzmans if they would be nice enough to try to get Frieda Lurie on the phone for me. I explained about our missed luncheon appointment and said I would like to ask her to dine and would they join us?

"We'd like to very much," Bernie said. "She's someone I've wanted to meet for a long time."

Marie Jeanne went at once to the telephone but even burbling Russian like a native she had no better luck than I. "Never mind," I said, "I'll have the hotel try again and we'll hope to get reservations at the Aragvi." This, we had been told, was the best restaurant in Moscow.

"We want to see the best of everything," we explained laughing. "How about the Czar's private apartments in the Kremlin? Could you exert a little pull?"

Bernie shook his head.

"*Nyet,* eh?"

"*Nyet.* They've been opened to British and French diplomats but never to the Americans, despite the fact that the Embassy has requested permission many times."

Later, when I was wondering about that, Norton said maybe we had denied the Russians visiting rights to someplace they had wanted to see and maybe it was tit for tat.

"Oh come on," I said. "You mean to tell me we refused them Mount Vernon?"

"I don't know but we wouldn't let Khrushchev go to Disneyland, remember?"

"That was different! That was a security problem."

He laughed. "Don't ask me to probe the Russian psyche."

Shortly after luncheon we left the hospitable Gwertzmans. We did not want to outstay our welcome but also we had to be back at the hotel to catch the bus for a museum tour. Bernie's chauffeur drove us and this time a native knew better than a visitor. We were certain he was on the wrong track when suddenly the vast bulk of the Rossiya loomed before us.

The museum was the Tretyakov Art Gallery, founded originally by two rival and rich art collecting brothers in the mid-nineteenth century. Most of the pictures date from that period too, although some of them were painted a little later.

One of Russia's most famous artists, Ilya Yefimovich Repin, is represented by probably his most renowned work, *Ivan the Terrible,* holding in his arms the body of his son whom he has just murdered.

Another gruesome episode depicts a maiden standing on a bed in a prison cell. Water is streaming through the bars of the window obviously flooding the cell and rats are struggling to clamber onto the bed to escape it but you know that there *is* no escape. Maiden and rats are soon to drown. That one is *very* popular.

There is a quite remarkable painting of a man, presumably Christ, seated in the desert brooding, so it is implied, over the fate of the worker. If this is so Christ knew something about Czarist Russia that nobody else knew at the time. Yet there is no denying the impact of the picture with its haunted and haunting expression of sadness.

All these canvases mean a great deal to the Russians, especially at this period when their art is sterile chiefly because it is state controlled. No matter how wiley, ruthless, or politically brilliant the men of the government may be their artistic background or interest is elementary. What they like, and what the Worker had better like too, is a good straightforward story telling picture of the old academic school. In the Tretyakov they've got acres of the stuff. They also

have something else and I would suggest that the traveler visit the
gallery without a guide. This is possible because it is in Moscow
proper and you can walk out of your hotel door and simply go
without benefit of monitored taxi or tourist bus.

The reason for doing it on your own is because if you are indifferent to academic art, the guide is not going to understand the
perversion, and will insist, willy-nilly, that you view the enormous
collection in its entirety. This, to many people, will seem a waste of
time but the treasures on the first floor are incomparable. There
they have some of the greatest icons that, I should imagine, are to
be seen anywhere. Incomparably rich, colorful, solemn, and even
gay.

At the desk we tried to buy postcard reproductions but at that
time none were available. There was, however, a charming collection of miniatures from old illuminated Russian manuscripts.

A little later, after returning to the hotel I sat at an Intourist
desk trying to work out the irksome business of reserving a table
at the Aragvi Restaurant for the following night. The restaurant
line was busy. Would I come back later? the Intourist girl asked.
I would not, not for all the caviar in Russia but I would phone her
from our room. She looked at me with open admiration. "You
are not afraid of it, the phone? Most foreigners are."

"I blanch at the sight of it but at least I can be sitting down and
all I have to do is dial these numbers?" I glanced at the slip of
paper on which she was scribbling the number of her extension.

"That is all. I will answer."

"And you speak English, you glorious girl."

I went off and the gambit worked. Provided anyone on the other
end spoke English we could get the outer world on our phone, it was
just that it didn't ring in our room. Other people's phones rang but
our bell was on the blink. To my delight she had secured a table. I
phoned the Gwertzmans with the news but there would only be the
four of us. By no amount of effort were we able to raise Frieda
Lurie.

All those arrangements, however, were for the next night. Our immediate goal was the Uzbekistan Restaurant. When I had got the reservations the young lady had requested $22 which struck me as high and I said as much. "Food here isn't cheap, is it?"

"Oh," she said, "that is because of the reservation. Without it you and your husband can dine for four or five rubles each but you will have to stand in line. Besides, this includes your drinks." I began to perk up. And she was right about the line. Others had warned us too. When we arrived in the with-difficulty-reserved cab it was to find a long line of Russians waiting outside the locked glass doors.

We went up and waved our blue cards and the doors were immediately opened by the headwaiter. The Russians courteously made way for us, but pushing through to the head of the line, especially in a foreign country, makes me extremely uncomfortable.

Another American couple arrived when we did and as they seemed to be having some difficulty about their reservation we asked them to share our table which, as it turned out, was set for four in any event, and I mean Set. Two carafes of vodka, four bottles of wine, two red, two white, and an infinity of small bowls holding varied and delicious hors d'oeuvres. These were followed by a rich soup further enriched by spaghetti, then the main course, an excellent rice and shashlik dish topped off by the inevitable ice cream. I couldn't eat it all but it was a lot for $11 a person and I was sorry I had been so chintzy as to have brought the matter up with the Intourist girl.

The restaurant was of fair size and there were only three or four tables of foreigners. The rest of the diners were Russian. There was a pretty good orchestra and lots of dancing and as the evening wore on things really began to swing.

A blond buxom girl moved to the center of the floor and started dancing alone. She was full of verve and the others fell back and started clapping in rhythm. Her solo went on for some little time and ended in a great spinning whirl and uninhibited applause and laughter. It was the first time we had seen Russians really having fun and we enjoyed it as much as they did.

I would happily have stayed for a long time but not knowing how spirited the evening would prove to be Norton had asked the cab driver to come back at ten. He had done this by pointing to the hands on his watch, pointing to the restaurant and pointing to us. *"Da da,"* said the driver pointing to ten on *his* watch.

At ten the doctor went out to check. Sure enough the man was there. Norton then pointed to 10:45. *"Da da."* All too quickly the hands reached the appointed number and this time we thought it would be unfair to delay any longer. We reached the hotel feeling we had put one over on the Secret Police. They hadn't the foggiest notion *when* we would be back. If that sounds childish the whole system of checking, bugging, and following is childish.

I seriously doubt that any of our party was followed but after we had been home for a few weeks I dined one evening with a friend in Chicago who told me that some friends of hers, who were Jewish, had been on a tour in Moscow and had asked to see the ancient Jewish synagogue. They received the impression that the Intourist guide was trying to dissuade them but they insisted on going. Shortly afterwards they noticed that whenever they got into their bus a man appeared who had not been there at the beginning of the tour. He never spoke to anybody and they never found out his name or who he was but that he was not a member of the group was certain.

When Norton and I got back to the hotel after dining at the Uzbekistan we went to bed but I was awakened about 4 A.M. by my tooth causing me considerable pain. When Norton woke up I told him about it and he said, "That cinches it. We'll have to have it looked at. I don't know how good the dentists are here but I assume a Moscow dentist is likely to be better than one in Samarkand. I'll go find out."

After breakfast we went to the Red Cross station where they had told him we should check in. With almost five thousand Congress people on their hands the Russians had set up a first aid post on the ground floor of the hotel. The doctor whom we encountered there led us across the courtyard to the dentist's office where a funny brusque little interpreter told us the dentist was busy. "Within, he has a Danish and from Iran comes another one next." Traffic seemed heavy but if we would return at noon she assured us the doctor would see us.

Norton went off to attend a lecture on a topic that interested him, and that was presented largely by the Japanese: the conversion of petroleum by-products into edible food. I departed for the Pushkin Gallery. I had great good luck because that morning a group of Americans on an art tour were being shepherded by a distinguished-looking man who obviously knew what he was talking about. I learned later that he was Mr. Gordon Washburn of New York's Asia House, a most knowledgeable art connoisseur.

Since I was not in the group I felt rather brash and did not like to stand there too openly listening. On the other hand I was fascinated so I strolled casually around, one ear out on a stalk, made quick little sallies to other parts of the gallery, came back and stared at other canvases while listening to what Mr. Washburn was saying about the painting his group was looking at.

This ostrich-like procedure did not pass unnoticed because when, at the end of the lecture, I went up to apologize for my eavesdropping and to thank Mr. Washburn for all I had learned, Mrs. Washburn said kindly, "Oh that's all right, Miss Chase. I was sure it was you but I thought maybe you didn't want to be recognized." She was too courteous to add, "for what you are: a non-paying snoop."

The Pushkin has several Picassos of the Blue period as well as Cézannes, Van Goghs, Renoirs, Degases, and Monets.

It also houses the classic giants: El Greco, Murillo, Rivera, Rembrandt, and Rubens. The last is represented by a gross female satyr with hairy goats' legs and hoofs and great flabby breasts giving suck to two ancient monkey-like men. Looking at it one's stomach turns over and one is tempted to say sharply, "Really, Peter Paul, it's all very well to lay paint on canvas with the hand of a god but enough's enough!"

Since it was nearing noon, the hour for our appointment with the dentist, I left the gallery and walked back to the hotel. We had a brief wait and were then shown into his office. It looked clean and well equipped. The proprietor was rather short with dark hair brushed across his brow, making him look as though he was wearing a little cap and his left canine tooth was a bright gleaming gold. I think it was a status symbol. Gold for teeth is hard to come by in Russia and very expensive. Most of the populace have teeth capped with silver or steel. It is only appropriate that a leading dentist should have something better than that.

I sat down in the chair and the interpreter explained about my biting down on a bone and my fear that the tooth was broken. The doctor nodded his understanding. "No speak much English but open please." I complied by opening my mouth and his English proved adequate. He peered inside and said, "Jesus Christ."

Since his tone was one of interest rather than awe or alarm I was not too nervous but I was distressed when he took an instrument, reached in and delicately lifted out half a tooth with a bit of pulp dangling from it. "Ah, well, never mind. Can fix but will take several days."

My husband volunteered the information that we did not have several days.

"The trouble is, Doctor, we are leaving for Samarkand tomorrow night."

"Jesus Christ. Well, we see. No go dentist Samarkand. No go." The warning was stern and we assured him we would not.

He set to work pulling forward, I was relieved to see, a modern high speed drill. Even so.

"Doctor, please. What about a little Novocain?"

A merry laugh greeted this infantile suggestion.

"No, no, you do not want Novocain."

"*Da da,* I do."

"Ach." He looked annoyed.

"I do think, Doctor," said Dr. Brown, "that Novocain would be a good idea."

"Ah, Jesus Christ. I do not like Novocain. Xylocain. Much better." I believe they are approximately the same but I was not interested in arguing their comparative merits. All I wanted was to have it administered.

The dentist got up from his stool, went over to a small cabinet on the wall and brought back the wherewithal. But even as he was filling the syringe he hesitated.

"Madame," he said pleadingly, "you do not really want?"

I understood what Bernie Gwertzman had had in mind when he said Russian dentists were a little rough.

"Yes, Doctor, I really want. *Da, da, da.*" I was sounding like an imbecilic baby but I wanted him to know I emphatically meant yes.

"Jesus Christ." He then proceeded in business-like fashion to drive the needle into the inside of my cheek. It hurt but only briefly and while waiting for the drug to take effect he opened up quite a snappy conversation. He acknowledged that American dentists were the best in the world and he said, a little sadly, that he could not get the equipment in Soviet Russia but he added, "I have study for thirteen year. My uncle learn me, he was famous doctor." I was glad to hear it.

He sighed. "Ah, Jesus Christ." This time the inflection was nostalgic as one who remembers the good old days.

There was a little pause. "In all Russia maybe fifteen, maybe twenty good doctors." And again "Don't let them touch you Samarkand." Again we reassured him. Suddenly he said, "You know Richter, of course."

I shook my head. "I'm afraid not." I glanced at Norton who shook *his* head.

The dentist looked astounded. "But you must. He is American, he is famous."

"Richter scale?" I offered tentatively. I was not trying to be funny but it was the only Richter I knew. And I had hit the bull's eye.

"Scale! But of course. He is great pianist," and his fingers ran up and down an imaginary keyboard.

"Oh, *that* Richter," I said. I was still in the dark. (To Mr.

Sviatoslav Richter who, I have since learned, is an outstanding artist, my sincere apologies for my ignorance.)

"He came to me, I took care of him and then you know what?"

"What?"

"He brought to me a famous impresario, Mr. Sol Hurok."

"Him we've heard of," I said quickly.

"Well, this Mr. Hurok, Jesus Christ what a man, by a friend he sends me from America, American dentist equipment. High-speed drill $1500, a present for *me*."

I glanced at the menacing form of the high-speed drill a few feet from my head. "No, no, not that one. Much better, much more quiet. I have it in my home."

By now the Xylocain had taken effect and it was obvious from the doctor's movements that the inferior specimen was about to go into action. I thought of Joan of Arc and the men of the French underground who had endured tortures during the war and opened my mouth. Besides, Norton was there to protect me. Well, it wasn't a picnic but it wasn't any worse than the same procedure at home.

When he had my mouth well filled with assorted equipment our man spoke up again. "Your dentist at home, he is Jewish?" Surprised I shook my head, no. "How very American," he said cheerily. With a mouth full of hardware I could not reply to this cryptic comment and although later Norton and I spent considerable time trying to fathom it we never did come up with an answer.

Was the dentist himself Jewish? Judging from his appearance he might have been but what of it? Was he referring to the left-wing Jewish Defense League, causing trouble in New York because of what they considered to be harassment of Russian Jews and thinking it ironic that if Americans carried on that way they should not patronize Jewish dentists? Who knows?

A few minutes later as he was working he volunteered the information that he was tired. I thought he looked so and when conversation was once again feasible I said, "It's lunchtime. When you've finished with me why don't you just sign off for a while? Have something to eat sent in and rest a little?"

"No, no I cannot rest. Work all day nine to six, is too much. And I am old man, forty-six. Jesus Christ."

"You are *not* old," I said indignantly.

"Yes, yes. Open up, please." More machinery, more hardware. When he saw that it was making me gag he swabbed the roof of my mouth with some sort of anesthetic. I must have made a face, for he laughed. "Does not taste good, eh? Not good like brandy."

I managed to gargle that I could not drink brandy. "What I like is scotch," he said authoritatively. "Johnny Walker but Black Label. Red no good. Ballantine Twelve, good too."

The doctor fancies himself as something of a connoisseur of scotch so they launched into a learned discussion of the merits of assorted brands.

Finally he announced that he was putting in a dressing. "Arsene, arsene," he said to my husband who looked, I thought, a little blank.

"Arsenic, dear, he means arsenic."

The dentist impregnated a little cotton pellet with some salve, popped it into the cavity and turned to Norton.

"Doctor, you must remove this in five days. No later, *no later*. You understand?"

My husband nodded.

"Here," and he gave him a little pick with which to pluck it out reiterating the injunction to remove it in five days.

When we got home I understood his insistence. I learned from George Lindig, my own dentist, that arsenic hasn't been used in this country for thirty years. It can be serviceable in a pinch but if left in too long it rots the jawbone.

As we were leaving the office Norton asked how much he owed.

"Nothing, nothing. In Russia nobody pays doctor."

"That's all very well for Russians," Norton said, "but we are Americans. Why shouldn't we pay?"

"No, no. No pay." A sigh. "Little present maybe. Maybe. I am here till six. Oh, Jesus Christ."

"Goodbye, Doctor, thank you a thousand times. We are greatly in your debt."

The reason for the conversation about liquor was made clear. We went to the Beriozka shop and Norton bought some scotch, brandy, and a carton of American cigarettes. While waiting for the Xylocain to take effect he had noticed that the dentist smoked steadily. Norton took him the merchandise in the late afternoon and said he almost had his hands kissed in gratitude.

When we got back to New York, Dr. George Lindig sent me to an oral surgeon, Dr. Andrew Linz, having in the meantime briefed him on what had happened.

When I reached the threshold of his office I hesitated. "Doctor, you *are* going to give me an anesthetic for this job, aren't you?"

He looked as pained as I would have felt without it. "Please," he said, "we are not in Soviet Russia."

Indeed we weren't. He gave me a local anesthetic and after he had been working for a few minutes he suddenly stopped.

"*Now* are you going to pull it?" I asked.

He smiled. "That is one of the nicest compliments I have ever had. It's out."

That evening in Moscow the Gwertzmans fetched us in their car and we drove to the Aragvi Restaurant, flaunting our blue tickets of admission as we had at the Uzbekistan.

There are two high, narrow, main rooms with a balcony at the far end of one of them, a perch for a small orchestra. The food and atmosphere is Georgian but although it is supposed to be Moscow's best Norton and I preferred the Uzbekistan. The atmosphere is more sprightly and we thought the food quite as good.

It was an early evening since Bernie had work to do and we ourselves were leaving the following night for Samarkand. But first we were going to see one of the notable museums of Russia, or for that matter, the world. The Kremlin Armory ranks high. Even if you are not an armor buff, and I am not, don't let the name put you off. To be sure there is armor but they don't overdo it and oddly enough their particular pieces were fascinating. There were shirts of chain mail composed of 17,000 to 20,000 hand-forged links that took years to make and were wonderfully supple. Breastplates came into fashion because they covered a larger area and could be hammered out in less time.

There were some exquisite Fabergé eggs, the loveliest to my way of thinking being one of pale green enamel clover leaves set with diamond dew drops.

One may also see an enchanting toy that everyone Oohs and Ahs over and that is a tiny little train of gold cars, the Trans-Siberian Railroad with a bright ruby headlight.

There was a collection of ancient coaches, one being drawn by six white horses (stuffed) superbly caparisoned, another, with panels decorated by Boucher and a third, a present from Queen Elizabeth to Boris Godunov. He died in 1605 before it arrived in Russia so he never saw it. Too bad.

These coaches are like richly upholstered rooms on wheels and imagining them in procession with their prancing horses and liveried drivers and footmen, carrying kings and queens and diplomats in brilliant attire, one can only sigh at the drabness of life today.

A procession of sleek black limousines may be quite elegant but colorful and spirited it is not.

A curious and beautiful exhibit was a great ivory eagle with wings outspread. He had 3000 ivory feathers and was posed against a silk screen of embroidered waves and foam in grays and white. It was a gift from Japan.

Ivan III, also known as Ivan the Great, had a large intricately carved ivory throne, the back embellished with a panel on which appeared the crowned, two-headed imperial eagle of Holy Russia. Originally, however, the eagle was Byzantine and in all likelihood Zoë Paleologus brought the throne with her as part of her dowry. Zoë, better known by her orthodox name of Sophia, was the niece of the last Emperor of Byzantium and a ward of Pope Sixtus IV who successfully promoted her marriage to Ivan.

Sophia not only brought along a throne but the old family traditions too and Ivan and the Russian court adopted the etiquette of Constantinople with the eagle tossed in for good measure.

Peter the Great's throne had a high velvet back with a square hole cut in it through which a courtier murmured to the Czar the name and country of the diplomat he was receiving. The royal prompter.

Peter's boots were on display and they give one pause. Where were that man's knees? The monarch was high rise. It is said he stood over seven feet and he wore seven-league boots.

The scale of the exhibits in general was large. There were huge books, mostly gospels, bound in what may literally be called hard cover for they were of gold and ivory with religious figures in high relief fashioned of enamel and precious stones.

There were jeweled scepters and crowns like peaked caps bordered with sable and stitched with gems, worth a Czar's ransom, and magnificent table services of porcelain and Renaissance silver with shallow scoops of gold from which they drank wine and honey.

There were two dresses that belonged to Catherine the Great, one worn when she married Peter the Ineffectual at the age of sixteen and had a waist like a willow wand, the other a gown of her maturity. It is doubtful if the legs of Peter the Great, had he been around, could have spanned it, let alone his arms. That diet of pure starch must have been à la mode in eighteenth-century Russia too.

From the world of Mammon in the museum we went on to that of God, visiting the Cathedrals of the Annunciation, the Assumption, and the Archangel Michael, all within the Kremlin walls.

The same Zoë or Sophia, who brought the eagle to Russia, was, in a sense, responsible for the cathedrals. She obviously had her husband's ear, but nature too was her ally. In 1472, the year of their marriage, Moscow was partially razed by an earthquake. This was her opportunity.

Having lived in the Italy of Lorenzo the Magnificent and Leonardo da Vinci she understandably found Moscow a bit on the crude side. Presented with the providential gift of empty space, she sent south and presently Italian and Greek architects and artists began arriving

in the city. The most gifted of these was an Italian by the name of
Rodolfo di Fioravanti, nicknamed Aristotle because he was so smart.
He built the Cathedral of the Assumption where the Czars were
crowned and colleagues of his designed the Annunciation, site of
royal weddings and baptisms as well as the Cathedral of the
Archangel Michael.

In these churches, too, there were fabulous frescoes and icons, as
much as we could see of them through the dense crush of sightseers.
They were painted in the singing colors of the Renaissance; pink,
raspberry and scarlet, sharp blue, light green and glowing gold.

That last day in Moscow we took Wanda for a farewell luncheon
at "21." Although she had been responsible for our joining the
Congress tour we had seen very little of her. After all, for her it was
a business trip, and also she was indulging in a bit of auld lang
syne. To her delight she had run into Egyptian friends. Part of her
childhood had been spent in Egypt where her father was involved
in the oil industry and a couple of the men she had known
then were attending the Congress.

Although she had originally planned to go all the way across Russia, as we were about to do, she was obliged to fly to Rome that
afternoon for a business meeting.

Not unexpectedly at the door of the dining room we ran into
difficulty. Wanda had her coat on. Furthermore she intended to keep
it on.

"Take it off," said the bully.

"No," our girl said sweetly, "I will not. I am shortly leaving for
the airport and besides this place is cold."

She was right. One of the few contraptions that worked in the
Hotel Rossiya was the air conditioning in the dining room. It ran
under the windows and if your table was beside it you froze to
death.

"Is rule. Take off coat," he shouted and advanced a step toward
her. Dr. Brown, who is no pygmy, advanced too. The enemy fell
back muttering.

"I call administrator" and he rushed toward the manager's small

office. We three advanced into the dining room, found our table and
sat down. When we congratulated Wanda on her indomitability she
grinned impishly. "You realize, of course, they may refuse to serve
us?"

They did not, however, nor did the administrator appear. I suppose his spirit had been cowed by the foreign boors who did not
appreciate the civilizing influence of coatlessness.

Be it said in defense of us boors, we weren't trying to subvert
them with our decadent capitalistic ways. The only reason we clung
to our outer garments with a tenacity reminiscent of the defense of
Leningrad was the fact that most of the time we were in Moscow it
was chilly.

As we were leaving "21," the administrator happened to emerge
from his sanctum and I said we were planning to dine there that
night before taking the plane for Samarkand, adding, "Since we
must give up our rooms in all likelihood I will have my coat. Will
you please tell the gorilla that I intend to keep it and that I don't
wish to be assaulted."

The administrator smiled wanly. "You are welcome to come,"
he said, "most welcome." Poor man, I felt for him.

That afternoon I went with Ann Weeks, Mrs. Lewis Weeks, the
wife of the distinguished geologist who was a member of our party,
to Gorky Street. It was far enough from the hotel to make the idea
of a cab appealing but there was none to be had and Ann is an
exercise enthusiast. Yoga and walking. "I *enjoy* walking," she said
briskly. "You should wear Jolly Green Giants, like mine and you
would too." She was referring to her Murray space shoes, that are
especially moulded to the individual's foot and although their es-
thetic appeal is low, they are thick and square and, in this case,
green. Everyone who wears them says they are marvelously comfortable.

We started off, diving into several pedestrian underpasses and at
last emerging on Gorky Ulitsa. A quite large souvenir store is
situated there but we found nothing particularly interesting or different from what was to be found in the Beriozka store at the hotel.

What we were curious to see was the supermarket which had quite
a reputation. When we found it it turned out to be somewhat smaller
than the one in our local village at home but, like the subway
stations that had eluded us, it was fancy. Imitation marble walls
and art nouveau light fixtures on mirrored columns. The merchandise was limited. Mostly dairy products and a few canned goods.
Some meat.

The customers did not help themselves but queued up at the
counters waiting for a sales person. When served they took their
purchases to a check-out counter where there were cash registers
such as we have at home but beside every register stood a girl with
an abacus, checking up on it. When you think of the trouble our
stores have with computers I don't blame them.

The supermarket employed the same system we had noticed before in stores and other public places. There might be doors at
either end but one of them was always locked. This makes supervision of people much easier and in case of fire insures a holocaust.

We returned to the hotel, were peacefully admitted to the dining
room and at 9 P.M. took off for the airport. Our splinter group
that had broken off from the Congress of nearly five thousand consisted of a busload of thirty-four people, plus John Gessner the tour
conductor.

In the plane Norton, Clem George, and I had the bulkhead seats
which give slightly more leg room but before us hung the inevitable
baby's crib that we were to find in all Russian planes. It was a good
place to stow cameras but we longed for little pillows and lightweight blankets, amenities ignored by Aeroflot.

We took off about midnight and settled down as best we could
for the five- to six-hour flight. At 2:45 we were shaken awake for
breakfast. It consisted of apple juice, a thick slice of brown bread,
three small prunes, some dubious sausage, a roll, a cookie, a smid-
gen of pressed caviar and tea. A meal planned by a child.

Ken George, who was stashed in the back of the plane, came
ambling up and sat down on the floor in the aisle. "Just thought I'd
check and see how you all were doin'."

."Why, Ken, how sweet of you," I said, thinking what a dear boy he was. He eyed the food, most of which remained on our plates.

"You people going to eat all that?" he asked innocently.

"I shouldn't think so."

"May I?" and with a beatific smile and a wind-swift gesture he scooped up the delicatessen. "These folks sure don't know how to feed a growing boy." We laughed and tried to go back to sleep.

Travel in Russia is confusing since every place functions on both Moscow time and its own. I don't know why this is. Maybe it was an idea of Lenin's for more togetherness.

What with the uncomfortable plane, the weird food, and the unspeakable sanitary arrangements at the airport it was a far cry from *The Golden Journey to Samarkand* of Mr. James Elroy Flecker:

> When those long caravans that cross the plain
> With dauntless feet and sound of silver bells . . .
> Away, for we are ready to a man!
> Our camels sniff the evening and are glad . . .

Such is the power of literature and the pull of history that we had found the idea of going there irresistible.

(Note: Re the Arrangements. In case of need the Asiatic toilets are a good deal less gruesome than the European.)

It is strange about Samarkand and Bukhara too. In the travel brochures the photographs of the mosques and tombs are extraordinarily provocative. As I write about the cities they seem to me fascinating. While we were there we were frequently hot, tired, and bored. I do not understand it.

The Hotel Samarkand was more third-class Hilton, yet in the city itself there was much that was exotic and colorful.

On first beholding it Alexander the Great is said to have gone into transports of ecstasy: "I have often heard tell of the splendor of this place but I never dreamt it would be so beautiful."

Of course in the fourth century B.C. the environment was probably different. There may have been streams and canals and fruitful orchards where today all is sand and arridity. Indeed the name Samarkand comes from two Uzbek words meaning fruit and sugar. Fruit ranks high among their exports as does rice, wheat, silk, and wool. One is immediately struck by the difference in atmosphere and physiognomy between the Russia and Russians of the west and the inhabitants of the original Moslem City. The latter are Uzbeks and Tadzhiks, the cast of their features Mongolian.

It came as a shock to meet Mr. Lenin's likeness all over the place in what seemed foreign territory and one was tempted to mutter querulously, "For God's sake, it's *you* again. What are you doing *here?*" There was a strong suspicion that the natives felt somewhat the same. The Communists moved into Samarkand in 1920 but the Sovietization of the population has taken time and their ways and costumes retain a strong native flavor.

On the day of our arrival we drove from the airport straight to the hotel and, refreshed by a restful morning, went sightseeing after lunch.

Timur Lenk (the lame) the Emperor and indefatigable warrior better known as Tamerlane was born in 1336 in Kesh some fifty miles south of Samarkand. His father Teragai was a scholarly man and in his youth Tamerlane or Timur—I like that name better, also it is more accurate since the dynasty is referred to as the Timurids— is said to have been a serious student of the Koran and gentle of manner. However, events and his own inclinations changed that and most of his life was spent rampaging through Asia, fighting, burning, and looting. He was poised to campaign against China when he was laid low by fever and ague and died at the age of sixty-nine on the banks of the Syr-Darya River. His body "was embalmed with musk and rose water, wrapped in linen, laid in an ebony coffin and sent to Samarkand where it was buried."

His tomb, the Gur-Emir Mausoleum, still stands topped by a fluted blue dome set upon walls of dark and light blue mosaic. It has been greatly restored but the restoration may be considered fortunate for the building is beautiful and it would have been a great loss had it been allowed to go to ruin.

The interior of the dome looks like filigree but closer inspection reveals it to be a delicately sculptured geometrical bas-relief in misty blue and gleaming gold. Like the bodies of Shah Jahan and his wife Mumtaz-i-Mahal in the Taj Mahal, that of Timur rests not in a sarcophagus under the dome but in an underground crypt.

In 1941 the body was exhumed and the legend of the Emperor's lameness proved true; the skeleton had one leg shorter than the other.

Beside him lay the body of his grandson Ulug-Beg who was reported to have been beheaded by his own son and the sorry tale also proved true. The skeleton was without a skull and on a cervical vertebra the nick of a blade showed clearly.

Ulug-Beg was an astronomer and his observatory, partially in ruins, may still be visited. It contains the lower part of a gigantic quadrant, two curving rails set in a chamber scooped out of the earth. Ulug-Beg had a little cart which slid up and down the great curve and from it, through telescopes aimed at slits in the roof of the observatory, he could align and count the stars. He issued tables on the sun, moon, and planets and from his studies estimated the length of the year. He did this in the first half of the fifteenth century with primitive instruments and his calculation was wrong by only one minute, ten seconds.

An excavation currently in progress near the observatory attracted Norton and several of the others who went to investigate it. I did not. It was very hot and Elaine Downing and I decided to rest in the shade of the museum.

In the museum itself there are some recently excavated murals which are interesting. One in particular caught my eye. Led by a white elephant with a blue tasseled harness a procession wends its way toward a castle. A woman is seated in a palanquin and there are men riding camels, and many birds. All the figures are rich and colorful, even though partially erased. At most times the murals must be a joy to see but on the day we were there the electric light

—characteristically—was not working and none of us had brought flashlights nor were they provided by the management.

The tomb of Timur was impressive and so too was the Shah-i-Zinda, the tomb complex of his family. Chambers walled in blue and green tiles and glazed terra cotta were set on either side of a staircase that mounted to a narrow little alley. An intimate affair which was both beautiful and cosy. It was not hard to imagine the family skeletons hobnobbing in the moonlight.

Shah-i-Zinda means living Shah and the mausoleum of a Moslem saint was at the end of the alley. Since he died in the service of Allah his disappearance was, of course, only temporary.

That he was extremely holy, not to say self-possessed, was testified to by the legend that an enemy crept up behind him as he was praying and severed the head from his body. Not in the least incommoded by this act of violence, the saint picked up his head, put it under his arm and finished his prayer. He then repaired to the bottom of a well where he has been living ever since but he is expected to show up on the day of judgment.

He probably will too. People in that part of the world have strange powers. Take the case of the Bibi-Khanym Mosque. Today, other than a great arch and a tower, there is not much of it left but it was built by Timur for his favorite wife who was Chinese. While he was off following his profession of warrior she was overseeing the building of her monument. Timur is said to have allotted ninety elephants brought from India to tote stone from far away quarries to be used in the construction.

Bibi-Khanym was fair to behold and so she appeared to the young architect in charge of the proceedings. He begged her for a kiss. This she chastely refused but she did agree that he might kiss her cheek through her hand. Such was his ardor, however, that his kiss burned through the fragile shield leaving a crimson mark upon her cheek.

When Timur came home and saw the desecration he demanded to know what had happened and on hearing the story gave a bellow of rage and sent his minions to destroy the architect. But the fellow got wind of the scheme so what did he do but make himself a pair of wings—after designing a whole mosque that was a mere bagatelle—and he flew away from the topmost dome and hasn't been seen to this day.

He must have been a better lover and aviator than he was an architect because the mosque was never too solid at best and after a bout with a couple of earthquakes most of it fell down.

In the courtyard is an enormous stone bookstand on which the largest Koran ever known was placed on holy days.

Religion is pretty much ignored by Russian communism but the great medersa of Tilla-Kari built in the seventeenth century still stands, its walls faced with a double tier of deep arches into which are set the windows of the cells where the young theologians studied the tenets of the Moslem faith.

Although we had been experiencing a merchandise and souvenir drought, in Samarkand this was assuaged. In the shops there we found two fine art books. One was a portfolio of loose-leaf reproductions of miniatures and calligraphy of the Timurid, Safarid, and Baburid periods: the other a bound book of miniatures of Babur-Nama. The prints are in delicate and lovely color and the text is in both Russian and English.

Babur was a poet, scholar, and statesman who conquered India in 1526 and founded the empire of the Baburids which lasted some two hundred years.

He died in 1530 at the age of forty-seven leaving behind a distinguished family of four sons and three daughters. His son Humayun ruled India for twenty-five years and *his* son was Akbar, one of the most enlightened men ever to reign over India or any other country.

Akbar was succeeded by his son Jahangir who in turn was followed by *his* son the renowned Shah Jahan who built great cities and forts and buried his beloved wife in the Taj Mahal.*

Akbar had been devoted to his grandfather and toward the end of the sixteenth century he gathered together forty-one of the most

* See *Around the World and Other Places.*

prominent artists of his court to illustrate the Book of Babur. They created the enchanting miniatures which are reproduced in the picture books I bought in Samarkand.

While the reproductions are not as fine as those of the *Tres Riches Heures* of the Duc de Berry, the exquisite illuminated manuscripts painted in France in the fifteenth century by the three Limburg brothers, they are marvelously vivid and give as graphic an impression of oriental life of the time as the *Tres Riches Heures* do of the European.

The evening of our first day in Samarkand, not having slept in the morning at the hotel nor the night before on the plane, Norton went to bed early and I went off with two couples from our tour, the Shambaughs and the Kellys, to wander around the city park.

We followed long tree-shaded paths to an amusement area of swirling activity. A canal which could be navigated by little rowboats flowed into a big swimming pool and there were swings and a merry-go-round and a small bandstand. The orchestra was not the Philharmonic but the rows of backless benches were quickly filled with eager listeners. There were restaurants, balloons, and a theatre with people standing in line to get in. We felt we were really in swinging Samarkand.

We strolled about watching the children. In Uzbekistan the little girls wore their hair in braids. They had as many as twenty or thirty shiny dangling pigtails, providing, one would think, irresistible temptation to small boys.

Many of the women wore long tunic dresses usually over tight trousers and the men wore robes and small square caps on the back of their heads. We looked at them and they at us, the women giggling and nudging each other as we passed in our quaint native costumes.

The following morning we went to the market which, like markets the world over, was colorful, noisy, and seething with life. We bought fruit, took pictures, and occasionally cajoled someone into posing for us. Primitive people everywhere are anti-camera and everywhere that we have traveled we have found Moslems, al-

though they are not necessarily primitive, to be antagonistic to
photography. Yet the traveler longs for a record of such a vivid,
vibrant way of life.

Dinner that evening on the roof of the hotel was quite good and
was preceded by a little festivity kindly provided by Mr. and Mrs.
Watson Wise of Tyler, Texas. Like any logistic-minded general in-
tent on living off the land Watson had taken the precaution of stock-
ing up on the best the country offered. In this case a kilo of caviar
which he and Emma generously shared with their bus companions.
We were doubly glad to have had it as the next morning, roused
at 6 A.M., we breakfasted on cheese curd before departing for the
airport and the flight to Bukhara, forty-five minutes away.

It used to take camel caravans seven days to cover the distance,
stopping every forty miles to water and rest the beasts at the
village wells.

Bukhara is a museum city, its origin dating back 2000 years.
Silhouetted against the sky crumbling fragments of the ancient adobe
walls still stand and the old medinas of the town are still inhabited.
Although at one time the façades of many of its buildings were
brilliant with the blue and green glazed tiles of Islam through the
centuries they have chipped off, broken and disintegrated and the
over-all color of the buildings is brown, the earth sandy and gray.

One of the most imposing architectural sights was the Kosh
Madrasah or medersa. In its heyday Bukhara was the recognized
center of the Moslem religion and the Kosh, which means a mirror
image, turned out to be two large theological schools facing each
other. One was erected in 1566, the other in 1588.

There were other medersas as well, one of them had been built
by Ulug-Beg, our friend the astronomer. They were all handsome
and it is impossible to remember one from the other. I realize this
is no help to scholars in search of accuracy but I suspect it is the
reaction of the average tourist.

A monument that does retain its individuality is one of the oldest
and largest, the Ark Fortress, a sort of Kremlin enclosed by thick

brown brick walls rising high and sloping inward, the entrance gate flanked by two round towers surmounted by a roofed pavilion.

The fortress fronts on Registan Square and during the reign of the Samanids in the ninth and tenth centuries when Bukhara was the capital of an extensive empire we read that "it was ringed by magnificent and luxurious palaces . . . hotels embellished with beautiful frescoes . . . splendid pools; and elm trees whose leafy crowns were like tents."

The glory has departed. It was bare, dusty, and hot.

A charming structure does remain. It is the Bolo-Khauz Ensemble and includes a mosque built in 1712 with a roofed wooden colonnade called an aivan. The columns are tall, slim, and delicate with elaborately carved capitols but they are not very old. The aivan was, in fact, erected in this century.

What is old is the Kalyan Minaret dating from 1127. Rising about 150 feet it was constructed of small burnt bricks and alabaster mortar divided into belts, each ornamented with an intricate and different design. From it the muezzin used to call the faithful to prayer and it was used as an observation post for spotting any advancing enemy. On occasion smoke signals rose from it into the sky to guide camel caravans lost in the surrounding desert. It was also known as the Tower of Death, for at one time convicted criminals were dragged up its 105 stone steps and forced to jump off. The top of the tower is now the abode of a fine family of storks.

Having absorbed the lore of the tower we were taken by our guide to the Emir's Palace some fifteen miles out of town. It proved to be a curious confection built in 1911 and, with one exception, was a triumph of hilarious bad taste. Fearful stained-glass windows, fearful *objets d'art,* fearful everything.

The exception was a reception room entirely walled with delicately carved white plaster curlicues which looked like starched lace and are backed by mirrors. There was a freshness and subdued glitter about it that was very pretty.

The Emir who built the palace was one of the more ignominious and brutal despots of the East and it is too bad he escaped to Kabul when the Communists conquered Bukhara in 1920. He richly merited being shot dead. His estate was now being used as a rest home for Soviet workers and it was deeply depressing.

The grounds were extensive but unkempt with long scraggly grass and flower beds overgrown with weeds. The enormous square pool where the ladies of the harem used to cavort was filled with deep green, slimy water in which floated sticks and rotting logs. The paint on the high carved wood pavilion overlooking the pool, in which the Emir used to sit observing his female slaves splashing about, was peeling off and a melancholy air of decay pervaded the premises.

We were told that it was the Emir's pleasure to toss an apple at the lucky lady who would that evening be favored with his attention. It was difficult for me to believe that being bopped on the head or breast by an apple could have been considered subtle courtship by the target or could have aroused much amorous response in heart or body.

Near the pool, a long, low shack housed some of the workers there on their holiday. As we entered the grounds we had been aware of a bit of a controversy between our Intourist guide and the gateman. When we asked what it was about she said the man didn't want us to come in because the inmates were having their naps but she had assured him that we were eminently civilized and would be *very* quiet. In the face of the evidence Dr. Brown still chose to believe that the people we saw there were caretakers rather than vacationers or convalescents. If he was right they were delinquents for the Lord knows nobody was taking care of anything.

As we strolled about a couple of men in pants and undershirts came out of the shack carrying long folding canvas chairs which they set up under some trees, where obviously they planned to while away the afternoon. On the ground floor of the pavilion two or three others were playing desultory pool on an old rickety table. It seemed a dreary kind of holiday.

I supposed they didn't want to work although they might at least have cleaned out the pool so they could swim. Maybe there wasn't enough electricity to pump in fresh water. Or, for that matter, enough water. Bukhara is desert area and in June it is dry and it is hot, the temperature hovering in the late 90s and low 100s. In July and August the thermometer does *much* better than that, clambering up to around 130.

Whatever the lacks or reasons for decrepitude the Emir's Palace was a sorry example of the Soviets highly touted free vacation resorts for the proletariat.

From the palace of the late Emir we repaired to the tomb of the late Ismail Samani who ruled Bukhara from 892 through 907. It was a simple structure of sun-baked brick, a cube surmounted by sphere, but the bricks were laid so as to form an intricate and beautiful pattern.

The tomb rose from a sort of square well, a depression four or five feet deep. Through the centuries sand sifted in, completely covering it, which was why it escaped destruction. Invading hordes from one or another portion of Central Asia swept back and forth through the area according to the fortunes of war. Destruction was relatively wholesale but because it was unknown and invisible the tomb escaped. Quite recently it has been excavated and restored.

Nearby a small outdoor cafe nestled in a grove of trees and although the green tea and cloying lemon squash sold there were scarcely tempting the place was an oasis from the burning sun and we sat down to relax and to admire the largest Rhode Island Red hen any of us had ever seen. She was squatting on the ground enjoying the shade as we were.

The ancient religious monuments of Central Asia are renowned and have in recent years, especially since Stalin's death, been publicized, the Soviet Government seeing in them a rich source of tourist revenue. Many of them *are* imposing but although I hesitate to mosque drop I have seen those I liked better.

In Istanbul, for example, we saw the splendid mosque of Sultan Ahmed I, better known to foreigners as the Blue Mosque and in the same city the superb Mosque of St. Sophia.

In Shiraz, in Iran, there was an enormous mosque and in Isfahan there were mosques of splendor: the Blue, the Ladies and the wonderful Friday Mosque.

I do not suggest bypassing Asiatic Russia. I only say that if mosques are your dish you can do better elsewhere.

As we sat resting in the shade, a gaggle of little kids clustered around us begging for chewing gum. It was the only begging we saw in Russia.

Normally I am as averse to gum as I am to Coca-Cola but at that time I had some in my possession because of my broken tooth.

Once the Xylocain had worn off I realized that our friendly neighborhood dentist in Moscow had left a very jagged edge which was badly lacerating my tongue.

Norton, without proper instruments, improvised I thought very well. He took a nail file and whittled away the sharpest point. It was an improvement but my tongue still hurt. By pure fluke we happened to have in the traveling medical case a package of Aspergum and I made little wads of this to cap the offending tooth. I had been anticipating, with no pleasure at all, the day that the Aspergum would be ended but two of our tour companions had come to my rescue.

Having heard of the Russian children's passion for gum, Ted and Marty Shepherd had lugged with them from home several plastic bags of ten packs each, enough to stick together the whole U.S.S.R. Learning of my predicament they had generously bestowed upon me an entire package. With such wealth at my disposal I didn't have the heart to refuse the clamoring youngsters. Especially when they brought me a rose and a geranium blossom. There may have been forethought in their guile, it was nevertheless endearing.

Having passed out the largesse, I caught up with the others who were already trudging the hot dusty road to the Mazar Chashma-Ayub. This was either a place of worship or a tomb but its main attraction was the spring it enclosed. It is said that here, in Biblical times, Job struck the earth with his staff and water gushed forth. The name Chashma-Ayub means "The Spring of Job." I was grateful for the coolness it provided.

Though a little footsore from having covered so much territory, in the evening we wandered through the Medina, the old section of the town, with Ruth and Hans Lang of Kansas City, a couple we found most compatible. The houses of whitewashed sun-baked brick fronted on narrow twisting streets and, through an occasional open door, we saw families at dinner in the courtyard. The whole atmosphere was relaxed, casual, and Arabian and the evening ended in a pleasant little climax when emerging from the Medina we came upon a clean shop where they sold cool beer.

There was a curious topographical feature in Bukhara which we had not been told about and that was the enormous heaps of cotton. Great mountains of cotton piled in open-air storage behind a high wire fence. This, I suppose, was not surprising since cotton was one of the areas exports but I had never seen a whole mountain range of the stuff before.

Karakul pelts were another big item. Bukhara has long been renowned for them and in recent years the town's fame, not to mention coffers, has been increased by the discovery of vast deposits of oil. It is also the starting point of the Bukhara-Ural gas pipeline, the largest in the world.

The Soviet Government has a system which might be considered a coony way of saving itself money. A good worker will be created a Hero of Labor. He may be a cotton picker, a factory worker, I was about to write, a plumber, but that's overdoing it. There can't be two in all Russia. If he's good at the job there's a little ceremony on the farm or in the factory; a medal is pinned on his chest; his picture is taken and appears in the local press and is exhibited in the local museum or town hall. This makes him proud and happy. For a day or so he is congratulated or envied by his colleagues and then life slips back to normal, including, I suspect, the normal number of rubles in his weekly pay envelope.

Yet here and there that ole debbil, Profit Motive, raises his dear old head. One of our most interesting and amusing excursions took us to an embroidery factory in Bukhara.

In a great cool loft with overhead fans, big windows down both sides of the room, and a huge portrait of Lenin at the far end, girls sat two, three, and four together at large embroidery tables. They were a colorful sight with their bright patterned smock-like dresses, their heads wrapped in gay silk scarves and veils.

Stretched on frames or lying flat on the tables were the pieces of cloth they were embroidering which would later be blocked into the square and round caps so favored by the Uzbeks. They also made scrambled eggs for the military—all that gold stitching—and worked designs for slippers, handbags, and velvet vests.

They chattered like birds and we were interested to see that although some of them had been there for twenty years not one of them wore glasses. Whether this was because Asians have the enviable eyesight of Africans or because they don't have occulists I couldn't say.

As we passed among the tables they would stop their chatter, smile at us shyly for a moment and then burst into giggles.

At one table we asked them their names. They told us and I then said my name was Ilka. This evoked such a spasm of laughter I could only conclude it was a four-letter word in Uzbek too but when I asked Tamara, our local guide, she said no, not as far as she knew. Some of them were attractive girls, their dark brows elongated and joined by a black crayon line drawn across the bridge of their noses; their answer to false eyelashes. We saw several pairs of pretty earrings and were told they were often given instead of engagement rings.

The factory employs about 530 women and their wages average 120 rubles a month plus, and this is what I mean about the profit system, extra pay for piece work. The government fought it but finally had to capitulate if it wanted to fill the quota it considered necessary.

The upper floor of the factory was all hand work, the ground floor machines. The noise on the lower level was deafening and I suppose they either must become oblivious to it or give up the job.

The women there seemed somewhat older than the upstairs birds
and they guided great squares of fabric around and under the
pounding needles with unimaginable speed and skill.

I was watching enviously, for my talents as a needle woman are
nonexistent, when Ken George came loping up calling out above the
din, "Hey, look, look what I've got!" I should explain that Ken and
I were the only ones in the party who were wearing hats. Mine was
white cotton with a fair sized brim, his was white canvas with a
plastic window in the crown and a narrow brim. One of the women
had just embroidered on his two bright yellow flowers. They looked
great and I at once wanted some for mine. He led me down the aisle
to his benefactress' machine. I held my hat in my hand and was
about to pantomime a plea for the same kind of decoration when
she snatched it from me, broke the thread she was working with,
substituted one of bright pink and within a minute or two had
stitched a wavy garland all around the brim.

As I watched with admiration and amusement I kept thinking,
what on earth can I give her in return? Money, obviously, was out,
in any event that wasn't why she was doing it, but what *could* I do?
Anne Weeks came up to me. "Don't you think you ought to give
her something?" she muttered.

"I want to but *what?*"

"How about a lipstick?" We had been told Russian women were
always glad to get them but one look at my artist revealed that a
lipstick was not her style. Suddenly I had it! Of all the women there
only she was wearing glasses. One of the sidepieces was broken and
she had to balance the glasses on her nose. The other sidepiece
was hooked, somewhat askew, over her right ear. I couldn't give her
a new pair of glasses but I did have a couple of quite pretty cases
in my handbag.

I fished about and pulled out the one I thought would appeal
to her more. When she handed me back my hat with a little grin
I thanked her, *"Bolshoi Spaseba,"* my one Russian phrase and held
out the case. She shook her head vigorously. *"Da da,"* I said. "Please,

you must." I pointed to her spectacles and laid it on the machine. She glanced about and with a swift gesture snatched it and stuck it in a small drawer under a shelf beside her.

As I looked up there stood the forewoman of the factory who had been watching us. In all probability she too was amused to see the Uzbekistan treatment so quickly applied to an American hat and was perhaps pleased by the American interest but also there was a moment's contact with foreigners. Was it her duty to be on the qui vive?

That is what makes a Russo-foreign relationship uneasy. Even when they are innocent of any ulterior motive there is so much in their world that is oppressive and regimented and policed that one is immediately suspicious. They too, I expect, are suspicious of us. And in honesty I cannot believe that that skillful, elderly woman was sent to the pokey or, indeed, reprimanded. She may even have achieved a minute transitory celebrity for having shown the decadent capitalists a trick or two. It was just that Big Sister was *there*.

That same afternoon we left Bukhara for Tashkent flying in a Dutch-built Fokker Friendship but the Russians had shoved the seats so close together the discomfort was acute and the heat for the first few minutes almost unendurable until we had gained altitude and begun to cool off a bit.

The Tashkent airport is a very decent one. The city was virtually wiped out by an earthquake in April of 1966 and is being entirely rebuilt. It is the capital of Uzbekistan, a cosy little area that covers as much of the earth's surface as Britain, Belgium, Holland, Austria, and Switzerland combined. The population of the city is about 1,200,000.

As we landed the manager of the terminal came to meet us, informed us that the thermometer stood at 106 and offered us very welcome cool mineral water.

At the hotel we were entranced to find that our rooms were air conditioned and the bathroom more than acceptable.

Transistors are known in Central Asia and several of the hotels had radios in the rooms. Our irritation with transistors was less than it usually is because the voices were, for the most part, rich and warm, not that fearful caterwauling or breathy nasal whining that assaults the ear at home. Also, since we couldn't understand the language the lyrics didn't seem so idiotic.

On rare occasions we turned on the radio in our room for a short time. We listened carefully but there was never the little click when you turn it off that tells you the connection has been broken. We assumed it was the most convenient way of bugging the rooms.

The first evening we went to the ballet. The big pleasant theatre was across the square from the hotel and the orchestra armchairs the most roomy we had experienced. We still had difficulty finding our places and still couldn't fathom why Russian ushers are so reluctant to show the customers to their seats. We weren't even wearing our coats!

The ballet, *Kopcap* in Cyrillic, *Corsair* in English, is a turgid tale of plunder, rape, and abduction just like an old Douglas Fairbanks movie. The sets and costumes were, as usual, spectacular, but the dancers although full of energy and good will lacked the finesse of those we had seen in Leningrad and Moscow.

After the second act we departed, thinking to get a drink on the hotel roof, which had a restaurant of its own, before going into the main dining room where tables had been reserved for us and where we had been told to foregather at 10 P.M. That's one thing about traveling with a tour. You are relieved of the need to make your own decisions about where and when you might like to eat. The voice of authority speaks and you comply. Or else.

We walked up the six flights to the roof due to the fact that there was only one elevator and it was jammed and inspired no confidence in its ability to reach its goal.

Once there, however, we seemed to be where the action was. It was refreshing to see people who appeared to be having a good time. The women had obviously made an effort. They had done their hair and had on their nice dresses. The men looked like thugs. Sweaty undershirts and dusty boots. It's hard to see why personal neatness should be considered synonymous with reactionary imperialism. Dinner that night was a big shashlik barbecue over coals and it smelled extremely appetizing. We were tempted to stay but realizing that would probably invite chaos with the planned meal downstairs we decided we would only have a drink. Like those of the mice of Mr. Burns that plan was not to be. The only drinks were brandy or Russian champagne, no vodka. "Vodka ground floor," said the waitress.

Downstairs a couple of long tables had been set up for us and while the orchestra was on the loud side it was good and there was a stalwart male soloist.

Suddenly, inspired by the music, two men jumped up and started to do a native folk dance together. Everyone joined in clapping and chanting and cheering them on. It was a lot of fun and trying to envisage two Englishmen doing the same thing I nearly choked on my boiled potato.

Later on the evening turned more serious when François de Chadenedes knocked on our door. Although married and the father of a large family he was one of the men we called our bachelors. That was another reason our particular tour was enjoyable. On any tour the women, usually American widows, greatly outnumber the men. On this venture the reverse was true. The husbands were really the stars, their wives along more or less as appendages. It meant that not only were we matched up as cosily as the passengers of Mr. Noah but because the trip *was* primarily a male venture we even had a surplus. Four men were along without their families.

That night François, poor chap, had the miseries. When Norton took his temperature and found it to be 103 he hauled him off to bed with heavy doses of some fever-breaking brew of which I am ignorant. I am happy to say he recovered.

One of the most interesting episodes of the whole journey took place the next morning when four or five of us, women only, went to visit the Lola kindergarten or day care center.

The building, which went up in 1968 was especially designed for the purpose it serves and can accommodate 140 children. They

were almost entirely the offspring of parents involved in petroleum
and gas who live in the vicinity.

They attend the center from 8 A.M. to 8 P.M. when they are
delivered and picked up by their families and their ages range
from one to seven. According to their means the parents pay between
two and three rubles tuition a month. The Lola has twelve teachers
and we were told there were fifteen hundred similiar schools in
Tashkent alone.

The care they get appears to be excellent. They have dormitories
with child-size beds, the toilets are to scale and, miracle of miracles,
clean, as is the kitchen. They are fed four meals a day and have
large airy nurseries to play in. They have toys galore. Dolls, merry-
go-rounds, tricycles, Teddy Bears . . . "We change their toys every
week," one of the teacher-nurses told us, "so they will not get bored."
Also, perhaps, so that no little Ivan will come to love a Teddy Bear
and think of it as his own. It is a People's Teddy Bear and he'd
better not forget it.

Here, too, as in the embroidery factory in Bukhara, the rooms
were dominated by large pictures of Lenin. There exists a well-
known photograph of him as a curly headed tot of four which, one
would think, might be more appropriate for such a location but
probably the authorities wish to instill a father image. They do, in
fact, tell the kids stories about Dyadya Lenin (Uncle Lenin) and
how much he loved youngsters. They must think that Christian
saying "Suffer the little children" has a nice sound.

Since the Soviet Government makes Machiavelli look like a child
plotting a move at checkers one must think that it deliberately
keeps wages so low that, in order to live with any comfort or small
pleasures, mothers as well as fathers must work. In fact about 80
percent of them do. And although it is not compulsory to send
one's child to a center many parents go along with the system because there is no grandmother or other relative to baby-sit.

Then, too, the child is undoubtedly happier being with his peers
than at home with an adult and no playmates. The state is pleased
because, like the Catholic Church, it too subscribes to the theory

"Give me a child until the age of seven and it is mine for life."
They can stuff its little brains with respect for the state and communism in general. Yet parental love dies hard. Despite the availa-
bility of nursery schools only about 10 percent of Soviet youngsters
under two are enrolled in them. Because of this they have plenty
of space for babies and toddlers but even with only 20 percent of
children between three and seven seeking admission the kinder-
gartens are overcrowded.

For these statistics I am indebted to Susan Jacoby who, with her
husband, lived in Moscow from August 1969 to May 1971. She
wrote a fascinating and informative article on the schools that appeared in the *Saturday Review*.

We obviously saw one of their show places. Russians are hardly
likely to take foreigners to a second- or third-rate institution but
they exist and Mrs. Jacoby quotes a couple who, much as they
wanted it, turned down a chance to move from a one-room to a two-
room apartment "because the kindergarten in their neighborhood had
an outstanding director who had attracted an unusually competent
teaching staff."

In the Lola kindergarten after we had been shown all over the
building and allowed to take photographs we were escorted into a
big room where we were seated at low tables laden with fresh
fruit, mineral water, and tea.

About twenty moppets then appeared, boys and girls ranging
from about three to seven. Accompanied by a teacher who played
the piano they danced and sang and played games. A couple of
the songs were about how Lenin wanted them to be good, honest,
and brave. One dance was a kind of march in which they carried
small red flags. A woman in our group leaned over to me. "Look
at that," she whispered indignantly, "they're carrying red flags."
What did she expect they would be carrying? The Stars and
Stripes?

One of the games was called Who Is Quicker? A girl and boy
each put on a voluminous smock and the object was to see who
could whip it off first. Chauvinistically, speaking as a woman, I

am happy to say the girl won. Maybe if the little boy had had to rip it off *her* rather than himself things would have gone faster.

Following the entertainment large cakes which had been baked by the children were brought in and we were then presented with collections of the same charming miniatures I had bought in Samarkand. Had I only known!

The teachers were candid in talking to us and we learned their salaries were 120 rubles a month, the same as the embroidery girls, and these were university graduates. After five years they got a raise of ten rubles. It seemed pretty slim pickings.

We thanked the teachers, waved to the children who were every bit as cute as capitalistic tots, and departed.

Since Dr. Brown's heart does not melt into a puddle at the sight of young children, he had not gone with me on the kindergarten excursion. He and a couple of other men had been driven around a huge area outside the city where high-rise apartments extended for miles. He said that hundreds of thousands could be housed there and that it was grim. Not a tree, only car tracks down the middle of a wide mall and not a car in sight.

He did accompany me to the hotel post office where with no confidence at all I watched an inept female wrap up one of my miniatures and a brightly colored picture book called *Through the Eyes of Children,* an engaging collection of youngsters' drawings. Not wishing to lug them the rest of the way around the world I was sending them home surface mail. I naturally hoped they would arrive but if they didn't they were the books I could best do without. It came as a real shock when they were delivered to me in New York some two months later.

As I have said, my husband is a patient man but, the day before, driven finally to exasperation by not having received any mail at all and wishing to make sure that our dentist, Dr. George Lindig, would be immediately available on our return to New York, he had placed an overseas call to his secretary with the hotel operator.

She had told him it would be coming through the next evening about six o'clock and blow me down if it didn't.

Irene Kurguzoff has been with Norton for twenty years and many of his long-time patients depend on her almost as much as on Dr. Brown himself.

Once, as we were ending a visit to a friend he had been looking after for a lifetime, I said, "Goodbye, Ollie. Take care of yourself."

"Oh I do, I do," he assured me. "I call up Irene and do just what she says."

Irene's parents were White Russians, so getting a call from the homeland sent her corpuscles scurrying. The boss, however, was firm. "Listen, Irene, this is costing a lot of money. Have you got a pad handy? Good. How are you? How is everything going? Why the hell don't we get any mail?" They chatted back and forth a minute. "Fine. Ask Dr. Lindig please to be *sure* to be in his office the morning after we get home. Wait a minute, here's Mrs. B."

I took the receiver. "Irene, it's good to hear your voice." I had given her power of attorney before we left New York and she gave me a prompt report. "All your bills are paid."

"Hurray. Tell me, how did the battle between the New York *Times* and the Pentagon come out?"

When we had lunched with the Gwertzmans in Moscow they had told us about the *Times* printing the Pentagon Papers and the uproar it caused although it was old information that could in no way jeopardize the safety of the country.

"Did the *Times* or the government win?" I asked. The answer seemed to me important.

The contempt in which the ordinary citizens of the United States are held by both the Pentagon and the White House is obvious. Dedicated to their own aggrandizement the two Goliaths, irked by the voters, those impediments in their paths to absolute power, have enthusiastically adopted the slogan, What you don't know won't hurt you.

I thought it encouraging that there were elements who felt people had a right to know of decisions and actions that jeopardized their very lives and I sincerely hoped the *Times* had won.

But Irene was still in a happy daze over speaking with Russia. "All the bills are paid" she said.

"Great. Many thanks. We'll be seeing you." I hung up.

The next day we left Tashkent for Alma-Ata. We had been told to sit on the right side of the plane as from there we could see the Ala-tau Mountains. There was even talk of the Great Wall of China! Poppycock. What we actually saw was desert nor were our spirits lifted by the refreshment served on the plane. Warm mineral water.

The hotel to which we drove on our arrival, the Kazakhstan, was pleasant. It is named after the vast area of which Alma-Ata is the capital just as Tashkent is the capital of Uzbekistan. We did think again about the Great Wall of China when, in the park, we saw twenty-odd ping-pong tables with, what we assumed to be future diplomats, hard at work rehearsing for their future posts *behind* the wall.

Alma-Ata means Father of Apples in Kazakh—they have a lot of orchards—and in the afternoon we drove around town. It's a big apple set in the foothills of the Tien Shan Mountains. To the south spreads the panorama of the Ala-tau range.

There are spacious squares and fountains, a huge pool where children splash, and enormous government buildings. It sounds rather attractive but truth to tell it was dull and the day we were there the air was hot, muggy, and close.

Yet it is a city that could have real quality. There are broad tree-lined boulevards, they have those open gutters, eighteen to twenty inches wide that are like little canals running along the curb through which the water flows swiftly and which are actually quite functional as long as you don't step into one and break your leg. They had them in Samarkand and Shiraz in Iran uses them too and they are equally ingenious and equally lethal.

As usual the grass along the public thoroughfares was not cut nor did the management see any need for it at the hotel and there they have a garden court. Were the grass to be tended and were they to put out some easy chairs and tables and parasols it would be an attractive spot.

Alma-Ata too has a kind of Palace of Congresses and I diverted myself by snapping a picture of a lot of young soldiers as they streamed down the broad steps, released from what I took to be a military lecture. A policeman reprimanded me for doing it but did not snatch my camera.

The one sprightly interlude was the party Clem George gave that evening to celebrate Ken's twenty-third birthday. There was an abundance of vodka, beer, and fairly good Russian champagne. I don't think anyone got drunk but the decibel count rose as the evening wore on and old college songs rolled out with all the gusto one expects of a Rotary Club meeting. Everybody toasted everybody else and at Norton's suggestion I rose and proposed a toast to Faina, the Intourist guide who had joined us in Moscow and been with us ever since.

She was small, slender, I should imagine in her late twenties, and very capable.

I said that as one against thirty-four we all felt that she represented her country with dignity, knowledge, and charm. Cries of "Hear hear" and clinking glasses. I was truthful about the dignity and knowledge. She did not have a great deal of charm. Her manner was, in fact, austere rather than winsome but she undoubtedly felt she had her hands full and should exert a little discipline. A raft of capitalistic oil men and their spoiled, idle American wives. One had to keep a sharp lookout.

Nor was she altogether wrong! On one of our departures from hotel to airport she stood up in the front of the bus and announced sternly "Someone has taken a towel from room 336. This must be replaced before the bus can leave."

There was a moment of startled silence, then an explosion of laughter as one of the party cried out in anguish, "Oh God, it was me. I took it into 334. We needed it to dry some glasses."

On occasion one can be tempted in a hotel to heist a pretty ash tray perhaps, or a clothes brush—all the hotels had quite good ones—but the bath towel from a Russian hotel, no! A thousand times no.

On another occasion her charge was a little more serious. One of
the party had been so ill advised as to offer the manager of the
hotel a tip. The man was quite naturally indignant and he had
reported it to Faina. She admonished the bus at large. "The man
is well paid, he is *not* a servant. This is not *done* in Russia." She
was right. It was an insensitive and thoughtless act and we all felt
a little embarrassed.

When the birthday dinner party broke up it was getting late and
we drifted off to our rooms where once again I pondered, without
coming up with an answer, as to why the Russians never spread
the top sheet on your bed. The bottom sheet is tucked in. The
blanket is folded back at the foot and on it lies the top sheet neatly
folded into a square. You take it from there.

Theoretically, the following day we were to have seen more of
Alma-Ata. Public Library, Academy of Sciences, etc. but we went
on strike. It was terribly hot and we were all fed to the teeth with
public buildings and museums in which the exhibits, either reproductions or machinery did nothing to galvanize our flaccid interest.

"Then what *would* you like to do?" asked John Gessner, our Man
from Cook's. "What *would* you like to do?" asked Faina, our
Woman from Intourist. We said we would like to go to the country
and have a picnic. They said we could do just that. So we did. Incidentally I am once more indebted to my friend Irving R.
Levine for the information that the word Intourist derives from the
Russian Inostrani meaning "foreign" or "other country." Tourist
means tourist.

Each of us tourists was supplied with a plastic bag containing
our lunch: hard-boiled egg, unripe tomato, brown bread, cheese,
and sausage. With the exception of the tomato, not bad, and at
least the eggs were hard. They were often served for breakfast too
and we had become accustomed to them. It was the soft-boiled
ones that stumped us. They cooked them sometimes before breakfast was served and put them in a big dish on the table. By the
time we arrived they would be quite cold and a cold soft-boiled
egg is not appetizing. Even less so when there is no cup of any

kind to break it into or to support it in so it may be eaten from the shell. Someday, when time hangs heavy, try breaking one, holding it in your hand and spooning it out. You won't be very happy.

Anyway, having been victualed by the hotel and watered, in a manner of speaking, with our individual bottles of whatever, we set off by bus for the mountains.

We passed a few small farmhouses outside of Alma-Ata that seemed cleaner and more attractive than any we had so far seen and we also passed a Young Pioneer's camp set on a narrow ledge where the ground sloped down from the road. It looked to me precarious and not as though the kids had much place for games and recreation. We also drove by a barracks-like camp. It was, said Faina, a rest home for adults. There too recreational facilities seemed slender. I guess they rested.

The road wound upward through the Tien Shan foothills until we came to a high level plateau where we left the bus and started walking. Tall firs marched up and down the mountainsides although occasionally a rock slide had broken open the ranks. Far below us a narrow river wound through a sandy bed. Painted signs indicated camping spots. Superintending nature's wonderland was Comrade Lenin on a large poster. On this one he was wearing a cap. Très sport. Like paper dolls they change his clothes to fit the occasion. Within reason. God forbid he should ever appear in a dinner jacket and despite some years of his young manhood spent in Europe he probably never did.

We came at last to a rocky grassy slope shaded by thick green branches and deployed ourselves for lunch. Fortunately we had passed a spring of icy water to blend with our vodka. It was all very pleasant and relaxed and infinitely preferable to the hot city and dreary public monuments.

Returning to the hotel later in the afternoon we established ourselves, as had now become our custom, in the four rooms John Gessner engaged for our group when we were leaving a city after our hotel's check-out hour.

As I emerged from the girl's department a woman in the room

across the hall beckoned to me. I went in and in pantomime and Russian she offered me a glass of tea from an electric samovar. I accepted it gladly although I did turn down the jam with which she wanted me to sweeten it. I knew that was the Russian custom but it is difficult for me to swallow sweet tea. I did, however, eat some of the jam and it was very good. She then offered fresh cherries pointing to herself, "My *dacha*," she said, so I knew they were home grown. We both bit into one at the same time. It was *very* sour. I tried not to show it but she burst out laughing, and, shaking her head, tossed it away. So I did the same.

She greatly admired my shoes pointing to them and clasping her hands to her breast in ecstasy. Having noticed that her feet were short and wide, whereas mine are long and narrow, I thought fleetingly of the gracious open-handed offer but it occurred to me that she might well recognize it for the specious gesture it was and I felt ashamed of myself.

Still, wishing to keep up my end of so friendly an encounter, I smiled and said we were flying to Irkutsk that night, holding my arms open and waving them about to denote distance and Aeroflot. We sat together for a while longer in the small cluttered room and between us poked a few more holes in the iron curtain. It was as cosy a little interlude as I had in Russia.

In the evening, after dinner, with time to spare before we had to leave for the airport, François de Chadenedes and I went up to the fourth floor where he had told me a wedding was in progress. Everyone, bride, groom, and guests, looked very Korean or Mongolian and seeing us standing at the door several of them urged us to enter.

Supper was in full swing and the orchestra was playing. There was a professional photographer at work and when he saw my camera he indicated that I might take pictures too but there was not sufficient light and I had no flash bulbs.

I was standing beside François when a young girl in a silver dress and with very dark straight hair came up to me and asked me to dance. I accepted and looking around saw that that was the way

they did it. Several girls were dancing together and a good many
men danced opposite one another, each weaving his own intricate
steps in time to the music.

When it stopped my partner led me to the head table, plumped
me down and poured me a generous vodka. Finally the bride and
groom got up, she wearing a veil and a long white dress, and
although they looked solemn they were obviously very happy. I was
too because it all seemed sweet and warm and simple, the way life
can often be when the Messers Brezhnev, Podgorny, Kosygin and
others of their kidney all over the world keep their noses out of
people's business.

The flight to Irkutsk took off at about 11 P.M. and in the course of
it we came down at Novosibirsk. Quite possibly the name means as
little to the reader as it did to me but the men of the party were
interested to know we were there as it is considered the capital of
Siberia and hums with industry which, judging from the display
at the airport, must include printing nine-tenths of the free propaganda literature of the country.

The Soviet Government fancies Novosibirsk because it and other
towns are living proof that Siberia is not all salt mines and snow
and wolves devouring babies tossed from sleighs, an occupation that
has always struck me as curious to say the least, but I was impressed
by a painting of such a scene in my childhood. From what I have
since learned of wolves, of their gentleness, courtesy, and generosity
they would be far more likely to succor the infant than to eat it.

We arrived at Irkutsk at 7 A.M. The airport was clean and, for
an airport, reasonably attractive. That was fortunate since we were
destined to become far more intimately acquainted with it later.

For the first time in a Russian domestic terminal we saw signs in
English. That is because Alaska Airlines fly in and out, the only
foreign carrier, I believe, to do so.

While waiting for the bus that would drive us to our hotel we
inspected a big lucite model of Lake Baikal, the main reason for
coming to Irkutsk in the first place, at least for the foreigner. For

the Russians the city is a big industrial and educational center with a student body of something like fifty thousand registered at the universities.

The Lake Baikal model is interestingly presented, as though they had lifted the lake out of the earth, so that one sees very well its contours and varying depths.

The Angara on which the city is situated, is the only river that flows out of Baikal for Baikal is a getter rather than a giver, being fed by 336 rivers and streams. Considering this intake it is not surprising to learn that it is the seventh largest lake in the world with an area of 12,150 square miles. The Russians themselves, with unaccustomed modesty, term it the eighth largest but that must be because they are counting the Caspian sea as a lake.

Without the Caspian, according to the World Atlas, the order runs Superior, Victoria, Aral (in Russia too, of course, how ignorant can you be?) Huron, Michigan, Tanganyika, and Baikal.

They do come out with the flat claim that it is the deepest of the lakes and that it contains one fifth of the world's fresh water reserves as well as an enormous number of plants, fish, and the unique and famous Nerpa seals. The Russians estimate there are about 50,000 of them and 3000 are allowed to be killed annually.

We had all hoped to see the seals but they were at the upper end of the lake and although we rode a hydrofoil we did not get that far.

We had a nice guide in Irkutsk, a man for once, and older than any of our girls had been. We suspected he perhaps remembered the old regime because he smiled when we commented on the charm of some delightful old wooden houses with carved shutters and elaborate gingerbread trim. They were almost the only private houses we had seen in the whole country.

"A general who was the chief of police used to live in that one."

Others had belonged to army officers, civil servants, and professional people.

"And who lives in them now?"

He shrugged. "Who doesn't? Many families, you understand, now share."

It was hot in Irkutsk, it had been hot in Samarkand, Bukhara, Tashkent, all the places we had been after leaving Moscow but there were never any flies or insects. That is one of the virtues of Russia. If it lacks a good many other things it lacks those nuisances as well and for this deprivation one is thankful.

After breakfast we showered and I tried to sleep a little while Norton went out to reconnoiter. He came back with the information that we were in Limerick on Sunday. This is a family joke. We once spent a Sunday in Limerick, Ireland, and split another one between Belfast and Glasgow.* If you ever feel that life holds no more and that you would just as soon cut your throat those are three cities in which you can bid farewell to the world without regret.

In the afternoon we wandered about heading toward the river. Here, too, the streets seemed covered with snow, the fluff from the cottonwood trees. It piled up along the gutters and in crevasses and a sudden gust of wind sent it licking like flame along the curbstone and swirling skyward in smoky gray twisters.

We joined the crowd leaning on the parapet that bordered the Angara River and watched a small boat with two red sails tacking back and forth. Later we strolled down into the park and listened to the band and two concert singers, a man and a woman, both with excellent voices. They were enjoyable but the really entertaining event of the day occurred that evening.

After dinner the Kellys, the Shambaughs, and ourselves stepped out of the hotel dining room into the cool of the street. I held a glass of white wine in my hand and was sipping it and chatting with the others when a young man passing by stopped a minute, looked me in the eye with cold hatred and hissed, "Fascist!" He was so comically ferocious I nearly dropped the glass.

The next morning we drove to the dock to catch the hydrofoil that would take us to Lake Baikal. There was a small buffet on board

* See *The Carthaginian Rose*.

but no tea or coffee; just buns, sausage, and the insipid sweet apple juice dear to the Russian palate.

"Boy, I sure miss that Tree Top apple juice we have at home," said young Ken George. "It's just like biting into a crisp cold tart apple. Man, is it ever good. That's the best!" Our tongues were hanging out but our thirst was not assuaged.

His father, however, was involved in an interesting bit of byplay with the woman who presided over the buffet. She offered him ten rubles for a dollar. In view of the fact that the going rate was one ruble for $1.10 the suggestion was interesting but Clem thanked her politely and refused. The transaction did not tempt him. Tinkering around with currency in Russia is a highly risky business and one which the prudent traveler will eschew.

We left the hydrofoil on the shores of Lake Baikal which are green and hilly and in parts heavily wooded and went into a small museum of plant life, skeletons, and stuffed fauna. The seals looked appealing and small but the most interesting exhibit was a Golomi-anka. This is an oily fish which, out of water, quite literally melts away leaving only a fragile skeleton behind. We also learned from our guide that a healthy sturgeon may easily count on a life-span of eighty years.

Another piece of news was more disturbing. It seems the Russians are seriously considering lowering the level of the Caspian Sea by diverting and rerouting the rivers that feed it.

Since it is the largest inland body of water in the world, 163,800 square miles, scientists are greatly concerned over what the results may be. One would imagine that Iran will have something to say about it, too, so maybe the project will be tabled until some serious study has been made.

My husband considers me impetuous but when it comes to fiddling around with nature I am all for having the old girl take her course and letting sleeping dogs lie.

As far as Lake Baikal is concerned let us hope they let well enough alone there. Its age is estimated at twenty million years so it may be said to have proven itself and while many lakes grow shallow and sometimes disappear entirely Baikal's level and volume have remained constant.

The next day we ran into something we wished with all our hearts the Russians would change. It was the plane schedule. We were routed out of our beds at 6 A.M., made a wild breakfastless dash to the airport, rushed inside, passports and tickets at the ready, to be informed that the plane was five hours late.

It is at times like these that those who spend their lives on the well-worn path between home and place of work seem endowed with the wisdom of the ages.

We spent as much time as possible breakfasting. We then investigated the Beriozka shop with the thoroughness of a mother monkey divesting her offspring of fleas. In the course of this procedure I did find three of the very pretty boxes that the Russians lacquer and paint in charming designs.

Bearing our loot we returned to the waiting room to sit. We read, we worked double crostics, we chatted. Those who knew how played bridge. Among these was our courier, John Gessner. Besides being a professional guide and courier for Thomas Cook, Mr. Gessner is also a professional bridge player and teacher so from his point of view perhaps the day did not seem as lost as it did to the rest of us.

At one we lunched. Tomato and cucumber salad, tough unidentifiable meat, chopped up green stems of scallions by way of a vegetable, a dill pickle, an apple.

At 2:35 a bulletin! The plane will not be in until at least 5:30. Where in God's name was it coming from? Kansas City?

On these occasions the limitations and irritations inherent in a non-competitive dictatorship are brought home with a vengeance.

Apparently there wasn't even another plane to be sent to replace the laggard one. Since no one could make a profit or enhance his reputation who cared when the tourists got off? They could damn well sit and rot as far as Areoflot was concerned.

I will say that Faina, spurred on perhaps by a few acid comments

from her charges, organized a sightseeing bus to drive us around
the neighborhood to view such sights as were available.

In a backwater of the Angara River an old icebreaker, the *San
Francisco*, lay at anchor, settling and rusting as the empty days
drifted by. She had been built in Britain sixty years before and
brought overland to be reassembled in Lake Baikal. Since the lake
is frozen from October or November until May an icebreaker has its
uses but I suppose today's contraptions are far more modern.

Stands of pine and birch line the shores and among them was a
group of shacks. Although somewhat larger, they looked not unlike
the temporary privies erected for gangs on construction sites when a
big project, a dam or something of the sort, is being built. It was a
camp for Young Pioneers and appeared primitive in the extreme.
Peeking through a window we saw there were four beds to a shack
and no further amenities. Apparently the Pioneers were truly that,
for they had to bring everything with them. Bedding, cooking utensils, food. There seemed to be no toilets and at first we thought no
mess hall although later we came upon a structure that might have
served as a teahouse.

We saw no fishing tackle and, other than hiking, amusement
seemed limited to splashing about in the shallow water or, as some
girls and boys were doing clambering about over the rusting old
hulk of the *San Francisco*.

When Russians say they have rest homes for the workers and
camps for the young people they are telling the truth. It's just that
what they have seems drab and dispirited and not much fun.

Back at the airport at six-thirty there was still no word of our
plane. Patience frazzled, the men of our group were finally galvanized into action. They formed a committee, put on jackets and
ties and, armed with a letter from an official in Moscow stating that
these representatives of the petroleum world were very special guests
of the Russian Government for whom *everything* should be done,
waited upon the management of the airport. Why they hadn't acted
sooner I can't imagine. Whether or not the visitation was responsible
for it, in the end we got results. Although by then it was 9 P.M.,

a plane finally did arrive and we had time for a reasonably good dinner before we took off.

One theory that was advanced for the all-day delay was that on the flight to Khabarovsk we would be only thirty miles from the Chinese border and the Russians didn't want foreign eyes to see the powerful military installations that the whole world knows they have there. If that is the case their delaying tactics would appear plain silly. Why not simply say: "We fly at night!"

I myself incline to the theory that the delay was due to inefficiency rather than precautionary military tactics. And I well remember an entire day spent in San Juan, Puerto Rico, when booked on a splendid American line we were not even permitted to leave the airport because "The plane may take off at any minute. Who knows?"

Who didn't know was the pilot, the tower, the ticket counter, the home office, and the passengers.

Khabarovsk is a spacious and airy city on the banks of the great Amur River. Our guide seemed a little miffed when we took scant interest in the points of interest on the Russian side and kept asking, "Which way is China? Is that it, over there?" That was it. We could see nothing but low distant banks yet there it was, the lair of the dragon. Go it, dragon! Go it, bear! Some day will it be Go to it, eagle? I shivered in the hot sunlight.

Our hotel was on an enormous plaza dominated by a statue of Lenin that was called . . . you'll never guess . . . Lenin Square.

In the old days the Khabarovsk Territory was the most sparsely settled of all the vast region that has since become the U.S.S.R. Its most notable discoverer was a peasant of Vologda, the Cossack explorer Yerofei Zhabarov who arrived there in the seventeenth century. He was a massive specimen if one is to judge from the rugged bronze statue of him prominently displayed in Vokzalnaya Square. On beholding the Amur he is said to have exclaimed, "There will be rich fields here . . . and this will be a place of greater beauty and plenty than in all Siberia."

Just what amanuensis were on hand to jot down the prophetic utterances of great men has never been made clear to me but there must have been far more Boswells in the world than we have been led to believe.

In the spring of 1858 a stretch of land on the Amur River was chosen as the site for the future city and its foundations were laid by the descendants of the pioneers who had explored and settled Siberia.

Today, according to the propaganda leaflets all is sweetness and light, this happy condition having been attained "When the fresh revolutionary wind of 1917"—which had started in Leningrad and Moscow—"reached the Far East, Soviet power was established in Khabarovsk."

The Russians do acknowledge that the following five years of foreign intervention reduced the city to rubble and in fact the region was the scene of some of the bloodiest battles of the revolution between the Red and White forces, the latter supported to greater or lesser extent, and for their own reasons, by the United States, Czechoslovakia, Great Britain, Japan, and France.

Despite this formidable opposition, and largely because it was uncoordinated, by 1922 the Soviets had gained complete control and began the rebuilding of the city. The final battle is depicted in a giant diorama in the museum. Today Khabarovsk is a center of power and industry and of many schools and universities. Their medical school alone graduates four hundred doctors a year as compared to the 150 of New York's College of Physicians and Surgeons at the Columbia-Presbyterian Medical Center. How expert they are is something else again. But even if only ten or fifteen are top rank, their knowledge and experience will expand and deepen and enrich those who learn from them.

Nor are schools all that Khabarovsk has to offer. It manufactures prefabricated apartment houses, it is the baby carriage center of the land and it has the Lenin Sports Stadium. Russians are enthusiastic sport fans and great admirers of statues, chalk white or gilded, of beefy athletes with muscles like cannon balls which spring out at passers-by from the most unexpected places.

Despite its dubious art, however, Khabarovsk booms, another aspect contributing to its prosperity being transportation. The city is the terminal of the long Moscow–Khabarovsk flight. It is provisioned by the broad artery that is the Amur River and, this was the reason for our own presence, it is a vital station on the Trans-Siberian Railroad.

Moscow to Nakhodka, 5700 miles, is the longest rail journey in the world. In computing track, the United States has about 225,000 miles, as opposed to Russia's 75,000 but in no single stretch can our long steel lines match that one span. Travelers who have made the entire trip contend that this is just as well.

Somewhere someone wrote a line which I deplore since it is about a land I love. He referred to "miles and miles of bloody Africa." Mr. Kevin Kinsella, in an article published in the New York *Times* in June of 1971, recounted his adventures on a trip between Moscow and Nakhodka. It was entitled "Traveling Hard Class on the Trans-Siberian," but one gets the impression he might well have called it "Miles and Miles of Bloody Russia."

Today a non-stop trip between the two cities takes eight days. It took the same in 1910. We were lucky. We were traveling only between Khabarovsk and Nakhodka where we would board a ship for Japan.

Since we were not leaving until late afternoon we spent the morning moseying about the city and climbing a high hill which overlooked the river and a small cove where they were building a bathing beach. I say building one because the natural strand was cramped and narrow and big dredges were dumping dark yellow dirty-looking sand into the shallow water.

We did not think it looked very inviting but a crowd of Russians, thick as flies on a honey pot, were splashing happily. In the afternoon we went for a cruise on the river but there was a dead calm, the sun beat down on the glassy water and it was with a certain lifting of the spirits that we at last set off for the station.

Everyone was rather keyed up over the idea of the famous train and there was much speculation as to what our accommodations would be like. I felt I knew and I said to Norton, "We have to brace ourselves. They have four berths to a compartment and I don't doubt we'll have to share with two other people."

If this were the case I think we both secretly hoped they might be Russians instead of our fellow Americans. By now our party knew each other pretty well and Russians would be a novelty. I am not so particular about whom I am asleep with but I am extremely fussy about whom I am awake with.

As it turned out our suspicions were wrong. There were four berths all right but only one couple to a compartment. We were first class. If there was a second or "hard" we did not see it but there was very definitely a de luxe. I do not know how clean the compartments were but en route to the dining car we admired their Western great-days-of-the-Golden-Arrow décor. Rich upholstery, mahogany, shining brass and heavily crocheted antimacassars. All the cars were terribly hot with the exception of the diner which, mercifully, was air conditioned.

The country between Khabarovsk and Nakhodka was some of the loveliest we had seen in Russia. Green, rolling, fertile—hills, woods, an occasional small hamlet. Interestingly enough every place not in the immediate vicinity of the railroad tracks is out of bounds. One is too near the coast and Vladivostok where the Russians have their mighty air and naval installations.

The next morning we said goodbye to Faina, having presented her with an amber something or other. We had all contributed small amounts for a farewell present. She had been an able little soul, a small tugboat nosing a large busload of Americans across the steppes of Russia and eventually into berth at Nakhodka.

As I recall, it was Ginny White who had chosen the bauble, and who composed an amusing rhyme using all our names, to go with it. Since we knew Faina was married and had a two-year-old son we discussed whether money would not be more useful but the consensus was that she might be offended or might possibly get into trouble for accepting it. From our point of view too this was more important.

Having completed her stint Faina turned us over to a colleague who rode with us in the bus the short distance between the rail terminal and the pier.

Since we were in nautical surroundings I saw at once that the cut of her jib was very different from Faina. This one was a Prussian Russian.

"You will go here." "You are to do so and so." "Sign these papers."

Norton watched her with objective interest and then murmured to me, "That one makes lamp shades out of human skin." I thought it more than likely.

Fortunately we were soon free of her and plunged unaided into the usual bustle and confusion of a seaport, going through the formalities of health, converted money, and passports. We at last passed a barrier and thought our troubles were over, but we had merely reached customs. It is when you are leaving the country that the Russians do their serious check-up work. Although others were scrutinized carefully we were fortunate: our bags were not opened.

The man looked at them, counted them three or four times as we nodded acquiescence and said yes, they were ours, our very own. Then he inspected our passports. He held them upside down for a while but it really didn't matter. He was incapable of deciphering them from any angle. He then asked to see our traveler's checks. We presented them. He shook his head. He shook it again when he saw the financial papers that had already been signed by a banker colleague in the outer office. With a sigh and a shrug he stamped our bags and passed us through. We concluded he had to be a Commissar's nephew or he would never have kept the job.

Our friends the Kellys had had rougher going and John's Irish face was scarlet, torn as he was between irritation and laughter. The Kellys' son Mike had accompanied his parents to the Petroleum Congress in Moscow and on across Russia. Because they amused him, and as a souvenir, the young man had kept his fancy engraved invitations to the opening ceremonies and the performances of the ballet.

These greatly impressed the customs man. To such an extent that when he learned John was Mike's father and that it was *he* who had transacted business at the Moscow meetings, he didn't believe it.

"If you are the important one, where are your invitations?" he demanded.

"I didn't keep them. I threw them away when we left Moscow."

"If you really had them"—a suspicious sneer at the unlikelihood of such an honor—"where are they now?"

"I told you. I threw them away."

"Why?"

"Why? Because I'm not a goddam kid that's why. I gave up keeping my dance programs a long time ago."

With a glare of disapproval the customs man waved them through.

To our happy surprise the ship, the *Khabarovsk,* was a delight. Fifty-two hundred tons, built in East Germany five years previously, she was clean, comfortable, and remarkably stable; far better than we had anticipated.

Though our cabins were small they were adequate and each shared a toilet and shower with another, although there were also several commodious bathrooms.

One of the enclosed decks served as a very pretty small conservatory with green and flowering plants.

The passengers were a mixed bag of Russians, Americans, and Japanese, including an enchanting little Japanese child whose head was patted bald by gushing ecstatic females of the West.

With the exception of a loud-mouthed, usually drunk American woman, the United Nations atmosphere was amiable. We concluded the tipsy compatriot must be a secret nipper since, for the rest of us, there was only one difficulty: getting to the bar. It didn't open until 7 P.M. which was the time dinner was served. From the American point of view this was scarcely practical.

A group of the oil lads went to one of the ship's officers and asked him to intercede with the barmaid, a formidable female, before whom her fellow countryman obviously quailed. However, in the interests of international good will, he did his best. She obstinately refused. Why *should* she open earlier? She wouldn't be getting anything out of it and Russians of that class we had found were not very accommodating.

The food was about what it had been on land but in the dining saloon there was something else to interest us. Norton and I were at a table for four and the other places were occupied by two Russian brothers, good-looking boys both of them. One was twenty-three, the other fourteen. They spoke English, the older of the two fluently, and they told us they were on their way to Tokyo to spend a couple of months with their parents whom they had not seen for a year and a half. The father, we gathered, was in a Russian firm doing business with the Japanese.

Igor was studying international finance and banking. As this was what Ken George was interested in, too, the young men quickly got on a friendly basis and Igor assured us that if he did well in economics he would be allowed to travel to other countries to learn their methods.

Norton and I tried not to pump him too obviously. We didn't want to be rude or to frighten him off, but he was educated, intelligent, and a real live Russian with whom we could communicate.

He himself was a student at the university but he told us that if, at eighteen, a boy could not pass the examinations he was automatically drafted into the army.

He and his brother Michael lived in Moscow with their grandmother. "I couldn't imagine living in any other city than Moscow," he said with a happy smile. We suspected that Tokyo would be the first other city he had ever seen.

He earned a stipend of forty rubles a month and he had to pay three taxes: to the trade unions, to the Communist party and one because he was not married or, just as we have, there were no tax deductions for a single man.

His grandmother paid fifteen rubles a month rent. Of course, since the value of the ruble depends on the country with which the Russians are dealing and since it fluctuates back and forth, up and down, like a bird in a badminton game, it is hard to say what his salary and his grandmother's rent actually were.

Having visited Russia, I now understand why financial tables pubished in the United States estimate the number of hours or days' work required for a Russian to buy a pair of shoes or a coat or whatever it may be.

From something Igor said we at first understood that the Soviet Government was paying for his trip to Japan. Later we gathered that we were mistaken. "We have been invited," he said. We assumed by their parents. In any event, whether because it was all he possessed or because it was all the money the state would allow him to take out of the country he, with his young brother in tow, was making a trip of several thousand miles with four rubles in his pocket.

To Americans that seems inconceivable but vouchers are the Russian way of life, for Russians as well as for tourists. Train and plane and boat fare, hotel rooms, food, everything has been paid for and they have vouchers to prove it.

And in case of emergency? Ingenuity instead of money presumably. Doctors and hospitals are free. If you break your leg and have to take a taxi to get to one that's your hard luck. If you'd like a sociable beer at a bar that's your hard luck too. You need a new pair of socks? You should have thought of that before you left home. It's imperative that you make a phone call? Let us hope reversing the charges pertains in Russia too.

We felt that if banking and finance were Igor's interests there was a rich vein to be explored. I thought of his American opposite number, Ken George who, to our certain knowledge carried on his person many, many, *many* more than four dollars. It would be instructive for young Mr. Suvoroff to learn how, under certain circumstances, one *may* be equipped for travel. I'm not saying it's the average American way but it exists.

We did ask him how the Soviets arrived at the arbitrary rate of exchange they applied to the dollar and he said that they knew what services cost in other countries and so for the same thing they charged the same rates.

The argument seemed ingenious enough but we tried, as tactfully as possible, to point out that labor's wages were not comparable to ours and that the quality of goods and services was, for the most part, very different in the Western World.

It was around in there that we got on to the subject of food and when he learned that in the United States green vegetables were normal fare throughout the winter and when he heard about deep freezers a wistful look mingled with a dash of incredulity came into his blue eyes. It is this kind of thing that makes the visitor so indignant with the Communist Government. Deprive the People is their code.

In the course of the voyage Igor told us their parents would be meeting him and his brother at the dock in Yokohama and after a year and a half without seeing their sons we could well imagine that neither hell nor high water would keep them away. Still, there are such things as flat tires, or drawbridges that stay up an unconscionable time, or a collision with another car and a cop haranguing you for an hour and a half even if you are the innocent party.

Norton had given Igor a dollar bill as a souvenir. "Presumably at the dock the Japanese will accept rubles and dollars, Igor," he said, "so now you're a capitalist but just in *case* . . . if your parents *should* be delayed for any unforeseen reason, promise you'll come to me and Mrs. Brown, we'll see that you and Mike get to their house in Tokyo."

They were sturdy boys with high fresh color and bright to boot but somehow, those four rubles and the one dollar bill . . . We half-expected to see them disembark with their worldly goods tied in a red handkerchief on the end of a stick.

It was on shipboard that we learned the tragic news of the three Russian cosmonauts who had perished in their capsule. When we commiserated with Igor he said offhandedly, "Oh I knew about

that in Khabarovsk." Norton and I were surprised and a little
shocked. Why had he said nothing? Did he think we would not
be interested? That, unthinkably, we would gloat? Did he perhaps
feel ashamed that it had happened, that it would show the Russians in a poor light? We never found out and did not dwell on it, yet
it was a tragedy for everyone.

Our second night on board, which was also our last since we would
be disembarking the following afternoon, we saw a marvelous spectacle, once more courtesy of Ken, who having gotten very cosy with
the young captain came to fetch us, saying, "Come on up to the
bridge. This is wild!"

Stretching for miles was what we took to be a lighted coastline
and it was so festive in appearance we thought it a sort of Coney
Island of Japan. Not so. It was the Japanese fishing fleet, over one
hundred brilliantly illuminated boats spaced at close intervals for
more than ten miles.

It occurred to me that if that density and intensity of human
predators held to the pace we were witnessing their quarry would
soon be eliminated. Maybe there are controls I know not of but
they certainly appeared to be killing the fish that laid the golden roe.

One of the ships, with third degree lights, passed within two hundred yards of us possibly drawing fish but certainly protests from the
blinded passengers.

It was a memorable spectacle nevertheless and with all those
experts at work we wondered why it wouldn't have been possible
to have something more palatable than the disheartening fish dish
we had been served at luncheon.

The next afternoon, as we drew near Yokohama, the sea was
rough and I marveled at the nimbleness, not to mention skill and
courage, of the immigration officials who approaching us in bobbing,
rolling tenders leapt aboard with split-second timing while their little
boats wallowed in deep troughs or rose on high crests.

As we were docking we stood at the rail watching the activity on
the quai. Suddenly Norton nudged me. "There they are," he said.
"They've got to be Igor and Mike's parents." I looked where he

pointed and agreed. There, eagerly scanning the crowding, waving passengers was a European couple beside a blue car they had managed to drive right onto the dock.

We had been right. A little later, as we were waiting at a customs bench for our luggage to be delivered, Igor came up to us, his parents following close behind him. He must have said something nice about us because they took our hands and in broken English thanked us warmly for our kindness to their two sons.

If it was kindness it hadn't been hard. The boys were charming and we were interested in them.

We said goodbye, wished them well and once more piled into a bus, clean and air conditioned, for the drive from Yokohama into Tokyo.

In this one too we had a hostess guide and a chatty little piece she was. Picking up the mike she smiled winningly and said, "First I tell you my name. It is"—some unintelligible Japanese sounds— "you know what it means?"

One of our gallants spoke up. "Pretty girl," he said. She dimpled and I sensed her ploy was a well-practiced one.

"It means Elegant Child," she informed us. "Elegant Child of Turnip Tree." Mr. and Mrs. Turnip Tree were her parents.

We learned quite a lot more about her, her parents and the kind of house they lived in and the rent they paid. Then she swung into action. Two or three times she reiterated her instructions about what we were to do when we reached the hotel, whom we were to contact, where we were to foregather, with especially strict emphasis on the timing of our movements.

The thirty-odd adults before her were a reasonably alert group. Through know-how, vigor, imagination, not to mention oil in the ground, these potentates of the petroleum world had arrived at enviable positions and, for the most part, even more enviable wealth. To little Turnip Blossom they were obviously a bunch of duds and once more she explained, as to backward children, the simple routine being set up for them. Smiles and nods became automatic and eyes fi-

30. Communist babies are every bit as cute as capitalistic tots.

31. Boy meets girl in a slightly more advanced class. Lola Day Care center.

32. Reid Brazell of Total Oil and Faina, our stanch little guide who shepherded us across her native land. She was helped out in various cities by local girls.

33. Gingerbread facade of house in Irkutsk. Once the home of the chief of police. "Who lives there now?" "Who doesn't?"

34. Ilka and Russian youngsters on shores of Lake Baikal.

35. Igor and Michael Suvoroff on board the *Khabarovsk* between Nahodka and Yokohama.

36. Norton Brown on the Ginza, Tokyo.

37. Tim Liversedge on the shore of Lake Ngami, Botswana. He was good-looking, charming, and knew more about animals than Mr. Noah.

38. African kids waiting for the big thrill. The arrival of Rodney's plane at Lake Ngami.

39. The "stage" at Khwai River Lodge. Lechwe and wildebeest.

40. The big cats. Moremi Reserve.

41. Lordly lechwe resting beside Larry's Lagoon.

42. Impala.

43. Bushwomen and children.

nally glazed but in the end we muddled through with true British grit.

For Norton and me this was our third visit to Tokyo but two previous times we had arrived by air. This time we drove along an elevated highway looking down on the city. The sky was overcast, the atmosphere smog-laden and the district through which we were passing crowded with small mean houses huddled along dirty streets yet interspersed here and there, unexpectedly, almost incredibly, with green gardens: flowering jewels in a dingy setting.

The streets of Russia had been immaculate, sterile. Those particular streets of Japan were distressing but the human touch survived.

Our hotel was the Imperial. Frequently in my life, both viva voce and in print I have held forth on the charms of small, local inns. "Why," I have demanded rhetorically, "why travel half around the world to sleep with Mr. Conrad Hilton?" Having by now traveled, I should imagine, a couple of million miles or more, I have the answer. He and his ilk are excellent bed fellows.

It was a Russian friend, a New York White Russian friend who first gave me food for thought on the subject. I had been riding my hobby, the small hotel, the picturesque inn, the local color when she, speaking English like a stage Russian demanded, "But Eelka, daarling, what is bad American hotel? Is warm winter, cool summer, hot water, tubs and tubs hot water, clean sheets, nice beds, so what wrong?"

Looked at from that point of view I had to admit American hotels didn't seem all that bad. Nor was Tokyo's new Imperial. Large? You bet. Commercial? Definitely. Good? Divine!

A huge lobby in which you sank to your ankles in luxurious carpeting. Extraordinarily large rooms admirably equipped. Great baths with superb tubs, showers, shower caps, washcloths and sheet-sized deep pile towels. Toilets, elevators, everything worked!

As far as the elevators were concerned I went a little mad. I rode up and down twice in one for no reason at all except the pleasure of seeing the lighted direction arrow go on almost instantaneously, in feeling the car rise and descend smoothly, the doors open sound-lessly at the correct floor. Happiness is a functioning elevator? On occasion it can be.

And then there were the shops! The lower lobby contained an inviting maze of exotic wares and in one of them I stumbled upon a real find: a packet of small, beautifully colored wood-block prints. In that obvious and well-known ploy designed to hoodwink the shop-keeper I pretended to be deeply interested in other merchandise and then casually, almost indifferently I held out the prints. "And these? They're not bad. What are you asking for them?"

"Seven-fifty," said the man. My heart jumped. I was candor itself. "That seems fair. I think I'd like to have them."

"Seven hundred and fifty dollars," he said gently.

They might have been living coals I dropped them so fast. A find indeed! I, too, know the folly inherent in buying from the shops in a hotel arcade but our one full day in Tokyo was Sunday and those were the shops that were open.

The evening of our arrival we dined in the hotel's tempura res-taurant. I have had greater tempura but this was delicate and crisp, a welcome switch from cabbage and potatoes, although our pleasure was a little dampened in discovering that while the dinner itself was included in our already paid tour expenses an extra and notably thin slice of melon cost $1.80. Gourmandising comes high.

The Imperial is pretty much in the center of town so after dinner I said to Norton, "Let's walk over to the Ginza." Knowing how I hate crowds my husband looked surprised. "I suppose the next thing, you'll be telling me you want to spend New Year's Eve in Times Square!"

"Not at all," I said, "that's silly. I was only in Times Square on New Year's Eve once in my life. Well, twice, but once I was in a play on Broadway and couldn't find a cab until after midnight and the other time, the authentic one so to speak, was because some friends from Paris were curious to see it."

My spouse accepted this and together with the Brazells and the

Langs who also wanted to go, we set off. The Ginza was brash, Broadwayish, vulgar, and altogether heaven. Lights were blazing, young people were sauntering up and down their arms around each other, even the juke boxes, normally anathema, played lovely tunes and our spirits rose like balloons. It was free, it was prosperous, it was gay. It was livin'! In Moscow by 10 P.M. Red Square was rolled up for the night, the streets silent and deserted.

That is the strange sad thing about Russia. The drabness, the oppressiveness and, the most frightening aspect, the rapidity with which one comes to accept them. We had been in the country only a little over three weeks and yet, although aware that the atmosphere was very different from that of home, we were already beginning to adapt to it as a way of life. My heart ached for those, especially the young, who know no other way and assume that that is what life is and has to be.

Later, back home, we got together with Wanda Jablonski to exchange notes and she told us that when, in the plane she had taken to fly from Moscow to Rome, the captain spoke through the intercom saying, "We are now crossing the border, leaving the Soviet Union," the entire cabin broke into a spontaneous cheer. That this should be so in a country that so many hoped would be Utopia is deeply sad.

In the morning of our Tokyo Sunday I did what every female traveler does at the first opportunity; went to the hairdresser, meeting Norton later for luncheon at the Suehiro Restaurant. The Suehiro is the traveler's dream in one respect. You are the only foreigners there. It is not far from the Imperial, nestling behind Matsuzakaya, the big department store.

It is a middle-class Japanese family restaurant with good food for average families leading their average lives. Norton and I smiled at one tableau apparently as common to East as to West. Mama, papa and a pretty young lady, their daughter. She was smartly dressed and we decided she must be the successful secretary

of an important executive. Sunday lunch was obviously the time allotted to honorable parents and good and bored the three of them
looked although father, at least, had a minor diversion. They were all
dressed in western clothes and the restaurant, to our way of thinking,
was agreeably air conditioned but he sat vigorously cooling off with
an elegant little fan.

We ordered beer but here one must take a firm stand. Almost automatically they will present you with a bottle of Suntory.
Suntory is not bad by any means but *the* beer to our way of thinking
is Asahi. We insisted upon it and it was produced.

After lunch we sauntered vaguely in the direction of the hotel,
passing at the junction of two boulevards a large and beautiful tank
filled with superb tropical fish and exotic plants. "The Japanese are
wonderful," we said. "What an imaginative thing to do." Our delight in the marine spectacular was slightly marred when we realized
that it was in fact an ad for our so recently relished Asahi. In the
bottom of the tank among the stones and flora, the labels cunningly
exposed, nestled three cans of beer.

This being Sunday a broad avenue had been closed to traffic. Down
the middle, chairs and tables had been set up, the tables shaded by
colorful scalloped umbrellas with Coca-Cola stamped around the
edges.

They have some lovely parks in Tokyo, we know because we have
been in them, and as the morning clouds had lifted and the day
turned hot and brilliant, we hoped they were being enjoyed too but
the great avenues were thronged.

The next morning we would be leaving for San Francisco where
the tour as such would be breaking up, members scattering in every
direction to their own homes. But that evening, still bound in
friendship by our mutual experiences, and at the Kellys' invitation we
dined with them in the theatre restaurant of the Imperial.

The large vaudeville show was not particularly good but it was fast
and where the girls weren't bare, and they largely were, the costumes were colorful.

Ken and Clem George were also at the table with us and while we all enjoyed our dinner, especially the poultry course which was excellent, from his expression as he watched the stage I imagine Mr. George Junior's last memory of Tokyo will not be breast of guinea fowl.

CHAPTER FOUR

Africa

At the opening of this book I observed that for us 1971 was the year of the Conducted Tour. September was the month of the Lindblad.

We had, of course, been making plans long before that, well before we went to Russia, but I said to Mrs. Lindblad, "If we do Russia I'm not sure we can swing Botswana."

Her dark eyes sparkled. "Oh, but you *must* do Russia," she said and this despite the fact that Lindblad would not be involved.

"You must go and you must wear your prettiest clothes. I do hope you'll decide on it."

If the reader has borne with me this far he will know we did go to Russia and happily we were still able to negotiate both Botswana and the "Extension" tour into Etosha in South-West Africa.

The whole area is well below the equator as everyone is probably aware. The new countries are sometimes the old countries with different names; sometimes they're not.

What used to be Northern Rhodesia,* is now Zambia. Nyasaland, that used to be known as Southern Rhodesia is now plain Rhodesia.

* See *Second Spring and Two Potatoes.*

Bechuanaland Protectorate is Botswana. North of it is the Caprivi Strip, which I had never heard of before, and to the left or west of Botswana, reaching up to the Strip is South-West Africa. North of the Strip is Angola to which we didn't go except for a brief touch-down in a plane.

Botswana has no coastline. South-West Africa has a long one and what used to be the Union of South Africa is now the Republic of South Africa and little old South-West is part of it.

Not that all that matters as far as the Lindblad tour is concerned but I like to get things straightened out in my own mind.

One strong appeal of the tour was its size. Small. We were to be eight plus one courier, although actually we had two, a male and a female, both excellent.

My husband and I can't be the only people who, confronted with a cosy number such as eight, say to each other, "Hey, let's try to gather a few chums. Make it our own party."

When we told our old friends the Kohlers what we were planning Charlotte sparked at once, "It sounds grand. How about it, Walter, how about our going?" Walter, though less sparky, didn't come out against it. Ruth Anderson, our South American stalwart couldn't wait. "Me too," she cried happily.

It was just before Norton and I were taking off for Russia that the long-distance call came through from Kohler, Wisconsin. Charlotte sounded disconsolate. "We're not going with you to Africa. Walter's changed his mind. He said he'd rather go to Europe."

True, his enthusiasm originally had not been ardent and it isn't that he doesn't like animals. When the deer come out of his own woods and pose on the great stretch of lawn in the mellow evening light he is a proud and contented man but that is different. They are his deer, viewed in comfort. Still, it wasn't even the travel per se that put him off.

What seemed definitely to decide him against the project was the itinerary. Studying it he observed that we were scheduled to spend one night at Victoria Falls. He looked puzzled. "But Charlotte, we've *been* to Victoria Falls."

So they had. So had Norton and I but I feel the spectacle is such that one may view it twice in a lifetime without undue boredom.* However, the ex-governor of the state of Wisconsin had spoken as effectively as Zarathustra.

With the Kohler defection we now remained a staunch little cadre of three. One Anderson and two Browns who felt themselves capable of standing off whatever other five people, fate and the Lindblads might deal them.

Never trouble trouble till trouble troubles you is wise philosophy. As matters turned out we were a congenial group, such minor tensions as did develop being dealt with well within civilized bounds. And the Lindblad office must certainly be one of the most congenial and relaxed in the business.

As our departure date drew near there would come every day or so a chirp from Ruth over the telephone. "I've got the brochures and all but have you people sent in your check yet? I haven't had a bill nor heard a word about it."

"Neither have we. I do suppose it's all set though, don't you?"

"God, yes. I'll die if we don't go."

We need not have worried. In due course we were courteously relieved of our money which, oddly enough, made us very happy for we were spending it for travel. We were as good as off!

We had been told that another couple would be joining us in Johannesburg: Dr. and Mrs. James Wicks from Tacoma, Washington. At Kennedy International in New York we met the other three who would be flying with us. They were Dr. and Mrs. William Saul from Emporia, Kansas, and another woman whose name, at first, we did not get. On introducing ourselves Ruth said, "I'm Ruth Anderson."

"*My* name used to be Nelson but I changed it," said the lady.

In the confusion and noise of the airport Anderson and Nelson didn't sound too unalike or at least that's how Ruth and I interpreted it. We, on our side, got the impression our companion's first name was Muriel and wondered why we couldn't catch her attention

* See *Second Spring and Two Potatoes.*

when we called it out. I should think not. Her name was Florence: Florence Mueller of Omaha, Nebraska, and she is one of the most traveled women on the face of the globe. She has been every place. To most of them twice.

It was pure coincidence that the three men of the safari were doctors although they worked in different fields. Bill Saul is a radiologist, Jim Wicks a pathologist, and my own true love an internist. When we weren't game viewing they held little conventions of their own so as not to get rusty.

We were flying to Johannesburg via Rio de Janeiro on Varig, the Brazilian airline which, until October 1, 1971 had been owned by its own personnel. On that date the company went public but the employees still control the majority of the stock.

When Ruth and I first heard what our route from New York would be we stared at each other in total disbelief. "Rio! But we were just there. In February. What are we going back for?"*

As far as Norton and I were concerned this was our fifth trip to Africa and we had *never* gone via Varig. On the other hand we had never flown to Johannesburg from New York. From Perth, Australia, yes, and when we did it in 1964, in an Electra turbo prop, it was the longest trip in the history of transportation but a look at the map will reveal why Varig is the line for the route we were taking.

You go straight south and you go straight east and the eternal L which you fly is, in this case, the shortest distance between two points.

I am not keen on night flying but that's when the plane went, so we did too. Of the stockholders in the company I can say that one of them, a stewardess, was a fine executive, promoting drinks and dinner nearly singlehanded while the steward owners lounged about chatting. Doubtless discussing their profits.

Incidentally, if traveling economy class in a Boeing 707 the places to try for are either the bulkhead seats, more leg room, or rows 11 and 21 where there are only two seats abreast, the evacuation shoots

* See *Chapter I.*

being folded beside them. These figures are approximate as the placing of the partition between first class and economy may vary with
the number of passengers but that is about the location for the desirable, more roomy seats.

We arrived in Rio the next morning after a flight of nine hours
and twenty minutes.

We arrived exhausted, as one is after a long night flight, to find
Galeao a remarkably inefficient airport. So much so that we decided
they really must have planned it that way. It couldn't have happened by pure chance.

They have set up rows of booths, in effect cubbyholes, manned,
more or less, by immigration officers and between these booths the
passengers move in single file. The 707 had been sold out so that
meant that 125 people progressed at glacier pace. The personnel on
duty helped slow us down too. The authorities had obviously been
in touch with Jane van Lawick-Goodall, the renowned young scien-
tist who has devoted herself to the study of chimpanzees in Tanzania.
She must have told them how to recognize the more backward members of a group. These they snaffled and imported to Rio de Janeiro
to staff the immigration centers.

What is especially maddening is that for a long time the cause of
the snail-like progress is invisible. You shuffle slowly, slowly, slowly
behind the person in front of you. It is only when you arrive at the
cubbyhole where your particular ape is sequestered that the reason
becomes apparent. He can't read. He takes your passport, pours
over it for an eternity, moving his lips as he examines it, turning
each page and turning it back again. Then he starts over from the
beginning. It was the port of Nakhodka in duplicate.

Norton and I were right behind Ruth Anderson who chin in
hand, elbow propped on the ledge behind which the creature was
officiating, watched the performance for sometime.

"That's the idea," she murmured appreciatively, "earn while you
learn."

At last, incredibly, he stamped her passport and passed her
through. An hour or so later we followed hard on her heels.

However, don't let our experience put you off. Galeao had been primarily an army air force base. Both the Brazilian authorities and Varig itself know that the amenities are far from adequate and they are now rebuilding for the future and with civilian traffic in mind. Probably already things are much better. Maybe the denizens of the treetops have even learned what they are supposed to be looking for in a passport.

When, in our case, the formalities finally were accomplished we dropped into the capable hands of the Lindblad agent, unexpectedly in that part of the world, a Dutchman by the name of John Hissink. He shepherded us into a mini bus and accompanied us to our hotel, the Leme Palace on the Copacabana.

There we breakfasted on our balcony overlooking the famous crescent beach but although the weather was clear the day was clammy and bed seemed far more inviting than a swim.

We knew our friends, Billie and Olivar de Araujo, were picking us up for luncheon so we tried to get a bit of rest in order not to look like walking corpses.

They took us to the Gavea Golf Club outside the city. The golf course edges the bay and there is a magnificent swimming pool. We were stopped at the gates, there was considerable pourparling and Olivar had to sign us in. When we inquired about the precautions he said it was because a good many foreign diplomats played golf there—we ourselves saw the French Ambassador on one of the fairways—and the government was leary of kidnapers. I noticed the de Araujos' chauffeur always locked the doors as soon as we were seated in the car which, to an uninitiated eye, seemed a little excessive but I suppose it's better to be sure than sorry.

And after all, who knows when kidnapers may strike? It was on a sunny Sunday afternoon after a good luncheon that Jim Thompson, the American who had done so much to revitalize the Thai silk industry, left a friend's house in the country outside Singapore to go for a stroll and was never heard of again.

Our own lunch was without dramatic aftermath. The French Ambassador could not have done better at Maxim's in Paris nor could

we. Heart of palm soup, great luscious *écrevisses* and fruta de
Conde, a round pale green fruit that looked as though it were
enveloped in small artichoke leaves.

Our friends took us for a drive along unfrequented beaches that
were wild and beautiful but we were too weary to appreciate them
properly.

To our dismay, on returning to the hotel for a nap, we were
greeted by marching troops and massed bands. September 7 is
Brazilian Independence Day but they chose to celebrate over the
weekend. Fortunately the festivities were not prolonged so we were
able to get some rest before being whisked off again by the hospitable de Araujos for dinner in what is a truly sumptuous apartment. It is an enormous duplex affair with a lovely loggia on the top
floor and a magnificent view over the glittering harbor with the
famous Sugar Loaf Mountain to the right.

Since Billie and Olivar had liked Ruth so much when they met
her the previous February they had asked her to dine too. She
had not been all that seduced by Rio the first time round but on the
way back to the hotel she said, *"Well,* if I could live like that and
eat that way all the time and had friends here, I would feel very
differently about the place."

Under similar conditions I imagine one would feel differently
about living even in Liverpool or Little Rock which, by and large,
do not echo in my heart like the silvery bells of far Cathay.

We were up the next morning at 5:45; breakfasted, dressed, and
rushed down to wait in the humid dawn for our mini airport bus.
As we were standing on the sidewalk a curious figure hurried by;
a tiny little man dressed in a bright green suit. "Look," I said to
Ruth, "a leprechaun."

Mrs. Anderson thought differently. In preparation for Botswana
she had been reading Laurens van der Post and in one of his books
about the Kalahari had come across a fascinating bit of information.
Bushmen, it seems, are usually in a state of semi-erection. She
eyed the passer-by greedily. Size-wise he could be a Bushman.
"Let's catch him and snatch off his pants and see."

He was too quick for us though so I am not in a position to enlighten the reader as to the truth or falsity of the assertion.

Getting out of the Rio airport was as tedious and long-winded as getting into it, nor was the ordeal lightened for Ruth who, catching sight of herself in a full-length mirror, groaned in dismay.

"My God," she said, "I look like Ilse Koch the Bitch of Buchenwald!"

I burst out laughing. Our friend is a chrysanthemum headed creature with a bawdy wit, a gentle heart and a sharply honed intelligence. It had not occurred to Norton or me that there was any resemblance between her and the unspeakable wife of the unspeakable administrator of the Nazi concentration camp.

The flight is long [seven hours and forty-five minutes] but fortunately the food on the plane, while late in coming, proved to be delicious. Varig had rounded up the steers and the medallion of beef was the best I have ever eaten.

We landed in Johannesburg on the dot to find it was 10:15 P.M. local time and to be met by Carol Martin, a pleasant bright young woman who was the Lindblad courier. She would be with us all through the Botswana section of our safari.

Our hotel was the President. Modern and comfortable, but watch the showers, they can knock you flat. The water gushes from the shower head with the force of Victoria Falls.

Although we were there on a Monday, it was a holiday. Nothing doing. This was a real blow to Margery Wicks. We met her and her husband, Dr. James Wicks, in the early afternoon. Margery is a pretty woman with fair hair, dark eyes, and small features. They are an attractive and affectionate couple still holding hands and walking with their arms around each other, although they have two children in their twenties. Madame's hobby, full-time occupation, and vital interest is shopping. To be in a new city and not able to get into the stores was a painful experience.

When we got to know them better we teased her about it but she claimed that she really only *looked* and never bought *anything* unless

Jim liked it too. Judging by the amount of stuff they sent home Jim's taste was catholic.

It may seem an odd pastime, but since it was the only thing open in the entire community, we went that afternoon to a snake farm, a short drive out of town.

The herpetologist was not only young, blond, and handsome with beautiful teeth but, to my way of thinking, his courage matched that of the defenders of Thermopylae or a mongoose.

With abandon and savoir faire he tossed his lethal charges about like paper streamers, winding them on a stick as though he were Mercury with his caduceus. Holding them behind the ears, if snakes may be said to have ears, forcing open their jaws so they spit their venom into the glass he held under their mouths, and keeping up a running commentary on his activities in English and Afrikaans, he held his audience spellbound.

Since it was a holiday parents had brought their children, for the grounds encompassed a small park with swings and trampolins as well as the serpents and a chap to whom I rather warmed, a lizard with a frill down his back.

After the milking performance we had tea and bought souvenirs in the park's small shop.

On our way back to Johannesburg we passed a colored township. It was better than the ones Norton and I had seen in 1964, at least there were some brick houses in place of shacks made of flattened tin cans but it remains depressingly sordid.*

They still have separate buses for colored and white people and when we saw a colored nurse wheeling a white child in a pram and asked Carol what happened if the nurse had to take a child on a bus she replied that it couldn't be done.

We still have a long way to go with our race problems in the United States but I am happy to say that particular kind of idiocy seems to be waning.

Carol did not speak English English so we assumed that she had perhaps been brought up in Rhodesia or Kenya. When we asked

* See *Second Spring and Two Potatoes*.

her where she came from, she giggled, turned quite pink and said, "Rhode Island."

If she thought we would be surprised she was right. Apparently, however, Africa had always fascinated her. She *had* been in Kenya originally but had gone to Botswana to study tribes and the anatomy of tribal life and she also taught school.

Carol herself was intensely interested in seeing justice done the Africans and of course not every South African white subscribes to the irrational and shocking nonsense which is so much a part of the country's daily life.

When we were there we read in a Johannesburg paper, *The Rand Daily Mail* an editorial entitled "People's Choice." It is encouraging and I quote it in its entirety.

There is something almost pathetic about the Minister of Labour's plea to Johannesburg whites not to go to that African bank teller who has been installed in a central city bank. There is no law against it, Mr. Viljoen agrees, but whites should respect the social pattern of the country.

Of course if the theory of apartheid were valid, such a plea would not be necessary. Whites, by a combination of instinct and tradition, shouldn't want to go anywhere near the black teller. They should feel explosively offended if required to do so. This is the assumption on which the whole costly business of economic apartheid is based. Now Mr. Viljoen is finding that when it comes to a choice between racial separation and convenience, ordinary South Africans unhesitatingly prefer the latter.

Which is what a number of people have been trying to tell him for a long time.

That evening at seven o'clock we gathered on the twenty-fifth floor of the hotel for cocktails and a little session of getting to know and love each other since we would be pretty inseparable for the next three weeks.

Florence was late. She had been having her problems. No one had told her where we were foregathering, she couldn't get her suitcase open, she hadn't been able to get in touch with Carol . . . However, once plumped down in the family group she relaxed.

It was here that the tenth member of our party joined us and we had no difficulty at all in cottoning to him at once. He was Tim Liversedge, our second Lindblad courier, a slim, handsome blond lad with delicate, square features. He had been born in England and taken by his parents to Rhodesia at the age of one year. Now twenty-seven, his knowledge of animals, reptiles, and birds was encyclopedic, as we were soon to discover. He was also an extraordinarily fine photographer of wild life.

After drinks we dined together, and went to bed early. Reveille next morning was at 5:15, everybody in the lobby at 6 A.M. in safari clothes.

That is one thing one must say for the hotels of Africa. The early-morning service is excellent. The staff is used to the safari-minded taking off at ungodly hours and the tap on the door is unfailingly punctual, the tea and coffee hot. Even hot rolls when they are spoiling you.

With two exceptions our group, though a little bleary-eyed, looked like the Messers and Mesdames Stanley and Livingstone in correct safari garb, a credit to Abercrombie & Fitch. The exceptions were Florence Mueller and myself.

Florence had on turquoise blue culottes, old sneakers, a sleeveless blouse, and a jacket from Guatemala. I had on bush green slacks, a shirt and sweater, my reputation saved only by authentic safari boots and my old game-viewing hat.

The boots and hat dated from our first African trip in 1962.*

The original slacks and shirts had finally lain down and died and I had not duplicated them because I had found through depressing experience that while admirably suited to the bush and the sand and dust of Africa, worn at home in the country that khaki color looks like nothing so much as prison garb. Hence a couple of pairs of pants that could do double duty and a silent prayer that the animals would not object.

At the end of this chapter the reader will find a suggested list of clothing that I hope will prove helpful.

* See *Elephants Arrive at Half-Past Five.*

Besides raiment there were, of course, binoculars and then there were the cameras! A quick count seemed to add up to people eight, cameras six hundred. If I identify them in some detail it is because most safari minded people are curious as to what their predecessors have taken along and have found practical.

My own true love had five: two Nikons, one movie, two Minox. That may not seem like much but let us not forget the lenses. There must have been easily eight or nine of those with cases and bags to carry them in.

I was allowed a Rollie. I was not expected to bother with quality, just keep a record.

The Wickses had two still cameras apiece, a 35-mm Canon movie camera and a 200-mm telephoto lense. Florence, who knows a great deal about birds and enjoys photographing them, had not only the best binoculars in the group but a quite staggering assortment of lenses for her Pentax. Then there were the Sauls. Thank God they were along because they were loves. But it was a near miss.

In the beginning we had received stern instructions from Lindblad about the weight limit we would each be allowed. Since from a certain point on much of our flying would be done in light planes we were restricted to thirty-five pounds apiece *including* cameras. The Sauls nearly went home to Emporia. Bill's Canon 16-mm movie camera alone had a whole little metal trunk to itself and weighed eighteen pounds. He and Mary also carried still cameras, a Pentax 35-mm with a 200-mm telephoto and a 35-mm Contaflex Prima, and if they were going to have any connection with the light plane at all they would have had to run underneath it, keeping in its shadow like an Italian dog under a wagon.

That any reasonable balance of weight was maintained at all was due entirely to Mrs. Anderson whose equipment consisted of one Instamatic.

Fortunately, Lindblad was later able to negotiate a bigger bird and, while we left in Johannesburg clothes we would not be needing on safari, we could comfortably accommodate all we would require in the neat brown suitcases they provided for us.

The plane from Johannesburg to Francistown, Botswana, while not of transatlantic caliber was of normal size and comfortable even though it was the scene of a humiliating moment as far as I was concerned. Ruth had been wondering about the altitude of Botswana.

"Oh," I said learnedly. "It's at sea level." And I turned to Tim for confirmation. "That's right, isn't it, Tim?"

"What?"

"That Botswana's at sea level."

"No, it's about three thousand feet."

My friend looked at me. "Sea level, eh?"

"They have high tides," I said and retired into a book.

It was on arriving in Francistown that we began the first of our shuttle flights. Since the plane could not accommodate us all we would go in two groups. In her very fair disposition of time and turns we thought Carol Martin's logistics were faultless. She and Tim would split us up between them so that we were never without a nanny.

On the first day the plane was big enough so that only one couple had to remain behind and Norton and I volunteered to do so. Since we were in Francistown we felt we might as well learn something about it and as Carol had lived there for six months she was an ideal guide.

Botswana has a population of only 650,000 but Francistown has the second largest diamond pipe or vein in the world. Tanzania has the first while the famous Kimberley in South Africa is relatively small. But Kimberley has the quality.

Diamonds from the other two are used mostly in industry. Botswana estimates that her pipe can be worked for twenty years or more and she also has deposits of copper and nickel.

Wandering along a dusty road we passed a friend of Carol's, an African politician who was about to leave for Gaberone, the nation's capital, in pursuit of political business. The country is a Republic with a president elected for a five-year term, the life of the

National Assembly over which he presides. The present incumbent is Sir Seretse Khama who became president in 1966 when Botswana attained independence and who was re-elected in October 1969.

The government also embraces a House of Chiefs which advises the government in tribal matters and whose members are drawn from the eight principal tribes of the country.

The flag is a pretty one: a pale blue ground signifying the sky divided by a broad horizontal band of black edged top and bottom with narrow stripes of white for the black and white inhabitants of the country. It is a dry land and the national greeting *Pula* means Let there be rain.

Botswana's economy is largely dependent on agriculture and the export of beef accounts for more than 80 percent of her foreign trade. Now, however, her game reserves are becoming a valuable source of income.

While one cannot say that poaching is nonexistent, Botswana's reserves are relatively free from it because the land is owned by the tribes themselves and poachers are more reluctant to steal from their own than they are from the white man. Also the tribal system lends itself very neatly to the profit motif since the land on which campsites are developed is only leased to the whites. The whites, at least in the places we visited, consisted chiefly of the well-known safari firm of Kerr, Downey and Selby, with Harry Selby very much the active star.

The hospital of Francistown is a focal point. It is staffed by Jesuit nuns and the head matron, a charming and I daresay highly efficient, Irish woman named Sister Mary showed us through it.

Turning a corner of the building we stopped in our tracks. The scene was like a flower garden. Perhaps seventy-five or a hundred African women were seated on the green grass, their brilliantly colored dresses and turbans clashing and glowing in the bright sunlight. They were laughing and chatting, many of them were pregnant, and a white woman was dispensing powdered milk and sage advice as they gathered round her.

Sister Mary told us the hospital was administered by three doctors;

two Chinese from Taiwan and one South African. Noting so many pregnancies I asked if they did not give the pill. She hesitated a moment then she said quietly, "Yes, *they* do." The heathen Chinese, perhaps.

We went through the wards, all very clean and all crowded. As in hospitals throughout the world their need for funds is urgent but it is a good place and many white women of the community go there to have their babies in preference to Gaberone the capital, or even, for that matter, a hospital in Johannesburg.

When we finished our tour it was time to go to the airport and our turn for a flight in the eight-passenger shuttle plane. The three men who were the other passengers, the pilot, and ourselves shared a picnic lunch as we flew over an enormous salt bed. We were not very high, it was very bumpy, I was not happy and I began to think to myself, What am I doing here? The animals had better be *good*. They were.

I would have liked to have had a peek at the Kalahari Desert, but we were well to the north of it. We flew to Maun where we were met by Tony Graham who runs the Okavango camp on the Thamalakane River.

We had been amused by the fact that Carol never spoke of a car or a Land-Rover or Toyota but always of a vehicle. When we saw what Tony Graham was piloting we thought her choice of words precise. It was an enormous kind of canvas-topped bus with old-fashioned comfortably upholstered railroad seats running down the sides, which Mr. Graham drove along the rutted sandy track at a speed roughly equivalent to that of a lunar rocket.

We did pause long enough in our trajectory to make a detour to a large depot where there were warehouses, lorries, and assorted safari equipment and where we met himself, Mr. Harry Selby. He was a vigorous man; dark hair, ruddy complexion, age unguessable, very much the white hunter.

Having for many years been instrumental in the needless slaughter of thousands of wild animals he is gradually turning to thoughts of conservation, to an appreciation of the fact that animals too have a right to their lives.

He has enormous hunting concessions and of these he has set aside fifty square miles as a permanent wild life reserve and for seven miles in each direction from his River Khwai Lodge, no killing of game is permitted.

When Tony Graham and Mr. Selby had finished their conversation, we resumed our landborn flight to camp and were surprised to see a great many Africans heading our way each leading a dog on a string. We thought we must be on the local Park Avenue but the reason for the canine parade soon became apparent. Parked just outside the camp gate was a large truck and painted on the side the word *VET*. Two or three African veterinarians were administering rabies shots for they had just had an epidemic. Fourteen cases had been reported, and everyone had been ordered to bring his dog for treatment. Okavango is a comparatively new camp and a few niceties, such as shelves to lay things down on were yet to be installed, but Tony Graham assured us that progress was in the wind.

Disposing of our possessions as best we could, the floor was a good place, we went out to case our surroundings; sandy ground patterned by the shadows of thorn trees and the wide, curving, lazily flowing Thamalakane. It is a very shallow river fed by another shallow stream, the Boro, and the three canoes, into which we divided ourselves, nosed their way through the thickly crowding reeds as the African boatmen poled slowly along. We came to great beds of water lilies and passed an occasional upthrusting branch bristling with clusters of birds. We saw the snowy, elegant egrets, darters, and a fish eagle. Sky and water were bathed pale gold by the late-afternoon light. When we watched vervet monkeys and saw our first baboons playing on the shore we knew we were truly in Africa.

That time of day is so incredibly lovely that were I to live there I would import gondolas, more comfortable than canoes, and invite my friends to picnic teas on the river.

Returning to camp the magic waned. The sky became overcast

and it started to rain. Oh God, we thought, the rainy season is going to start unseasonably early. Norton and I were low in our minds.

Our last African safari* had been passed, not actually so much in rain, although we had had that too, but in rivers and quagmires and morasses of mud owing to rains that were just terminating.

The Okavango camp people, on the other hand, were delighted. Their need for rain was acute and our own fears proved groundless. From then on we were blessed with perfect weather throughout the safari.

We drifted into the big airy rondawel which is the dining room-bar and made the acquaintance of a delightful young man, aged four, Master Robert Graham, son of the manager. His parents were separated and when we were there Daddy was having his innings. He was an enchanting little kid, formal as a penguin, and when someone was ill-advised enough to address him as Bobby he said with dignity, "My name is Robert."

The rooms were whitewashed cabins with indoor plumbing, running water, lamplight, and high picturesque roofs of thatch. In the middle of the night I was awakened by the gentle rain from heaven pelting down onto my cot through an imperfection in the picturesqueness and although I tried to ignore it and burrow deeper under the covers, I realized the time had come for action when I began sloshing rhythmically to and fro.

My roommate, being bone dry, slept blissfully on as I struggled to move the cot into more arid territory out of the quickly forming small sea.

In that climate moisture, indeed sopping wetness dries very quickly and when next morning I reported the leak in the roof, although he had been well aware of the rain, I could see Mr. Graham was inclined to put my tale down to foolish feminine fancy. I was able to prove my point by showing him a somewhat darker patch which, providentially, still remained on the floor.

By now, I am sure, the leak is mended and shelves in place. I

* See *The Varied Airs of Spring.*

would still recommend to every manager, even in those camps where one stays in tents, that they install, not larger tables, usually there is not enough space for that but tall *étagères*. When the traveler is garlanded with cameras, lenses, binoculars and dark glasses, shelf space is a vital requirement.

The next morning, hot and sunny, we were grateful for the rain since, unlike the red clay of East Africa, the roads of Botswana are sand. They had been packed down and for once we were dustless.

Tony Graham was again driving coached by Robert who, proud and efficient, sat close beside him. Two of the camp Africans came along for the ride and to help out at Lake Ngami where we were going. One of them, Smash, had quite a story.

He had saved the life of an American hunter, who having shot poorly was being mauled by the lion he had wounded. I myself was sorry the lion hadn't finished the job but Smash, with only a small dagger, rushed in and killed him.

The hunter, understandably grateful, had stood his rescuer a trip to the United States. Smash traveled to California and New York and when asked in a TV interview what he thought about the city he said, "It is full of very rich people."

Perhaps, conscious of his own salary, the interviewer asked in some surprise why he thought that. To Smash it was obvious. "Have to be rich. So many people walking about in streets can be no persons in offices working."

En route to the lake we passed through the village of Toteng: a group of rondawels surrounded by bomas, fences of thorn and brush for keeping animals in and out. Also there was a well equipped general store.

It was the home of members of the Herero tribe and the women wore charming dresses with long flounced skirts and handsome, skillfully draped turbans on their heads. One dress was made of a very pretty print, green, black and oyster white.

Forty miles more brought us to Lake Ngami and we were lucky to find it because it is a very catch as catch can body of water. When David Livingstone discovered it in 1849 he estimated it as anywhere from one hundred to one hundred and seventy miles in circumference. On the other hand when Thomas Baines saw it in 1860 it was more of a pond. In 1950 it wasn't there at all, in its stead was a sea of grass but by 1952 it had transvested itself back into water and was a lake four miles long. Today it has stretched. It is ten miles long by two wide but its depth makes one suspect it may change its mind again. In the center it is only five feet deep. Even so, there are cogent reasons for going there.

Lindblad has established a rough camp on the shore; two or three blue and tan tents, and two emerald-green toilet tents. Very chic. They had portable seats, a roll of paper on a stick and all in all were infinitely superior to like facilities in Russia.

After cold squashes, and beer for the more depraved members of the party, we set out in a fifteen-seater rubber life raft with pontoons and an outboard motor which had been snitched from the M.S. *Lindblad Explorer,* the one class passenger ship, 250 feet long, 2300 tons, designed for cruising through tropical or icy seas. It is owned by the company and was especially built for pioneer service combined with a little decadent comfort and convenience.

Florence Mueller recognized the raft as an old friend. "We had the same kind when we went ashore in Antarctica," she said. She had done that trip with the Lindblads and was going on their cruise to the Seychelle Islands at the end of the present safari.

Although we could easily have waded from the shore we were luxuriously transported to the raft by canoe. People used to go out to the raft piggy-back, carried by one of the African helpers but one fine day a Lindblad client arrived who weighed in the neighborhood of three hundred pounds. The custom was abandoned.

Our movements disturbed only slightly the big marabou storks who, standing about or walking stiff-legged along the beach, looked like a caucus of old men.

We crossed the water and came upon a wonderful sight. Pelicans, thousands upon thousands of them, a pale army massed in serried ranks on the shore of the lake. There were dark ones too. They

were the youngsters which turn white as they mature like Lipizzaner horses.

They rose in great flights, tucking in their feet as they gained
altitude and planing against the sky.

Tony Graham cut the outboard and in the hot bright stillness we
listened to the beating of their wings.

Noticing a tiny floating island he steered toward it. That is what
I love about the men of Africa. They are aware of everything;
they notice life and, in this case, death. Our island was a dead pelican. Tim Liversedge said that occasionally, when diving for a fish,
pelicans cut their mouth pouch. If the fish is small he drops through
and the pouch heals quickly but a big one will destroy the skin to such
an extent that the pelican cannot swallow and dies of starvation.

Returning to camp we watched great flocks of flamingoes rise
and wheel in the high air, their wings flashing pink and scarlet in
the sunlight.

After a picnic lunch we strolled around waiting for the small
plane that would fly us to the Khwai River Lodge.

The sun was hot and African kids, eager to see the great bird,
sought shelter with their African dogs in the shade of the Yellow
Peril, our big vehicle. Tony was roaming about over-seeing something or other and little Robert up in the caboose was sobbing,
"I want my Daddy, I want my Daddy."

Along posts set in the earth men were stretching fish nets to dry.
An old woman with naked hanging breasts came by to ask for
tobacco—now it was the pipe smokers who were the Great White
Stars. A young chap appeared with a curious musical instrument
which we learned was called a hand piano. Flexible metal strips
had been wired together on a small board, the board held over an
empty can for reverberation. The resulting melody was plaintive
and appealing.

About three o'clock our plane appeared, a distant speck in the
sky. Great excitement on the part of the children, a certain sense
of anticipation on ours.

There was no authentic landing strip at Lake Ngami, the whole terrain might serve, and we noticed with pleasure the smooth touchdown. The plane rolled to a halt and out hopped Rodney Hopkins, a young pilot with a cheerful, efficient manner that inspired confidence.

On this flight the Sauls, Ruth, Norton, and I were on the first shuttle. The plane, one of the Esquire Airlines fleet based in Johannesburg, was smaller than the one in which we had flown the day before from Francistown to Maun. It carried only six or, in a pinch, seven, but it was nicer and the flight was nicer too. Shorter and not so rough.

In about an hour we put down on the airstrip of the River Khwai Lodge. That night I wrote in my diary. *This is it!*

Of the lodges in which we have stayed Norton and I have always considered Samburu in northern Kenya to be the best* although recently Keekorock, in the southern part of the country has acquired a good reputation and the time we spent a few hours there we were impressed.†

The only shortcoming at Keekorock was that, aside from a swimming pool, there was no water. Samburu was built on the Uaso Nyiro river and was not far from the Isiolo. In Africa where water is, there too is game.

The Khwai Lodge was on the Khwai River. Not the one of Bridge fame which is spelled Kwai but a charming stretch of water nonetheless. That was typical of the place. It had an ambience of charm that seduced the heart.

The river shores were flat and grassy, the whitewashed, thatch-roofed cottages were set among thorn and fig trees and across the river, before the woods begin, a broad stretch of grass invited the local game, much of which was lechwe. Lechwe are small members of the antelope family, not unlike impala in coloring, but their coats are more furry. They are good swimmers, leaping into the water to evade marauding predators.

* See *Second Spring and Two Potatoes.*
† See *The Varied Airs of Spring.*

There was a blind on the edge of the river and Bill Saul spent a couple of hours in it with his movie camera shooting lechwe and a cooperative baboon who hammed it up in most gratifying fashion.

Ruth and I, not to be outdone by lechwe, leapt into the water too, a very pleasant swimming pool, but I was in a decidedly makeshift bathing suit. In the list of clothing suggested by Lindblad, bathing suits had been mentioned but looking at the map I couldn't imagine where we would be needing them and as weight was such a problem I did not want to take what I wouldn't use.

When I called the office to inquire about it someone as ignorant as myself assured me she couldn't see any need for one either. We were both wrong. Take a suit with you. There are *several* places where you will have an opportunity to wear it.

That evening when Norton and I had changed for dinner we stepped onto our terrace to watch the sunset and saw, emerging from the trees, a herd of sable antelope. They are comparatively rare and they are beautiful creatures with deep sable coats, slim legs, and long slender backward-sweeping horns.

As we watched them we became aware that flying against the evening sky were literally millions of little birds, the quelea. They are the color of pale autumn leaves and they travel like wind-blown scarves in vast undulating flocks; swooping, dipping, and turning in unison, their secret radar system keeping them from ever bumping into one another. Though they always seemed to be flying in the same direction they must fly full circle. There *had* to be *some* repeaters otherwise they would number in the trillions and mantle the earth.

Still, Nature knows what she is about and she must love the quelea. The reason she creates them in such profusion is because they are destroyed in such profusion. On one of our game drives we saw their nests. Thousands of them, little round baskets like Christmas ornaments hanging in the branches of the thorn trees, but the nesting season was over and they were torn open and deserted. It is during that season that so many of them perish because

the eggs and the babies are devoured by birds of prey and by
snakes who lie in ambush in the branches.

About six-thirty we strolled over to the main house for drinks
and to greet the Wickses and Florence who were just arriving on the
second shuttle, Mrs. Wicks a bit petulant because she was tired
and Rodney the pilot had had to come down at Maun to refuel.
Really they thought they would *never* make it.

The lodge was run by Mr. and Mrs. Beveridge. They were well
named but not only were the drinks satisfactory, the food was excellent. Our first course was a salmon dish, a kind of combination
delicate fish cake and light mousse followed by a roast. It was a
game animal, *not* killed in the reserve and killed for food not sport
and the taste, a cross between pork and lamb, was delicious.

I concur in the opinion that shooting to eat is not reprehensible in
the sense that shooting for trophies is but he was a nice animal and
as I do not want to betray him I shall not tell what he was.

Early the next morning we took off, and a nippy early it was, 58
degrees which shortly dissolved into beneficent warmth. When in the
mood African weather is incomparable. Lyrical mornings and evenings, hot, dry, brilliantly sunny days with almost always a little
breeze and at night warm blankets under the blazing stars.

We were distributed between two Land-Rovers for our game
drive through the Moremi Reserve adjoining the lodge. That was
one of the extremely pleasant features of the Lindblad tour. In
their contracts with other managements such as Kerr, Downey and
Selby in Botswana and Grosvenor Tours in South-West Africa they
stipulated two vehicles so everyone would have a window and
equal opportunity for photographing. Also the Land-Rovers had
hatches in the roof, sometimes two, which were ideal for game viewing.

The Moremi Reserve is a gem. Situated in north west Botswana
it lies just to the east of the Okavango Delta. The Delta branches
out over 6500 square miles and is fed by the Okavango River
rising in Angola. The vast network of rivers, streams, and pools is
ideal for game.

The reserve itself was created by the Botswana tribe on their own land. It is they who administer it and they are to be congratulated on their refusal to allow any tourist facilities to be set up. People may sometimes camp there, and we later met a couple who had done so, but there are no permanent installations.

Also, one of the joys of Moremi, which does not obtain elsewhere, is that the visitor may get out of his vehicle if he wants a closer look at some animal. Obviously, if he has a grain of sense, and wants to see another sunrise, he will not get out when there are females with their young about but on occasion, especially when photographing birds, being ambulatory has its advantages.

Moremi, roughly triangular in shape, spreads over seven hundred square miles and our first morning we were lucky for not only did we have an experienced African driver we had Tim in our car. He had served as the warden of the reserve for a year or more so it was like going back to the old homestead, especially when he pointed out a sandy road stretching between the north and south gates, dividing the reserve from the rest of the tribal land. He said he had employed sixty Africans and it had taken them about six months to build it under his direction.

Once through the reserve gates and across a log bridge held together by steel wire we drove through a sea of golden grass, spotting all sorts of game.

There were entertaining and, for me, beloved wart hogs, with their long slab faces, curly little tusks and dachshund legs, impala, and an accommodating hyena who lolled beside the road for a long time, turning his better profile for the photographers.

The word exquisite was coined for impala—swift, graceful, and gentle. And in actuality hyenas are not all that ugly. Their pug-nosed, round-eared heads are rather beguiling. It is their gait when in motion that is unpleasant. There is something shifty, mean, and underhanded about it and their reputations, deservedly, are not good.

For the first time in Africa we saw tsessebe—the T is silent—big antelope not unlike the hartebeest. Birds too were out in numbers:

long-tailed shrike, white heron, the saddle-billed stork, well named
with the saddle of color just below his eyes, the Birchill starling
and a black female ostrich.

Florence Mueller and Tim were hard at it, matching bird lore
and snapping pictures of specimens, perched and on the wing. Although spring was coming on the color of the trees was autumnal
and millions of small copper leaves patterned the sandy soil.

About eleven we broke for cold drinks and beer, everything efficiently chilled in big thermos containers, and set off again coming
upon cape buffalo with their horns like handle-bar mustaches, wildebeest, their improbably slim legs supporting hefty torsos, handsome
gray-black water buck and the kingly greater kudu.

At lunchtime we joined up with the other Land-Rover at an
appointed rendezvous. Settled beside a big pond we counted eight
hippo but they were not cooperative, exhibiting no more of their
formidable bulks than their little round ears and round bulging eyes.

When we said, "Listen, you fellas, we've come thousands of miles
to have a look at you," they silently submerged, the widening ripples
on the pond's surface the reflection of their smiles.

Among the ten of us we had an abundance of hunger but even
without that widely touted sauce the picnic lunch would have been
excellent. Not only had Bob and Millie Beveridge supplied genuine
goodies, but they were served up in most professional fashion. Trays
in racks, the basic food already in place, the canned accessories,
passed by Carol and Tim, all good products and with more taste
than most canned food. The asparagus and salmon, pears and
peaches were delicious with the home-baked bread the *pièce de
résistance*.

After a rest we started off again and late in the afternoon saw a
big herd of elephants. Unfortunately the ground was too swampy
and bumpy for the Land-Rover to navigate, so closer contact was
not feasible, but we knew they were there and could hope for better
luck next time.

Later on we saw several ostriches. When ostriches drink it is
funny to see the lump the water makes slipping down their long

throats. One was squatting on the ground enjoying a dust bath and a few minutes later a large pair scooted ahead of us down the middle of the road, ten chicks swirling about their feet. In their own good time they got out of the way, the chicks rustling and scurrying in the leaves.

Ostriches are like Muslems, multiple-wived. In the breeding season the ideal family consists of a cock and three hens, with the cock sitting on the nest at night and the chief hen, or I suppose favorite wife, taking over in the daytime. The nests are almost ten feet in diameter and the number of eggs is usually between sixteen and twenty-three.

We learned that shortly before the eggs are hatched the chicks communicate with each other and with their parents and that they have more than forty different sounds when they converse. I had never before thought of ostriches as being chatty but they're regular Martha Mitchells.

By sundown we were exhausted but it had been a wonderful day and even in East Africa, with the possible exception of the Ngorongoro Crater, we had not seen as large a variety of game so close together.

At the end of such an exhilarating experience a hot shower, a cool drink, and a good dinner rank among life's major pleasures. They were all ours.

It had been decided that the next day would be spent at the lodge, resting, catching up on correspondence, swimming in the pool . . . whatever we wished.

I had planned vaguely on sleeping late, although I am not good at it, but by sunrise there was far too much activity to make sleep even remotely desirable.

As usual the morning air was chilly and on the flat stage across the river were beasties full of beans. Lechwe and wildebeest, tsessebe and impala leaping and frisking and switching their tails. Big sperling geese stood contemplating the river, their mouths watering for fish. The light was marvelous. In the bush every African sunrise is the first sunrise of the world.

I dressed hurriedly and went over to the dining room to find Norton and Florence Mueller half through breakfast and discussing birds. In a few minutes Ruth came in and joined us. When I asked her how she felt she said, "Well, I feel better now but I don't mind telling you that yesterday I was a little out of my depth. All that learned talk about birds, it made me feel *ignorant* so last night I decided I'd jot down some birds I know to show Florence and Tim they aren't the only ones."

She handed me a piece of paper with a list of names written in red ink. It was headed: Birds Indigenous to New York and California.

Peeping Tomtit
Red Eyed Video
High Tailed Whoopee
Least Crested Horn Pecker
Carmine de Sapio
Swallow Tailed Seer Sucker
Round Heeled Road Runner
Top Lofty Frigate (extinct)
Yellow Bellied Fourflusher
Ruby Throated Blow Hard
Low Darting Snatch Grabber (a predatory bird)
San Quentin Quail (highly protected and always out of season)

We felt humbled by our friend's erudition and had a fine time explaining some of our native American birds to Tim Liversedge who could hazard a guess at the others but did not know about Carmine de Sapio or San Quentin Quail.

Needless to say, Mrs. Anderson's list started a flurry of bird naming but most of them are not fit for a family library. Someone mentioned the African bird, the honey diviner, who will always lead you to honey but when he does you must share it with him.

I said to Tim, "It's a nice idea, isn't it?"

He laughed. "Yes, but what really happens is that the diviner will squawk and flap his wings over anything that excites him so you may find you are being led to a snake or a leopard."

According to the natives, however, this only happens if you don't give him his rightful share of honey at those times when, thanks to him, you found it.

In chatting with Mrs. Beveridge I learned that the lodge is closed from January 15 to March 30. The rainy season usually starts at the end of October or in early November at which time it is terribly hot. In May, June, and July the nights can be bitterly cold. August is probably nice too but I should say our timing was perfect: September 3 to September 29.

Since we were on a tour everything had been prepaid, as is usually the case, but should an individual wish to get in touch with the Khwai River Lodge the address is P. O. Box 100, Maun, Botswana. The price is $28 a day per person for full board and lodging. A game viewing drive of about five hours runs to $9.80 a person. A full day with an African driver and a guide costs $49. The car may be shared by two couples.

With luck one may get the services of a young chap who sometimes works there. Like Tim and some of the others we met he too was very knowledgeable and looked as though he were a member of the stork family: a blond boy, very thin with long, long legs that went up and up and up.

There are obviously many books, some of them very learned, on the wild life of Africa but he was writing a simple handbook for the average tourist which would give succinct information on the game he was most likely to see and never mind the critters unlikely to cross his path. It struck us as a practical idea.

We were all impressed by the three young people who were with us: Carol, Tim, and Larry. They were in their mid-twenties, full of exuberance and enthusiasm, dedicated to their way of life. They had so much. They had achieved it themselves and were achieving more. To see them was to feel grief for, as well as irritation with, the drop outs, the cop outs, the wastrel, drug-sodden, self-pitying youth who play so large a part in American life.

And, almost too good to believe, in some miraculous way their young bodies were whole and safe. There was not a war going on in

which they were involved, a war created by old men who so glibly
send the young out to die for their poor judgment.

Our second day in the reserve we were the same group, Ruth,
Florence, Norton and I but Larry was our driver-guide and we also
had Carol while Tim went with the Wicks and Sauls.

We passed through a lovely park-like area of the reserve we had
not seen before. The trees, receding almost like those of a coffee
plantation, grew up from the sandy soil with no clutter of underbrush.
They were mostly mopane trees with silver gray bark, and leaves
like butterfly wings, dark green and copper pink.

There were many giraffe, for herds were gathering because the
mating season was drawing near. We learned they were once known
as camel leopards. They are, of course, related to neither but the
name is not so inappropriate. To some their marking might be
reminiscent of a leopard—if you had never seen one up close—
and they do have a camel gait, both legs on one side moving in
unison.

For our eleven o'clock soft drink, beer, coffee, and drainage break
Larry led us to an enchanting pond on a small open plain, the
home of happy herons, thousands of ducks and a herd of lechwe.
He said, "Not many people come here but it's my favorite place in
the park." We asked him if the pond, it was really a small lake, had
a name and he said no. Ruth and I went into conference. "Now it
has!" we said triumphantly. "It is Larry's Lagoon." He smiled
vaguely but did not seem overcome by the tribute.

A little later, during our picnic lunch, we learned why. Ruth and
I had been mistaken. Our lad's name was not Larry but Barry.
Barry Unwin. That blew the nomenclature. Lagoon obviously was
out. "Well," I said, thinking aloud, "maybe we could change it,
maybe it could be Barry's Bond or something."

"That's silly," Norton said. "You can't call a pond a bond."

"You can if you have a gold in your dose." As far as I know the
pretty splash is still untitled.

The other carload had seen a white lechwe and were all agog over
him. Barry knew him well, so after lunch we went bumping off to

catch up with him. We succeeded, too, but truth to tell he was no more white than a white rhino is. He was, in fact, the same dirty gray and we thought little of him but Barry looked at him admiringly and assured us he was unique.

Farther on we met up with seven or eight wild dogs. They were engaged in no nefarious activities at the moment but Mrs. Anderson was depressed because of their reputation for cunning and cruelty.

She is a devotée of the canine species in any form and wants no self-betrayals of its heroic lineage nor to have damaging imputations cast upon it.

Her household now numbers three of her loves which she considers the irreducible minimum. "There was a time though," she said with a nostalgic sigh, "when if you were cold in bed in our house you threw on another dog."

More appealing than the pitiless hunters of the bush was a troop of baboons leaping across the track in front of us, two tiny babies rushing to keep pace. Never breaking stride the two mothers reached down and scooped them up under their bellies where they clung like burs.

On the whole, however, that particular afternoon was on the bland side, although we were pleased that the tsetse flies seemed to have retired for the day. In the morning we had been briefly plagued by them.

They do exist in the Moremi but in a curious way it's lucky they do. There can be no question of tribes trying to impinge upon the reserve to turn it into grazing ground because domestic cattle cannot tolerate them. Wild game is immune.

Humans, I think, should take certain precautions against the tsetse. With this in mind Norton had equipped us to do battle with them. He had ordered cream from the Cutter Laboratories in Berkeley, California, which has been sending its product to Vietnam to protect the troops against the malarial mosquito. The cream is pinkish and pleasant and comes in small plastic containers and should be applied to face and hands and any other bare area. This does not completely discourage flies from landing on you but they usually glance off immediately. A mere touch doesn't do any damage. It's when they settle and dig their long spike noses into you that trouble may ensue. Don't let them do that.

We also had with us two fly fisherman's head nets, the kind that fit over the crown of your hat with a draw string at the bottom so that face and head are completely protected. I think they are a good idea although I only used mine once for about ten minutes. Both vehicles were also equipped with spray cans of insect repellent, courtesy of the lodge.

We had been told it was a good idea to wear light-colored clothing, the reason being that tsetse flies live in the bark of trees and are attracted to the dark.

How much of this is fact I am not prepared to say. I had on a light shirt and they lit on me and some of the others had on darker things and they lit on them too.

Actually when the car is moving one is hardly troubled at all. When it is stopped for viewing and photographing they will swarm in if they are around, but they disappear as soon as the car starts up again.

When we met in the evening to compare notes we found that the Sauls and Wicks could lord it all over us. They had seen a great herd of sixty elephants and three lions. We were crestfallen but that is the luck of a safari. Now you see 'em, now you don't, and we were to have some pretty fine luck ourselves.

During the night we had taken a good deal of sass from the birds who apparently were holding an ornithological congress but even disrupted slumber could not assuage our regret at leaving Khwai, an enchanting spot. It was all the harder to go as we left around noontime and game was gathering on stage, as we called the opposite bank of the river. Animals are like French businessmen. Home for lunch.

The flight to Shakawe, Rodney again at the controls, was just an hour. We landed near some tin-roofed shacks and buildings and I was a little disillusioned. That place, we quickly learned, had nothing to do with the camp. It was just an airstrip and depot and recruiters of labor came there to get men to work in the mines.

The camp itself was farther down the Okavango River and we went to it by launch. The river is lovely. Winding, in places quite wide, and lined with great stands of papyrus and sweet-scented acacia trees, home of egrets and sharp-eyed fish eagles with their glossy white heads and rich brown plumage. Against the blazing blue sky the patterns of birds, stark naked branches and branches in flower were like exquisite Japanese prints.

Crocodiles inhabit the river and later on we saw one or two but at the time of our arrival they were having a siesta. Ruth and Norton trawled for tiger fish and in short order Ruth caught one; about three to three and a half pounds. Tiger fish are quite pretty to look at, silver with orangey bits but their round mouths are full of sharp teeth and whites do not consider them good eating. The Africans relish them or at least they eat them.

The camp, when we reached it, proved to be as appealing as Khwai. The atmosphere was different but its own magic was potent. Nestling in a curve in the river the lodgings were tents rather than cottages but well designed and convenient. Set on low concrete platforms each had a kind of little anteroom or veranda, equipped with a couple of comfortable chairs and a washstand. Inside were cots, a bed table, dressing table, and clothes rack. The plumbing facilities were in separate huts and there were a couple of good-sized cabins with tubs and showers.

It was run, most efficiently, by a young couple, Bernie and Daphne Trutha, but since we were there I have learned with regret that they have left. They seemed to like it very much but they had a three-month-old baby and perhaps they felt it was a little remote in case of emergency.

The main structure was walled with mabinda, a pretty, decorative matting but, in theatrical parlance, everything could be struck in an instant because, by law, in Botswana in the reserves proper, all buildings must be built to dismantle quickly. This may be for the sake of the game and also because the tribes only lease the land. Outside interests are not allowed to buy.

For anyone interested in a visit the address is: Shakawe Fishing Camp, P. O. Box 12, Shakawe, Botswana. The price is $21 a day per person, all inclusive with the exception of laundry and liquor.

We went over to the terrace in front of the main building, which was also the bar, for tea and met two pleasant couples and a fine greedy goose whom Norton named Guzzle, since that was his life's work. To head him off from the cookie plate one had to be nimble.

One of the couples left immediately after tea, the other, Angela and Peter Mostert, stayed on overnight. They were interesting people who lived in Rhodesia and had a game reserve of their own, bordering on the Kruger National Park. I don't know how they keep the inhabitants from visiting back and forth unless they have a sort of Berlin Wall and Checkpoint Charley. Or possibly gently electrified fences.

We had arrived at the Khwai River on a Wednesday. The Mosterts told us they had spent the two previous nights camping in the Moremi and that they had had wonderful luck, seeing two lionesses and fourteen cubs of various ages and later a beautiful young pair mating. That is one of the things that draws people back to Africa. I saw such and such this time but maybe next time I'll see *that* and *that*.

The Mosterts were leaving the following morning for an eight-day cruise down the river to Maun. They were dedicated conservationists and he was doing research for the government to ascertain the effect of a mine, then under consideration, which was meeting with support and opposition equally strong. The owners wanted to divert the Okavango to bring water to the mine site but there was a great chance that in so doing they would also do irreparable harm to the ecology of the area.

We were surprised when we saw the boat they planned to travel in, a launch with a gaily striped blue and white awning scarcely larger than the one we had used to come to camp from the airstrip.

They were taking with them one African as handy man and planned to sleep ashore on small islands. I assume they knew some islands that were more substantial than the papyrus stands which were all we ourselves saw the whole time we were there.

They told us a grisly adventure of a friend of theirs, a safari manager named Lloyd who was in a canoe on the Okavango when a large and unpleasant crocodile assailed him, wrenching the paddle out of his hand. He drew a gun and shot him point-blank and just managed to do in an accomplice who was swimming rapidly toward him. I was relieved that our craft was a sturdy Fiberglas launch with an outboard motor.

The only drawback to the camp was that it was set in a grove of high dense trees which in themselves are lovely and are the home of myriads of birds but they do, to some extent, shut out the sky. Fortunately, in one place, the perfect place, there was a break. Lying in my cot at night, I could look up into the darkness and the blazing stars of Africa through the big screened aperture in the back wall of our tent. I even saw the Southern Cross, although I am not one of its ardent fans.

We saw it for the first time when we were on a cruise in the Fijian Islands.* It always sounds so romantic but in actuality it is a rather paltry affair. To my way of thinking the Big Dipper has far more to recommend it.

Nor was it only the video aspect of Shakawe that was superb. We had audio too. A great slapping around in the river in the blackness and a sound like boards banging down on the water. Ah ha, I thought, crocodiles! I said as much to Tim in the morning but I was being too dramatic. "Fish," he said.

Besides the river and the camp itself the special attraction of Shakawe is its reasonable proximity to a Bushman village.

Early in the morning of a glorious day Rodney drove us about eight miles along a bumpy sand road to the airstrip.

As we went along we saw, standing in a field, two Africans with pails on their heads. They were as immobile as statues and indeed, so

* See *Second Spring and Two Potatoes.*

lean and elongated were they, they might have been statues, sculpted by Giacometti.

From the strip we took off for the Tsolido Hills, site of the Bushman village. I sat up front next to the pilot so I can report that we were flying at 4500 feet, ground speed 150 miles an hour. Having piloted planes himself, my husband likes to know about such things. The flight is not long but it is necessary. No roads lead into the area.

One picks up the hills while still quite far off and they form three groups, large, medium, and small. They are called, reasonably enough, male, female, and child.

Bushmen are probably the oldest members of the human race, older even than the aborigines of Australia. They were always nomadic and some of them may have drifted southward from Tanzania and Rhodesia. They were also driven by European and Kaffir encroachment from South Africa into the most barren part of the continent.

When we landed we were met by a Land-Rover driven by a big black fellow in a green jersey. He was a loud-mouthed party, I gathered sort of head man and manager of the compound. He spoke a tiny bit of English but Tim was fluent in Setswana which is the language of Botswana. There may be a Bushman dialect. That I don't know but if there is he was fluent in that too.

The community is on the periphery of a conventional village; rondawels and reed fencing, and contains, we estimated, fifty or sixty people. They were small of stature but not pygmies. The skin of the authentic Bushman is a deep luminous orange-brown. There were some black-skinned ones too but they were of a different tribe.

Several dogs were running around but although thin they were not emaciated as were the dogs we had seen in India and Nepal.*

The babies were tiny and there were many children, a few young women and several wrinkled crones who really were Lilliputian. They looked to be eighty or ninety. They were probably thirty-five to forty-five which is already an advanced age, for their life is harsh, their span brief.

* See *Around the World and Other Places.*

They had shrewd, humorous faces and their attitude was both hospitable and indifferent. They did not seem to mind that we were there and they went on about their business.

Stooping to get under a branch, I caught my sweater on a thorn tree. They burst into gales of laughter and two or three of the women rushed to free me.

They live in low, bell-shaped huts of reeds and grasses, completely open on one side. Their possessions are slender. A rag or two, a couple of pots and the vital ostrich egg containing water that they draw from a nearby spring, sucking it up through a reed straw, then either bending the reed or spitting the water into the empty egg. When water is scarce they are dependent on moisture-laden roots and succulents. The ostrich eggs serve not only as vessels but as ornaments as well. They break them and string the pieces into necklaces and bracelets.

The women were, for the most part, bare breasted; the men wore breechclouts and nothing else. Since they have little subcutaneous fat the skin of their stomachs and around their joints falls into deep folds.

Although we were not aware of the physical phenomena described by Mr. van der Post, a mild steatopygia seemed a universal characteristic.

Many of them, including the babies, suffered from a deplorable eye condition since, in that part of the world, there are no doctors, no missionaries, no one to help them.

They live in small bands and are scrupulous about not trespassing on one another's territory. Since cooperation is vital for survival their social customs, as we had learned from the Lindblad people, are geared to exclude, as far as possible, anything which might cause friction or dissent. There is no private property, indeed in the accepted sense there is no property of any kind, and the game killed is divided according to age-old custom.

They are the primitive of the primitive yet their legends are legion. They have myths and stories for all the animals. The stars, they believe, are great hunters. In *The Heart of the Hunter*, Laurens van der Post sketches a charming vignette of a Bushman mother holding her baby high above her head singing a reverent little song as his Bushman companion explains to him that she is asking the stars "to take from her little child his little heart and give him the heart of a hunter."

When a collection was made of their folklore and oral literature it filled eighty-four thick manuscript volumes of 3600 pages.

We were told that Bushmen are sometimes kidnaped by bigger and stronger tribes who coerce them into settling outside their villages and working for them. They are, in effect, slaves but they may get a little better food than they have in the wastes of the Kalahari, where they live largely on roots and berries, insects, lizards, and meat when the hunt is successful.

Bill Saul bargained for a bow and arrows and quiver. Carol, who could also speak their language, intrepreted and Bill got it for two rands, $2.80.

The arrows are cunningly devised with poisoned metal heads and a slim tail attachment that fits into the shaft. When shot into an animal only the head penetrates, the tail drops to the ground. It seemed to me quite like a module leaving the command ship but Norton says that system is different.

Jim Wicks was the most popular member of the party. He had a big package of tobacco which he doled out as they crowded eagerly around him. They did a little dance for us to the accompaniment of a hand piano such as we had seen at Lake Ngami and Carol handed out food and candy.

We left shortly afterward to drive to the rock paintings, Tim carrying with him a thermos of water and his snake-bite kit.

"I hope we're not going to need that," I murmured.

"Don't worry," he laughed. "I've got enough stuff here to immunize an elephant."

Furthermore he knew how to use it but happily the occasion to exercise his skill did not arise.

To my mind the rocks towering high against the sky and the enveloping silence were more awe-inspiring than the paintings themselves although they are believed to be approximately 2000 years old. The outlines of an eland, a giraffe, and a rhino were clearly visible. We were told there are several thousand such drawings but many of them are high up and inaccessible.

Some of our party, however, were keen to do a little rock climbing so that they might see those that were on top of the cliffs and invisible from below. The rest of us were not so intrepid and asked to return to camp. An African driver met us at the Okavango River airstrip and Rodney, our Doublemint sprite, flew back to pick up the climbers.

In the late afternoon we went fishing on the river. Bill Saul brought in the first one, a good tiger fish and my heart sank. In his recent fishing expeditions, and they weren't very many, Norton had had rotten luck. This induces trauma in him and I was afraid he would be very glum. But that was not to be. In a couple of minutes he started pulling them in himself. Bing, bing, bing, bing, just like that! Four in a row.

I then began to worry about Bill. He was a dear and I didn't want him to be feeling underprivileged. Fortunately he got another and even I hooked one. I was pleased in a way but it was a tussle, the thrill of battle marred somewhat by the fact that as I kept hauling in my victim I kept cracking my elbow on one of the joists on the launch. I developed a bruise the size and color of an eggplant from which I still feel an occasional twinge.

Finally, Mary Saul caught one too so we felt the expedition had been a success and hoped the African staff would enjoy the fruits of our victory.

That night our own dinner was especially good; chicken, shish kebab, and sausages barbecued over coals. There were beans and salad and assorted other yummies which we helped ourselves to generously. Three or four of us carried our plates to the bar to eat and as she gazed at her own heaping portion Mrs. Anderson observed happily, "A snack like this is as good as a meal."

I suppose everyone has certain phrases that seem glamorous to him although they may have no appeal at all to others. To me, the nautical expression "Bound east for . . ." Singapore? The Celebes? It doesn't matter so long as it is some exotic far-away port. "Bound east" is such a phrase. In my youth "To clear customs" was another. It had a sophisticated, romantic ring. With the passing years I have now cleared so many that the gilt is off that particular ginger-bread but one that still piques my fancy is "Bringing in the nets."

Therefore when Mary and Bill Saul said they'd like to go out on the river early the next morning to see it happening, Norton and I said we'd join them. The Wickses wanted to come along too.

Secretly I was anticipating the repetition of a scene we had witnessed in the harbor of Alexandria where there were many men and rowboats and a great net strung on bobbing cork floats that was gradually drawn up against the jetty where the catch, easily a couple of thousand, was seized and tossed into baskets according to size.*

They do it differently in the Okavango. One or two puny little nets were stretched across the mouth of a narrow channel and in them eight or ten hapless fish were entangled. The Africans disengaged them and tossed them onto the floor of the launch and we went home.

A fishing party did take off after breakfast but sitting in a hot launch, on a glaring river, under a blazing sun is not my idea of pleasure. Several others also stayed behind including Tim who wanted to get some bird photographs and Margery who wanted to wash her hair. She had short blond hair and was by far the best-coiffed member of the group.

Later on I followed her example but first I went for a walk. The cleared space of the camp blends into a small forest, a lovely place of great trees, clear of underbrush and a reasonably well-defined path winding along the river's course.

I came upon a fisherman and a man planting pawpaw trees and farther on a bent-over woman dressed only in a ragged skirt searching the ground for berries or roots.

The path and forest ended on a high peninsula jutting into the

* See *Elephants Arrive at Half-Past Five.*

river, the site of a reed shack. It was the home, I imagine, of the Africans I had just passed.

On my way back I sat down to rest on the bank. Propped against a tree I watched the shining river and absorbed the silence, stirred from time to time by bird song or the leap of a fish.

Presently I became aware of a disturbance in back of me; leaves scattering and cracking branches. I got up quietly, binoculars at the ready. I had been told that there were small antelope in the forest and I hoped to see them. I could discern brown and white shapes moving in the bushes through the shadow and sunlight. This was exciting. Impala? Lechwe? Maybe with great good luck, an enchanting steenbok! I raised my binoculars and focused. A herd of brown and white goats. Exotic Africa.

When I returned to camp I found Margery still sitting in the sunshine waiting for her hair to dry—she was very good at the rollers, I am hopelessly inept—and reading the paperback copy of *Zelda* which I had finished and passed along to her.

In the afternoon we went to Qhoboya, a native village about six miles from camp. It wasn't far but the journey took time due to the condition of the sandy track and we were kept busy opening and closing the Land-Rover windows because of the branches of thorn trees that reached out to scratch and snap at us.

Most of the men of the village were off fishing. Surrounded by small children, a group of women sat on the ground in the shade of a big tree dandling babies, all of whom seemed to be boys.

At Qhoboya I experienced an infinitesimal triumph of communication. Having been assiduously coached by Carol I had learned two or three words of Setswana. I used them and they worked! *Dumelama,* good day to a woman. To a man, *Dumelara. Sala sentle* for goodbye. When I tossed in a *Keatumetse* (thank you) the women laughed and Ruth Anderson looked at me in awe.

"For God's sweet sake," she muttered.

"It's nothing," I said airily, "I have the gift of tongues."

Near the group under the tree a couple of youngsters with long stout sticks were pounding corn in a deep stone mortar. Farther off three women were beating stalks of grain on a small threshing floor. They struck alternate blows to the rhythm of a grunting song.

Carol asked permission and the village women were hospitable, letting us wander through their rondawels behind bush and reed fences. Each had its own courtyard insuring privacy. Made of adobe faced with thatch, the houses were notably cool under the very hot sun.

In one we saw a hammock, others had skins on the floor which served as beds. There was no furniture. There were a good many iron pots and Africans are extremely adroit at keeping low, low fires burning continuously. They use long logs, gradually shoving them farther under the pots as the flames consume them. Hanging on racks were strips of biltong, smoked meat. It did not look appetizing, but also they had chickens, fresh eggs, fish from the river, and corn beer. They offered us small fruits, about the size of a cherry, with a brittle dust-colored shell. We cracked the shell and the meat surrounding the pit had a very good date-like flavor.

Carol arranged to have the women sing a song and collected 50 cents Rhodesian or 70 cents U.S. from each of us. Having heard the songs, I felt that Messers Rodgers, Lowe et al had nothing to worry about.

The next day the Sauls and Browns spent a leisurely morning while the others departed on the first shuttle for our new camp, Savuti. Wandering about we listened to the birds. The bird song at Shakawe is a symphony, liquid and lovely. When I first heard it I thought, I could listen all day. And I did. They keep it up all day and all day it is a delight.

We were going by launch to the airstrip and just as we pushed off we saw a small crocodile and later on a flight of hundreds of white-faced geese. Piling up his movie footage with abandon Bill Saul was a happy man. We were amused and touched by the way Mary would help him. His eye glued to the viewer his vision was necessarily limited, but Mary would say, "Now, Bill, there's a giraffe coming in from your right," or "Get ready because off to the left, we'll be passing him in a minute, there's a fine fish eagle."

They had been practicing this team work for a long time and I hope someday to see some of the results which I suspect are very good. I asked them if they ever showed any of their films on local television and they said no but they do sometimes show them in schools and hospitals and service clubs.

Our flight to Savuti was only an hour but we left in the heat of midday. It was very bumpy and poor Mary needed the paper bag. After that we insisted she go on the first shuttle.

We were met by John Bennett, the camp manager, and I thought it nice the way he waited to make sure Rodney was safely airborne before driving away from the airstrip.

Savuti is a primitive camp and we fell in love with it. We fell in love with successive camps the way one falls in love with a succession of men and women.

They are loved not only because of their qualities but because of timing and because they are there. Yet their absent predecessors are not deprived of the affection they had evoked. And just as there is always one whose memory lingers like a fragrance, so for us there will always be Khwai River Lodge.

Savuti is primitive in the sense that there are tents rather than cottages and, unlike Shakawe, they are not set on concrete platforms but directly on the ground under the trees along the bank of the Savuti channel.

However ground cloths are attached to the canvas sides as they had been when we had been on safari in East Africa.* This gives a feeling of security. No unwanted creeping strangers can meander in. Of course, you can't be narrow-minded about it, there are exceptions to every rule.

Each tent had its own adjacent toilet and shower tents and there was a commodious and comfortable mess tent with a big gas refrigerator, ample ice, cool drinks and an honor system bar. You made your own drink and wrote it down in a book.

The exception I mentioned above had occurred shortly before the Sauls and Norton and I arrived in camp. Margery had gone into

* See *The Varied Airs of Spring.*

44. Bushmen.

45. Carol Martin, our courier and children outside a rondavel in Qhoboya village.

46. Savuti. All the tents had walking water.

47. Class picture taken our last morning in Savuti.
Left to right: Norton, Tim Liversedge, Ruth Anderson, Mary Saul, Bill Saul, Carol Martin, Ilka, Florence Mueller, Jim Wicks, Margery Wicks.

48. The Spectacle! Victoria Falls.

49. The Beau Gests lodge of Namutoni in the Etosha Pan, South-West Africa.

50. The bridal pair.

51. Enjoying the fruits of his labor. The water hole he dug himself.

52. Eight of the thirty-three decorative derricks at breakfast.

53. The bonus twosome. They were completely unexpected.

54. Social weaver nests.
The kind that bring down trees
in heavy rains.

55. Guess who's coming
to dinner?

56. Homeward bound.

her tent and shot out again like a rocket. Coiled around one of the iron legs of her cot she had seen a boomslang. She hadn't stopped to learn his breed at that moment for one glimpse of him was enough. But the boomslang is a reasonably deadly serpent. Tim had been summoned by her shrieks and had done his stuff; capturing the enemy with a forked stick and dumping it into a bag.

When we got there he exhibited it. Not very large, pale green and deadly. The three men took pictures and Tim took it away. When I asked Norton later what had happened to it he said, "Tim killed it." The men all told the women that and we felt better. When we left camp we learned it wasn't so. To begin with nothing is supposed to be killed in a reserve. Snakes are living creatures like any others. If one can be objective about them I suppose they balance the ecology and Tim had taken the boomslang about a mile from camp and released it.

I will say, though, the lesson sank in. We locked up everything; suitcases, toilet kits, especially shoes. We kept our tents firmly zippered at all times and at night before we went to bed we women took our flashlights, peered under the cots, especially in the springs under the mattresses and peeled down the blankets one by one to make sure no terrifying lodgers had cuddled in. The procedure was successful and there were no unwelcome sequels.

The eviction of the boomslang was not the only time Tim had been called upon to render bouncer service. He had had a curious experience some months before, involving a man of the cloth.

He was a little vague as to the gentleman's correct title, "Canon or Deacon or something," he said and if I am equally vague in recounting the story it is because my theological connections are tenuous in the extreme.

Tim's adventure came about because he was shortly returning to England to be married and a posting of the bonds in Rhodesia was apparently necessary or at least customary. I gathered the announcement had to be made for three consecutive Sundays, a procedure which, due to one thing and another, our hero had neglected.

Tim was trying to get himself organized and his papers in order for presentation to the Canon-Deacon who, he had heard, was a martinet for protocol and was testy too about the unprecedented delay when a friend of his came dashing into his room.

"My God, old boy," he gasped, "drop what you're doing and come with me. I've just been with a bloke down the street and he's discovered a mamba in his closet. Big bugger too as far as I could see. We were both terrified but I told him to hold hard, I knew a great snake man, that's you, who'd help us out. Come on."

Tim was irritated by the interruption but being humane as well as a herpetologist and curious he dropped what he was doing and hurried off with his friend.

They got to the house and there, sure enough, coiled in a closet was an eight-foot snake. Tim banged the door shut and went to round up sticks, hooks, a sack, whatever equipment was needed for such a job.

Returning he proceeded to secure the mamba. He dropped it into the sack, fastened it securely and dumped it on the floor. He then turned to the rescuee. As you have perhaps guessed, by a twist of fate far too strange for fiction, the chap he had benefitted was the very Canon-Deacon whose favor he was courting.

With a winning smile and a significant glance at the gently undulating bag in the corner he said, "I'm Tim Liversedge, Canon-Deacon. About those bans . . . I was wondering . . ."

He was beaten to the draw. "Think nothing of it, my son," burbled the prelate. "Consider the matter closed. Go with God and may your marriage be a long and happy one."

Savuti is in the Chobe National Park, a district some 4500 miles square, and in the late afternoon of our first day we went for a game drive, one of our best.

Fording the channel, mounting a fairly steep bank, we drove a considerable distance from camp to a great marsh and came upon a picture of extraordinary brilliance. The coarse blades of marsh grass stood tightly ranked like glittering green bayonets, blue water glinting between them. White egrets of dazzling purity flashed in and out, the whole scene dominated by the great dark shapes of elephants lushly dining.

We met another herd later on but couldn't imagine why any elephant would exchange the riches of the marsh for the arid bush in which these particular fellows were strolling.

Farther on was another swamp, the home of hundreds of openbill storks and spoonbills, well named with their long scoop bill so like a spoon. In their midst black and white sacred ibis.

We thought that what we had just seen was wonder enough but we were building to a crescendo. Tim and Bill, our African driver, pointed in unison to a fantastic spectacle off to our right. A vast herd of buffalo was milling about and then suddenly, silhouetted against the sun they took off. Their galloping feet churning up great clouds of golden dust, three thousand, four thousand buffalo streamed by in a never-ending line. Bill had cut the engine and we sat mesmerized, listening to the pounding rhythm of their passage. That sound might have been expected but there was something else too. Perhaps their flowing motion evoked fluidity, for there was another sound that seemed like rushing water but soft, at a distance. It was like a trillion dry leaves rustling and whispering in the wind as they brushed against each other in their headlong flight. They poured past us on and on until finally they were gone. Not only was it a unique spectacle, it was an unforgettable emotion.

And yet it was not the day's last wonder, the coda was to follow. Bill turned the car, heading home. We had gone perhaps a mile when we saw, standing on a ridge, immobile as a carving, his whorled spiraling horns silhouetted against the fiery pink sky, a great male kudu. He was inexpressibly majestic. He regarded us, his subjects, dispassionately and, at his leisure, turned and disappeared.

It was a subdued group of game viewers who returned to camp.

The next morning I awakened about 4 A.M. The light streaming from the stars was almost palpable and half an hour later the crescent moon rose above the trees to the accompaniment of a grunting symphony, courtesy of the hippos in the channel just below our tents.

Tea arrived at six. Our lodgings might have been simple but the service was unfailing. Meals well cooked and well presented, one day laundry service, abundant hot water heated over great log fires for our evening showers, the water itself drawn from the river and carried in pails on the heads of a file of Africans. If that's roughing it, it's not a bad life.

About eight o'clock we took off, Mary and Bill Saul, Ruth, Tim and ourselves. Again Bill drove us and I looked at him with interest. His head was quite beautiful: delicate bone structure, finely drawn features and, like all bush-trained Africans, his eyesight was incredible.

Our first draw of the day was bountiful. Tsessebe, wart hog, wildebeest, and any number of giraffe.

Probably the most incredible animals are giraffes, elephants, and rhinos. Hippos don't seem very likely either but the first three are creatures of legend. How they did they ever get off the drawing board? How did they ever get on it? They are miraculous.

In a way, giraffes are the most fantastic, with their extraordinary composition of disdain, tolerance, and curiosity plus the physique of a child's toy.

Then there were the guinea fowl. Guinea fowl amuse me. Their polka-dot plumage, gray with white dots, is tucked up like a short full skirt, a sort of ballet dancer's tutu, pressed flat in front, puffed out behind.

Finally the impala. As they race across the plain, spanning the track in front of the vehicles in great arcing leaps, the heart leaps with them. Even when safe from what they must consider danger, they keep on leaping, their little white scuts flashing. They keep bounding as from a trampolin in the sheer joy of living and one feels that on a wave length inaudible to the human ear they must be shouting in exultant Impaleese "Look at me, look at me, whee, whee!"

That morning we saw our first pride of lions: four cubs and a female. We bumped along after them until they gathered in the shade of a bush. For a long time we watched them rolling about, playing gently, lying down, yawning and finally falling asleep. The urge to get out and stroke them was almost irresistible. Almost but not quite. Were one on foot their good nature, especially Ma's, might evaporate, but I never cease to wonder at how near one may approach them in a car without any of them turning a hair.

A few minutes later we spotted another pride of eight but they were moving too swiftly through the undergrowth for us to catch up with them.

Eleven elephants in single file passed in slow majesty and we saw a limping male in a herd of stately waterbuck. Mary was concerned because an incapacitated animal is easy prey for lions and we wondered if the reserve wardens ever sent for a vet to tranquilize the animal and do what was necessary to help it recover. Tim, less sentimental, felt it would be a waste of money. "Better a lion should get a faulty beast than a healthy one," he said. Survival of the fittest. Like it or not, the natural law is the one hope for maintaining a viable balance.

Just as we had had Barry Unwin at Khwai so we had Daryl Dandridge at Savuti. He too was a member of the stork family. He was a young chap, tall, thin, *very* long-legged and as dark as Barry had been fair.

He co-managed the camp with John Bennett who had only recently arrived and was just getting settled in. Despite his inexperience Mr. Bennett set a good table. We even had fresh green salad! In the bush? In Africa? The man was a genie.

Like the others, Daryl was a knowledgeable game scout but he took out hunting parties as well as photographic safaris and much of his talk around the evening fire was of bores and guns and rifles. Since I was ignorant of the equipment and antagonistic to the pursuit, I shut up.

I was less censorious of his activities with elephants. They are marvelous creatures but country through which they travel is left a shambles. They crash through bushes, they uproot trees to eat only the top-most leaves. Upended roots and gray, naked trunks and branches are the stark testimony of their passage.

It is true that sometimes, with the trees gone, the grass comes back and this gives nourishment to the smaller plain animals. Almost all the reserves can survive some destruction if it is limited but limitation is the key.

Just as indiscriminate breeding in humans will destroy the planet so with elephants. If they overbreed they will ruin their own habitat and starve to death. It is for that reason that they have to be controlled—which, of course, means killed.

To my way of thinking it would be preferable to have a good many cows and bulls rounded up and sterilized. But probably the job would be considered too time-consuming and costly. Failing that, I suppose killing them is the only way.

This is part of Daryl's work. But at least he goes about it with compassion and intelligence. He doesn't pick off one here and another there and throw a herd into panic. He rounds up an entire family group and shoots his way through it. It is a sickening, ruthless, and necessary business and having to decide which shall die and which shall live must be a traumatic experience.

Usually we gathered together in the evening by the fire but living as we did we had early-morning socializing too as we waited for breakfast. Dressing was informal and fairly communal. I remember one morning in particular when Bill Saul and Margery were darting about like *paparazzi* snapping pictures of the rest of us brushing our teeth, washing and shaving in the basins set outside our tents.

We tried to shoo them away but they weren't having any. "It's for our blackmail work," they cried gleefully.

That particular morning's game drive was notable for giraffe. We saw a great many. They would stare at us, rock away, stop, turn and resume their gaze at once curious and courteous. They are endearing animals.

From time to time as we were driving about I had been aware of the most delicious fragrance, a pungent bittersweet aroma permeating the air. That morning when I remarked on it Daryl hopped down from the vehicle and gathered me a handful of a low-growing green weed. He did not know its name but it looked very like alfalfa with a similar small round purple flower. I crushed it in my hand and the odor was delicious.

In the middle of the day the heat became intense and even the animals too took to the shade, the exception being that sometime, thirsty from the heat, they would congregate at a water hole. Unless parched they were likely to refrain from even that activity until late afternoon.

When our two vehicles met for the coffee break Carol announced we would be lunching early at a water hole where sable and elephant were approaching.

Daryl was with us but the other car was having engine trouble which Bill, the African, did not feel he could cope with. Daryl therefore left us to go with the others and Carol joined him.

Ruth, Norton, John Bennett and I were on our own and by the time John had backed the car and turned to start after them they had vanished.

There then ensued a wild comedy of errors as we started off in all directions each of us being convinced that "*that* way, over *there*," was the way they had gone.

The ground was dry and although there was a maze of tire tracks in the powdery, pale sand it was impossible to tell whose they were or when they had been made.

We came to a couple of water holes and in the distance even saw some antelope and elephants but no trace of our chums. John was all for driving farther to get a closer look at the game but Ruth and Norton were adamant. "No," they said, "the first rule you learn in camping is, when lost return to where you were last together."

The difficulty was John was new in the area and finding our way back to where we had been was not all that easy. We finally made it, however, and Mrs. Anderson and Dr. Brown had spoken with the voice of experience. There, sure enough, patiently waiting under a tree for the loiterers to show up was Bill.

We hauled him aboard and within minutes, under his guidance, joined up with the others. Daryl had gone off in another direction to look for us so we kept tooting two shorts and one long on the Land-Rover horn to notify him we had been found. He eventually appeared and we resumed our picnic lunch in the shade of a grove of thorn trees.

Mary Saul was radiant. "Oh," she said, "the most wonderful thing happened. We raced an ostrich. We clocked him at thirty miles an hour! He was neck and neck with the car and then he won! He tore ahead and dashed across the track in front of us. Wouldn't you say that was winning?"

We agreed that his was the victory and that he deserved the laurel wreath of an Olympic champion of Ancient Greece. "I was so glad," Mary said, her brown eyes shining. "He was so wild and free and he won."

In another grove, not far away from the one in which we were sheltering from the sun, we could discern a large mother elephant with a small baby. We admired them through binoculars, where they loomed startlingly near, and decided to leave quietly. That particular madonna and child combination is not one to tamper with.

By one of those fantastic quirks of memory, seeing them reminded me of my father. I have friends who assure me their fathers frequently uttered remarks rich in wit and philosophy. Daddy's comment was perhaps not all that good but it was not without wisdom and it was trenchant. Shortly after I had learned to drive, he was with me in the car when I chose, imprudently, to challenge the right of way of a hefty moving van.

"Stubs," he said—he called me that because as a baby, I had only a stub of a nose—"Stubs, never argue with a Mack truck." Gazing at the mother elephant I thought of dear old dad.

Driving back to camp we came upon a scene, very different but as remarkable in its way as the galloping buffalo had been: a whole herd of sable antelope. Seeing them in numbers is unusual but there they were. With their pointed cream-striped faces, long backward-curving horns, their rich brown-black coats, the short thick black hair like a ruche down their necks, dappled with sun and shadow, they moved quietly through the trees like faery creatures in an enchanted grove.

Late that afternoon Ruth and I went on a private little game drive of our own. We wanted to see hippo but patient watching on the channel bank by the camp failed to produce them. We accordingly dragooned Bill and the three of us set off. We didn't see hippo that time either but we didn't mind. Other creatures made up for them.

Standing near his burrow staring at us was a father wart hog. Ma was close beside him, her head sticking up above ground her two front paws resting on the edge of the family hole. Some slight movement of ours must have startled him for he suddenly took off at a gallop. She dashed out of the hole hard on his heels to be followed a beat later by junior, scampering hell for leather after them. They were so comical that Ruth and I dissolved in laughter.

As Bill nosed the car toward the channel, seven buffalo came picking their way down the opposite bank. We cut off the motor and sat very still watching them. They bent their great heads and drank for a long time. There was nothing to startle or disturb them and I thought how moving it is to see animals drinking without fear. Usually they are so vulnerable to predators or to man, that their survival is ever in peril. Of course very few forces other than man *can* attack buffalo, unless they are incapacitated or young and weak. Just the same it was good to see them quenching their thirst at the end of a long hot day.

While waiting for them to finish we watched a bee eater. Since where there is one bee eater there is another bee eater, we watched his mate balancing on a twig jutting up from the ground. They are entrancing little birds, brilliant green with touches of black and yellow.

When the buffalo had drunk their fill and started back up the slope Bill turned the key in the ignition and we headed toward camp, passing on the way a fair-sized baboon colony. There were lots of babies and mothers frolicking about and an elderly grandfather sitting on a log watching them with a combination of distaste and resignation. If ever I saw a "What is the young generation coming to?" expression it was on that old baboon's face.

As we turned west the great blazing ball of the sun slipped slowly down the neck of an enormously tall giraffe. Down and down until his whole body was in dark silhouette and he became Ra, the sun god. It must have been like that, I thought; the first sunset of the world.

Back at camp we had hot showers and as we gathered for drinks around the fire I commented on how long the wood burned. In the morning there were always embers and ashes from the night before. Tim said it was the wood of the camel thorn tree which is very hard. The leaves are pod-like, the shape of human ears, with a coating soft and gray as moleskin. The Afrikanners too call giraffes camel leopards and the tree got its name because it is their preferred food. The early Romans knew that too and in Latin it is called *acacia giraffae*.

We were sitting in a wide semicircle around the fire chatting and sipping our drinks when there was a sudden hubbub from the direction of the cook tent and five or six Africans came running, shouting and jabbering as they jostled and crowded together.

I don't know what the others thought but Ruth, Norton, and I are New York bred and our reactions were instantaneous and identical. A rumble!

Tim, Daryl, and John may have had that impression too because they jumped up and ran toward the group. "What is it? What's the matter?"

Just then one of the women tripped over a guy rope of the mess tent, did a complete somersault and picked herself up unhurt and giggling, whereupon they all burst into shrieks of laughter.

"What is it? What's happened?" Tim demanded.

"Hippo. Hippo, he come!"

"What? Where?"

"There. There"—and they pointed back toward the cook tent. At that moment we couldn't see anything but it was true. They had been busy preparing supper when, drawn perhaps by the light and movement as well as the appetizing smells, a large hippo had loomed from the shadows into the bright light of the tent lanterns. Confused by the commotion he evoked, he hastily retreated and as Tim grabbed his flashlight we caught a glimpse of a large dark rump vanishing around the sleeping tents, making for the channel.

African breakfasts are sometimes confusing. As we sat at the table early next morning Mary Saul was telling of how sorry she was because she had had an opportunity to go to London for a ten-day theatre tour but had to pass it up as Bill couldn't get away at the time. The point was that they had a joint passport.

"I'm rectifying that," she said, "it's an awful nuisance. I was crazy to go to London."

I had never even heard of such a thing. Two married adults and only one passport?

Margery Wicks spoke up. "We have only one passport. I don't want to travel without Jim."

"But supposing for business reasons, or there's an emergency and one of you has to get some place fast, what do you do?" I asked.

"We'd go together."

"That isn't always feasible."

"I wouldn't enjoy it without Jim."

"It isn't necessarily a question of enjoyment."

She had a pretty, petulant pout and now she pouted prettily. "I don't want to go around with a lot of girls."

By this time I was completely at sea.

"What's that got to do with it? Who said anything about girls?"

Mrs. Anderson in assorted stati—single, married, divorced—has covered a good deal of the globe and her patience was wearing thin. She began muttering into her cereal. "Never heard such damn nonsense in my life. No passport of your own."

"Obviously I'd rather be with Norton," I said, "but if I have to, I travel by myself and hope to meet some fellas."

My husband grinned. "Ilka's had a passport since she was sixteen," he said, "and she's been married three times. Your system would make her life very complicated, Margery."

Such impasses, however, were infrequent and for the most part we were on common ground.

That morning was our last at Savuti and as the others had asked Norton if he wouldn't take the "class" picture he rounded us up after breakfast, snapped us a couple of times, then the Sauls, Wickses, Tim and Carol took off for the airstrip and the flight to Victoria Falls.

Ruth, Florence, Norton, and I hung around camp trying to evoke hippos with song and mesmeric passes but we had no better luck than we had had at the big pond in Moremi: scattered pairs of ears, bulging eyes and nothing else.

When we saw Rodney's small plane approaching John drove us out to the airstrip. It was about noon and the flight was rough but we could see the meandering Chobe River and then followed the Zambezi until we sighted Victoria Falls.

Flying low Rodney banked and turned to give us an uninterrupted view of the mighty cascade and the water rushing and eddying through the gorges. It was powerful and it was beautiful but I preferred the sight of the airport, the hot bumpy ride having done nothing to settle my stomach.

Rodney made one of his perfect landings at the very modern terminal and we were impressed by the gentlemen of the passport control, smart in starched white shorts and short-sleeved white shirts with gold epaulets. What must the Rhodesians do for their generals?

We four were the only people around and there was no red tape although our man did make a note of Ruth's profession. Writer. In Rhodesia and South Africa they're not too keen on the written word. A permanent record perhaps but criticism—who needs it? The new passports, which no longer require professional identification, make for greater relaxation.

There is a precautionary note the traveler should remember about Rhodesia. Do not let them stamp your passport. If they have to stamp something ask them to stamp a card which they are perfectly willing to do. Because of the racial discrimination practiced by Rhodesia if there is a record in your passport that you have been there you will have great difficulty getting into other countries of East and Central Africa. It's like Israel and the Arab lands.

There is another little eccentricity too. When you cash traveler's checks you must not, as you would normally do, write in the city and country in which you are cashing it. Just put the date and sign it. You'll get the money but avoid our mistake! With tips in mind we got several rands in change but the rands of Rhodesia are not those of South and South-West Africa where they will accept paper money but not silver. Rhodesia gives one a curious feeling. It is like being in an invisible country.

Our hotel was the Victoria Falls Casino, highly visible and extremely attractive. However, as we drew up to the door, Florence Mueller was loud in her protestations. "We're supposed to go to the old Victoria Falls Hotel. It says so in the brochure. That's what it says, The Victoria Falls Hotel." It did say that but Carol appeared, explaining that there had been a change and one could not complain. The Casino is clean, comfortable, well run and altogether pleasant.

We dropped our luggage in our rooms and joined the others at luncheon in the garden on the edge of a big swimming pool. Victoria Falls is another place where you will want a bathing suit.

After luncheon, the Spectacle! The Falls themselves in living color. The Zambezi River rises in northwest Zambia, flows into Angola, crosses back into Zambia, heads south and then east to where the Falls are, continues on its way forming the border between Zambia and Rhodesia, pushes through Mozambique, develops at Chinde a delta three to four miles wide and empties into the Indian Ocean after a journey of 1750 miles.

The Falls drop 350 feet down a sheer black basalt cliff into the boiling gorge below. The curtain of water is a mile and a quarter wide with a mean average volume of 47,000,000 gallons a minute.

The roar, the billowing smoke, the glittering spray and the great rainbow spanning the chasm are marvelous to hear and to behold.

The rushing, foaming water is dizzying and it is almost impossible to believe that David Livingstone lay on his belly on a little island at the very brink of the drop, his head hanging over the edge as he let down a line weighted with bullets from which fluttered a small white cloth. When it came to rest on a projection he found he had played out 310 feet of line and still hadn't reached bottom.

Mrs. Anderson was skeptical about those bullets and the line claiming that greater accuracy would be achieved if you were lowered in a britches buoy with a tape measure.

We agreed that regardless of what some nuts might do at Niagara Falls going over Victoria in a barrel was not a sound idea.

Arab traders knew of the Zambezi for hundreds of years and it is considered likely that Boer farmers visited the area seeking ivory but Livingstone was the first white man to charter the river's course and it was he who named the Falls after his roly-poly queen.

Almost as marvelous as the Falls themselves is the spray. There is an extraordinary grandstand view of the fabulous phenomenon because across the narrow gorge, directly facing the cliffs down which the water roars, is a companion cliff. Walking along the top of it you are drenched with spray and mist but the view is unparalleled. From Rodney's plane we had seen the spray, rising into the sky like a great plume, before we could see the water.

When we were there, there was a fairly large crowd of sightseers, among them many spinster ladies carefully wrapped in raincoats and plastic raincaps, carrying umbrellas.

Their outfits were not inappropriate but I would not say such gear was vital and I would recommend taking raincoats only if one is planning to be in that part of Africa in the rainy season.

You can pick up a bus or car at the bridge that crosses the gorge at the far end. You can cross the bridge too if you want to. Or at least go part way. There is two-way traffic with a narrow-gauge railroad down the center and bisecting the middle two yellow lines about two feet apart separating Zambia from Rhodesia.

Norton and I took the information on hearsay since we wanted to return to what might be called the town although it is more a center of activity and shops.

We knew that our friends the Jan Allans whom we had first met in the Serengeti, in Tanzania,* were now running a curio shop in Victoria Falls and we were eager to see them.

Mrs. Allan, Lasse, was not in but Jan was. There were several other curio and handicraft shops in the vicinity but the Allan stock was much superior to any we saw. There were some fresh and imaginative batik prints designed by Lasse and we bought an ancient Congo mask, simple and decorative. It was arranged that they would come to the hotel that evening to dine with us.

Tim had secured a conference room and when they arrived shortly after seven we went downstairs to see some of his slides. He is a talented photographer and he showed beautiful animal and reptile shots and a remarkable series of pictures of fish eagles, from the hatching to the hunting stage.

Because of their years in the lodges and reserves the Allans are keen about game and I watched their reaction with pleasure.

Jan, although he is Scandinavian, is very dark, Lasse silver topped and patrician of bearing. She is a beautiful woman in a lean, economical way and extremely intelligent.

When they left the Serengeti they had four months to wait before taking over the management of Keekorock Lodge so they had gone to Treetops and thus they figured in a story told me by a friend. She had spent a night there sometime after *Elephants Arrive at Half-Past Five* had been published and had seen a copy on the bookshelf. In it I had described our own night at Treetops so she said cheerily, "Weren't you pleased by the nice things Ilka Chase said about you?"

They said yes they were but my friend sensed a reservation.

"Was there anything you didn't like?" she inquired.

"Well," Lasse said, "what Miss Chase said was very nice, of course, but a great many people seem to have read that book.

* See *Elephants Arrive at Half-Past Five.*

They come here, they have tea, they look at their watches and when it gets to be half-past five they say, 'All right, where are the elephants?' We can't bring them in on *cue*," she added a little desperately.

That night we were laughing over the story but Lasse shook her head ruefully. "Oh, Ilka, if only you hadn't given your book that title! I always knew when trouble was brewing because you remember you said, 'Take woolen gloves to Treetops, your hands can get very cold!' Any time I saw a pair of mittens I knew we were in for it."

I tried to persuade Jan to open the shop after dinner because Ruth had not been with us in the afternoon and she was eager to see the merchandise. I knew it would be child's play to persuade Margery to come along and I was sure the others would want to too but for reasons of his own he was reluctant. Perhaps he did not wish to commercialize on a social occasion.

They would be open in the morning but we would not be there. Indeed our schedule was the cause of considerable irritation.

At this point Grosvenor Tours had taken over from Lindblad. They were nothing like as able, imaginative and thoughtful, and in this particular instance their scheduling struck us as ridiculous, although, as we later learned, they were not entirely to blame. There had been a change of plane schedules and we were not supposed to be on the flight we took.

This did not change the fact that we had to be up at dawn Sunday morning to fly to Johannesburg to spend a long dull day in a completely shuttered city where we had already spent a long dull day on our arrival.

The spectacular Falls fall on the Sabbath too. The most rudimentary common sense would dictate staying there and leaving Monday morning for Johannesburg where one would still have a whole afternoon for shopping and the hairdresser. That's not how Grosvenor did it, but I understand they have since pulled themselves together on matters of that sort.

Still, the ill-timed Air Rhodesia flight was pleasant and we en-

joyed the view of the Falls from the large plane more than I had
from Rodney's bumpy little buggy the day before.

We returned to the President Hotel which is well run and comfortable but one little matter I still have to get straightened out. I
was on the phone ordering breakfast from room service the next
morning. This is my chore. The doctor, who can remain calm in the
face of fatal cardiac infarction or massive hemorrhage, comes as-
sunder when faced with Mr. Bell's invention.

In cultured, dulcet tones I was making known our wants.

"One tea and one coffee, please."

"Yes, sir."

"Two orange juice."

"Yes, sir."

"One order of two poached eggs, one of one."

"Yes, sir."

"Toast and jam."

"Yes, sir."

My patience snapped. "God damn it, I'm a woman." A startled
silence. "Yes, *sir!*" The receiver dropped from my nerveless grasp.

It could not be said that our group was shot with luck in Johannesburg. Although this Monday was not a national holiday it *was*
Yom Kippur and searching for alcoholic supplies Ruth and I discovered that all the liquor merchants were apparently Orthodox
Jews and their shops tightly closed. We looked at each other in
wonderment. Although not a drinking woman herself, Ruth was concerned for us, her chums. "My God, are there no Christian lushes
around here?" Well, yes. We came upon the Western Province
Cellars and I bought what I thought Norton and I would be needing.

We made more worthy purchases too. A book by Eugène N.
Marais *My Friends the Baboons* and one of beautiful photographs
by Helmut zur Strassen, *Land Between Two Deserts,* the animals
and country of South-West Africa. We also visited the Bushman, a
reasonably good souvenir shop. The masks, I thought, were com-
monplace but they had some amusing bead work.

Quality came in the afternoon when Carol guided us to a diamond factory but it was not as glittering a locale as one might imagine. It was in fact a humdrum machine shop and madly noisy.

The machines for grinding, cutting, and polishing made a terrific din intensified by super-loud piped-in music intended, I gathered, to soothe nerves already shattered by the original racket.

At 2:45 came a tea break and a couple of chaps leapt to the ping-pong table for a quick game. They have the table as a relaxation from the tensions that can form when the precise and intricate cutting of a valuable stone is involved.

I was pleased to learn that although the business is costly no waste is involved. The diamond dust, a sort of carbon, is gathered up and used to polish other and grander diamonds.

Since I prefer to look at the finished product in a jeweler's window I wandered out of the shop and back to the small office we had been ushered into on our arrival. Ranged on a shelf were six or seven little wire stands each supporting a showpiece; a large obviously glass diamond. As I picked one up to look at it it slipped from my fingers and dropped to the floor. It rolled under a chair so I had to kneel down, then flatten out to retrieve it.

At this unpropitious moment the door opened and, led by the plant manager, my pals came trooping in from the machine shop. I knew the stone was glass, the management knew it was glass and they had to know that I knew it. I nevertheless blushed scarlet. Caught in *flagrante delicto!*

At the sight of me Mrs. Anderson doubled up with unfeeling laughter. "My God, what a moment to have left the Instamatic at the hotel. What wouldn't I give to have a picture of you groveling around down there!"

I rose with as much dignity as I could muster. "I'm sorry," I said, handing the truant gem to the chap who had been showing us around. "Naturally I knew it was a fake." The chap looked at me with what I considered a rather queer expression. "Naturally," he said.

I was relieved to get out of there and to drive to the Botanical

Gardens although they specialize in succulents over which I do not enthuse. The gardens were set on a steep hillside and from the looks of them were fairly new. Kindly old Father Time can only bring improvement.

Back at the hotel the more swinging members of the tour decided they would dine on the roof at the 6000 Club but with a 5 A.M. call hanging over us our timorous trio, Ruth, Norton, and I, decided on a quiet meal in the first-floor dining room and early bed.

The reason for such matutinal highjinks was our flight to Windhoek, South-West Africa, and the beginning of the extension tour. On this one we were only six, the Sauls having stayed behind to visit friends in Durban. We missed them. Without them we felt shriveled, in reduced circumstances, but they would be joining us in Rio for the flight back to New York.

The breakfast on the plane was solid Boer stuff. Cold rubber omelet, mushrooms, slice of tomato, and steak.

Windhoek, the name means windy corner, is a cheery little city with a population of about 80,000, of whom 47,000 are white. Carol Martin and Tim Liversedge had stayed behind in Johannesburg and we were met by our new courier, Tommy Samson.

The Grand Hotel of Windhoek was plain and comfortable and the weather in Windhoek superb. Norton and I laughed because, when we did our bits of laundry, they were practically dry by the time we stepped onto our balcony to hang them on the line he had rigged up, à la Chinese.

The hot sun was fanned by a little breeze in the daytime and at night our doors and window stood wide open with nary a fly or mosquito to mar the balmy air.

The next morning we took a 320 mile drive along good roads bordering the Eros Mountains. The Wickses and Florence were with Tommy in another car and our guide was George von Klackstein, one of those men who emanate an aura of freedom and dependability, the result of life spent largely in the open among wild free animals.

If I speak more of him than of Tommy Samson it is because

although Ruth and Florence sometimes switched cars the Wickses stayed with Tom and Norton and I were with George. Both men knew Etosha well and both were admirable guides.

George told us a comical story about the problems common to emerging countries struggling to emulate their more sophisticated neighbors.

Uganda and the Congo along with the Sudan share a common border. The Congolese drive on the right, the Ugandans on the left. The question arose in the Uganda Congress as to whether Uganda might not switch in order to comply with her neighbor and her Minister of Transportation came up with a bright idea. Why not have public vehicles—buses, trucks, and taxis—take to the right for a while to try it out? Private cars would still keep to the left. Then, if that worked, they could move over too. If the citizens survived they would emerge as super men but one suspects the transition period would be tricky.

We stopped for a coffee break at the hotel Hamburger Hof in Otjiwarongo where I bought a bathing suit. It was a gay print, very light in weight but considering the quality of the fabric and the limited area covered I did not think the equivalent of $14.45, the price I paid for it, was the greatest bargain I'd ever struck. They have inflation in Otjiwarongo too.

We set off again passing on the way a truck loaded with Hereros in their brilliant costumes. They made me think of those flat horse-drawn wagons loaded with pots of flowers that used to appear in the streets of New York in the springtime.

Skirting another mountain range, the Otavi, we reached Tsumeb and the Minen Hotel where we lunched in a garden, surrounded by bougainvillea and lovely jacaranda trees in full purple blossom. It was the spring of the year and the thorn trees too were in bloom; fuzzy, furry flowerets like cotton blossoms.

As the name of the hotel implies, Tsumeb is a mining town. It is surrounded by eucalyptus groves because the trees are strong and fast growing and the wood is used for props in the mines.

We entered the Etosha Pan Park at four o'clock after about eight hours on the road.

The guardian at the gate, a friend of George's, was a vigorous upright man with a fresh complexion and a twinkling eye. It was hard to believe he was eighty-two. He was though and George said he was still a marvelous shot.

We had asked if there were no light planes flying to the reserve such as the one we had used in Botswana and George said no. The three lodges where we would be staying had airstrips but business did not warrant the use of planes. Since we found them to be all pretty full we concluded it wasn't so much lack of business as that South-West Africans go every place in buses and in their own cars.

The atmosphere is very different from that of Botswana. There the lodges are British and the country is independent. One has a sense of freedom and of a relaxed kind of sight-seeing that does not prevail in Etosha Pan or "Big White Place."

The big part was certainly accurate. At one time the Pan embraced 22,000 square miles, the largest reserve in the world, but because of politics half of it was officially ceded to the tribes. They don't do anything about it other than hunt and poach but it is a sop to those who think there is something wrong in devoting all that space to wild life.

Man may be a political animal but thank God animals are not political men.

South-West Africa used to be under German domination. That was when they also had the Caprivi Strip to the north and the intention of pushing it all the way across Africa to the Indian Ocean. The scheme misfired.

The Germans are no longer there but a kind of Achtung! Verboten! aura lingers on. Our immediate reaction was one of disappointment because, instead of riding around in the flexible Land-Rovers which can go every place and have the handy hatches for viewing and photography, we would be doing all our game viewing in a kind of station wagon mini bus. Not too bad, especially as there were only four of us including the driver, but no hatch. The real blow came when George announced that the cars could never veer off into the bush but must at all times keep to the roads and passengers were *never* to get out.

Oh, darling laissez-faire Botswana, where are you? The road, even after we entered the reserve en route to our first camp, was tar topped and the likelihood that any game would approach it to look at us seemed slender. If we couldn't go off searching for them what would we do?

I am enchanted to say that my dour prognostications were one hundred percent wrong. Game was drawn to us as though we were magnets. We saw certainly as much, perhaps even more, than we had in Botswana.

Our first prize was a pair of Damara dik-dik, enchanting little creatures which are I think the smallest of the antelope family. They are less than eighteen inches in height and weigh about eleven pounds. Their Afrikaans name, duiker, means diver and they acquired it because their movements through the grass are similar to the arching and diving of a porpoise through water.

Brownish in color, with rumps gray-speckled like guinea fowl, they have great liquid black eyes, slender legs, and hoofs the size of gumdrops.

Our pair were very tame and most obliging, letting themselves really be viewed. We were lucky as they are shy and fleet and usually, before one can say, dik-dik, they have vanished.

We drove along and presently sighted Fort Namutoni, our first lodge, a vision of gleaming white sugar cubes rising from the flat dun-colored plain. Its romantic Beau Geste exterior is not matched by its interior but that, let us hope, will improve with time and experience although we learned, somewhat to our surprise, that it has served as a guest house since 1957.

The fort is a big quadrangle of crenelated walls with square towers at the corners and is entered through heavy wooden gates facing three points of the compass. A row of bedrooms forms the fourth side of the quadrangle and light comes from windows set high in the walls.

Outside the enclosure is a small inviting swimming pool but that geste, though beau, was not practical. When we returned from our afternoon game drive we wanted a dip but it was verboten because the sun had set.

The rule was not without a reason but we felt the reason didn't apply to us. It seems that a couple of years before, and before they had installed a kitchen, a group of tourists had arrived to spend the night. Rooms were provided for them but they had to supply their own utensils and cook their own food.

The men of the party departed to view game, the women were preparing dinner and the children were splashing in the pool. This pastoral idyl was rudely interrupted by the appearance of three lions who, seeking to quench their thirst, strolled casually across the compound in the direction of the water and the shouting children.

Wild maternal shrieks rent the air and the startled lions departed at a gallop but from that day on es wurde verboten zu schwimmen nach Sonnenuntergang.

The fort's history is colorful. In 1897 the outbreak of a cattle plague resulted in a cordon several hundred kilometers in length being drawn across that part of the country in the hope of arresting the rinderpest. Okaukuejo, at the other end of Etosha, where we also stayed, was established as was Namutoni. When the plague was over both camps remained as frontier posts.

By the end of 1903 the tiny settlement of reed huts where the men lived was abolished and the fort completed. In January 1904 the garrison consisted of seven white men and a large herd of cattle.

Early in the morning of January 28 they were attacked by about 550 members of the Ovambo tribe, three hundred of whom were armed with rifles. Five were on horseback and thirty rode oxen.

They stormed the fort, their object being to kidnap the cattle and riddle the storeroom. The attack was apparently well ordered. The Ovambo poured in and began looting and piling crates on top of each other in an effort to reach the beams supporting the corrugated roof of the western tower where the defenders had taken refuge.

Their situation was dicey until their companions on another tower were able to fire on the storeroom door and the space in front of its windows.

As the bullets began raining in on them the Ovambo, scooping up as much tobacco as they could hold on to, took to their heels, while their unarmed companions who had remained outside drove off the cattle.

Those who still had guns continued shooting at the fort from such shelters of reeds and hummocks as they could find. The garrison, uncertain of the outcome, had removed all ammunition to the top of the towers, planning as a last resort to blow themselves up with as many Ovambo as might be in range. Happily they did not have to. The Ovambo continued to fire until about three-thirty in the afternoon and then retreated into the bush to the north. It was just as well. By that time of the 1100 rounds of ammunition with which the garrison had started the day only 150 remained.

When darkness fell the soldiers descended from their towers and softly and silently vanished away to the south. The following morning, surprised to find their birds flown, the Ovambo did a bit more looting of the empty fort and then set fire to it. The entire building was burned to the ground.

It was subsequently rebuilt or, more accurately, evolved into its present style but documentation as to who planned it and exactly when it was done is scanty. The files of the Imperial Colonial Troops of South-West Africa, which could have supplied the information, had been taken back to Germany in 1919 and destroyed completely in 1943 during a bombing attack on Potsdam when the Reichsarchiv was burned down.

In the largest of the towers there is an engaging scale model of the original fort at the time of the battle complete with brave defenders, dastardly Ovambo brandishing tiny rifles and minuscule cattle being surreptitiously driven away.

On our arrival, after unpacking and a brief rest, we set out to try our luck with the beasts. Almost immediately we came upon a cheetah but he was off the road a bit, lying in the shade of a tree and at first we couldn't believe it *was* a cheetah. He was so still and his head was so large we thought we must be mistaking a rock or a log for a creature we longed to see. George assured us we could believe our eyes and when we returned that way some time later he was proven right. The cheetah had finally got up and was moving gracefully away into the bush.

The first water hole we came to was well populated. Giraffe—when they drink their splayed out knees look as though they must be dislocated but they seem to feel no pain—wart hogs, springbok, and zebra.

At the second water hole a lion and lioness. Inevitably they are the stars but this time I resented them a little. There they lay, on the far side of the pool, a pair of great lazy lugs while a whole herd of thirsty zebra hesitated on the near side. They would approach a few feet, stand, and back away again. They wanted so much to get to the water but their hereditary enemy held them in thrall. Finally they turned and disappeared, thirst unslackened.

Back in camp we had showers, the plumbing facilities were very adequate, and pre-dinner drinks. In all the camps of South-West Africa if you want a bit of hard liquor take your own. Beer, and usually wine, are obtainable, spirits no.

We then dined. The one truly ignominious meal of our entire safari. Like the air of New York City the food of Namutoni was unacceptable. A mess of inedibility with a fried egg on top.

In defense of the cook it must be said that the kitchen was unacceptable too. Conceivably, with enough tourists screaming loudly enough, the situation may change but judging from the apathy of the staff and the standards of the tourists we saw that isn't going to happen soon. Never mind. The lousy food eaten pales into insignificance compared to the superb game seen.

The next morning we were up at 6:15 and out of camp by 6:55 but not before a military reveille, the playing of the national anthem of South-West Africa on a rusty record.

Irked by the rasping sound, Mrs. Anderson observed that she was going to organize a live orchestra; the Etosha Panhandlers.

This kind of rigid ritual prevails all over the world and although by and large I am indifferent to it, when I look around the streets of the city I live in, I am not all that sure that a little ceremony, the stiff upper lip, black tie for dinner in the bush, the jungle and the desert, is such a bad idea. An emotional and intellectual corset is sometimes salutary.

That morning we drove only a short distance from the fort, joyfully abandoned the hard-topped road in favor of natural dirt, and came upon three beautiful lions, two males and a female.

One of the lads, apparently getting the message that three was a crowd, wandered off but the loving couple remained, gently caressing and nuzzling one another. They were a handsome well fed pair, not scrawny and mangy as they so often are when victuals are not abundant.

They good humoredly put up with our voyeurism until they had had enough of it and then strolled off passing within five or six feet of the car, in search of privacy for the culmination of their affair.

A little farther on a small water hole provided a wildcat, but curled up on a heap of stones exactly the color of his fur, he was not easy to spot. When our binoculars did zero in on him we saw that he bore a strong resemblance to our Abyssinian puss, Spice.

The drive also produced four gemsbok or oryx, magnificent fellows, gray, black, and white with black and white masks and long backward-sweeping pointed horns. The crimson-breasted shrike is the emblematic bird of South-West Africa, the gemsbok is the animal. They are well suited to dry areas where they dig for tubers, bulbs, and water roots and can survive without any other water for months at a time. They do not produce litters as do lions, their calves come singly, but they have a lion-like family life in that the young are left under the supervision of an adult though not necessarily their own parent. They are great squabblers and it is not unusual to see a broken horn, souvenir of a rugged brawl.

We returned to camp for a breakfast on a par with the previous night's dinner, with the exception of good freshly baked bread.

The Lindblad Tour had spoiled us. We were accustomed to a

thermos, cold soft drinks and beer on the drives. Grosvenor Tours were make of sterner stuff, not even water was provided.

Later that morning we saw a great herd of zebra drinking at a water hole. They were better off than we except that their legs were black with mud. George said they enjoyed that. Perhaps it kept the flies away.

Farther up the road we found a steenbok. Let us pause for a moment of silent admiration and love. They are exquisite little creatures, larger than the dik-dik but still small animals, with squared-off behinds and intelligent winsome faces. Both antelope are fashioned with the delicacy and precision of the finest watches and while I respect expert craftsmanship, the dik-dik and steenbok are more beautiful.

When the sun is high they seek the shade of the thorn trees. The trees are coated with a kind of rime from the sand and dust of the Etosha Pan, giving them the appearance of northern trees on an early winter morning. With the pale sandy roads glimmering in the bright light the effect of snow in so hot a world, is weird and beautiful.

Looming over this snowscape was a large dark elephant with tusks surprisingly small for his size and George said sadly that the heavy ivory had all been slaughtered long ago.

He went on to say that mid-June to mid-July was a fatal time to visit the park because that was the period of the school holidays. "Bus loads of tourists go honking along the roads and the animals disappear." I should think so! The reserve is closed on October 1 and reopens March 16 but the rainy season usually continues through April. The rain is by no means continuous, perhaps a few hours in the middle of the day. However through April the grass is high, water plentiful and the game dispersed and hard to see.

After the elephant we saw some glossy starlings, blue-green and brilliant, and then a group of superb male kudus. Their protective coloration is a remarkable paint job. Standing in bushes or in a grove of trees, the play of sunlight and shadow on their coats makes it almost impossible to spot them at even a few yards.

Our next water hole was what makes one say *"That's* why we

came to Africa!" About fifty animals clustering on the shallow banks: antelope, kudus, springbok, giraffe, zebra, a battler eagle, an impressive chap with plumage, red, brown and dark steel blue and seven great eland.

Plans are afoot to domesticate the eland. Their meat is quite flavorful, and apparently there is already a successful eland farm in Rhodesia.

George von Klackstein told us that once in Angola he had seen a herd of three thousand. It was high noon at a big water hole and must have been a marvelous sight.

His dream was to establish a reserve in that country. He knew a place where two rivers converged and game was plentiful. "It would be ideal," he said, his eyes filled with longing, and I wished I were rich and could hand him a large check and say, "George, go to it."

Back at camp we received a real shock when, at luncheon, we were served a *delicious* chicken. At Namutoni? None of us could believe our palates.

We left the fort after luncheon heading for Halali, our next lodge which is farther down the Pan—on the fifty-yard line—or halfway between the fort and Okaukuejo. We detoured a little to one of the morning water holes in the hope of seeing elephant. On the way we passed a steenbok lying on the road in the long shadow of a tree trunk. Reluctantly he moved but when we returned, having found no elephant, he was back in place, his legs curled under him, his tiny horns as upright as exclamation points and the sunlight glowing through his flower-petal ears. I thought of the Bushmen's belief that steenbok are protected by great magic for they are too gentle to suspect violence.

We drove on and a couple of miles down the road the other end of the animal spectrum was suddenly represented by two enormous elephants. And I saw them first! My secret dream on every safari we have ever made has always been to be the one who sees *something* first. I know when I'm outclassed. I do not hope to compete with an African scout or with men like Tim Liversedge or Daryl or George von Klackstein but I wanted *once* to be ahead of Norton or

Ruth or Mary Saul who had been so quick to point out game in Botswana. Or for that matter Margery Wicks who had seen a leopard's tail dangling from a tree. That may not sound like much but don't knock it. It was the most leopard we saw on the whole trip.

I was always Johnny-Come-Lately. "Where? Where is it?" and every one would point. "There, there, dummy, just follow my finger." "Oh yes, yes, now I see it."

This time, only because Ruth and Norton and George were casing the bush on the other side of the road, I had my chance. To be sure it had to be something the size of an elephant for me to spot it but I could at last shout proudly to the others, ignorant of the superb animals not twenty yards away, "Look, look! Elephants!"

George had already driven past them but he backed up and we admired my trophies as they went peaceably about their destructive work of eating the leaves from the trees and breaking off the branches. They demolish nature as efficiently as U. S. Army Engineers but their reasoning is more intelligent. They do it for survival.

We spoke of the intelligence of animals in general. George said it was curious that the four species of the highest intellectual attainment, man, baboons, dolphins, and elephants, all practice homosexuality. I hadn't known about the last three.

A little farther on we came upon more straight-laced types, a herd of giraffe. Most of them stretched their long incredible necks upward to nibble leaves but one was so tall he had to arch his neck downward to reach the top of a thorn tree.

There was also a herd of hartebeest, the first we had seen in this part of the world—they are more prolific in East Africa. They were handsome creatures with coats of burnished bronze. At a water hole we drew a martial eagle, three blue crane and a springbok of a lovely fawn color with white and chocolate stripes.

The game of the Etosha Pan is prolific and a visit there is marvelously rewarding despite the unhappy fact of many buses, mini and maxi, full of people. The miracle is that the game is so varied and so visible.

We arrived at Halali around five-thirty and found it attractive if rather large and public with a big area of tents for campers. However, we had comfortable cottage rooms with private baths, there was a nice dining room and a fine big swimming pool.

Ruth and I went for a dip and I christened my bathing suit from Otjiwarongo, causing Dr. Brown to emit a long low whistle when he saw me.

Halali, by the way, is the traditional tune blown on the bugle by German sportsmen to indicate the end of the hunt. I never knew *that* before.

The shop at Halali was a good one, which held true in all three camps we visited, and we quickly realized that while they sold post cards and souvenirs that interest was secondary. They were primarily little markets where campers bought fresh eggs and butter, milk, although for the most part that is powdered, tinned food, wine, and beer. One could also buy ice sold in small plastic packets for five cents.

That night at dinner we battled it out with George and Tommy Samson telling them we wanted a jug of water in the back of the vehicles and why on earth should there be any song and dance about that?

Well, it appears they once had had a bad experience. They did carry an ice chest and some clients, doubtless Americans, insisted on stopping every few miles to partake from it.

This, our South African friends considered perfect nonsense. Not only was it time consuming but it meant getting out of the vehicles which was, we gathered, a heinous crime. I couldn't help wondering what would happen were one to feel an irresistible urge of nature.

Unlike Botswana where one follows one's needs in these matters, there are, at rare intervals along the roads of Etosha, sign posts with an arrow pointing to two discreetly placed little huts half-hidden in the bush. Heaven help the traveler whose peristalsis does not coincide with the Park Administration.

George and Tommy were getting really indignant over the water question whereupon I am afraid I lost my temper. "If we were insisting on chilled vintage champagne," I said, "you would have every right to say 'Come off it' but a drink of water for God's sake, what's the problem?"

They implied that Grosvenor Tours did not provide for that but when the rest of us left the table Norton stayed on and the next day both vehicles had five-gallon plastic water jugs. It wasn't cold but it was wet. Maybe by now they will have graduated to a thermos.

The weather was hot and we all drank a good deal but whenever we offered any to George he refused. Maybe he wasn't thirsty. Maybe like the gemsbok, he could survive without water for months.

Despite the number of cars cruising about our early-morning game drive flushed a huge herd of zebra spilling into the road from either side, eland, giraffe and three lissome cheetahs as well as fish eagles and tawny eagles at a water hole.

A little later on we were treated to a charming Lilliputian puppet show. George stopped the vehicle at a plover's nest built on the ground right beside the road which, fortunately, was empty of all other traffic. A plover is a pretty bird with a black and white head, coral legs and a body gray, beige and cream like a skillful water color wash.

This one got up, chirped at us a bit, moved a few feet away, returned, stood over her nest for about five minutes then squatted down again on the two small eggs. They always lay their eggs on the ground and they are incubated by both the male and female parent.

Scurrying busily about the plover were any number of ground squirrels. They are sweet little creatures and very tame. They came right up to the car, sat on their haunches and stared at us inquiringly and when George leaned down to tempt them with bits of apple they nibbled greedily from his hand.

Okaukuejo—and it took us all the time we were there to learn to twist our tongues around that name—is the main administrative camp of the park and one of the nicest. Years ago the site served as a German border post. Our rooms were in long bungalows but the camp also has separate rondawels, the best of which overlook a spring and a big pond around which game frequently gather in great numbers. Indeed we met some people who told us that the night before they had counted seventy-two elephants but when we hurried over there, shortly after our arrival, there wasn't a soul in sight.

That day for the first time we drove out onto the Pan proper. It was my idea of hell. The conventional hell, with those leaping, flickering flames and devils busy with pitchforks and crowds of people, some of whom one is bound to know, has always struck me as a rather stimulating place. The Pan is total desolation, miles of nothing stretching to the horizon. There no bird sings, no insect scurries, no blade of grass brightens the floor of cracked colorless clay.

The area, nearly eighty miles long and forty-two wide, is actually a shallow dried-up inland lake which was formed some twelve million years ago by the Kuene River flowing east from the Ruacana Falls into a natural declivity in the earth's surface. Through the millennia the river shifted its course, the lake eventually dried up and the soil of the lake bed was blown away by wind erosion.

Today all life is leached out of it although in the rainy season large parts of it may still be covered with water. This, however, does not produce vegetation. When the water evaporates it leaves a salt crust of a greenish tinge, reminiscent of the sickly green paint at one time used on the Long Island Expressway with some mad intention of simulating grass. The color was horrid on the Expressway and it is not much better on the Pan, the one virtue being that there, at least, it's natural.

And in certain lights the arid clay is unbelievably like water, like a flat steely sea, and the golden grass on the far side is like a beach of yellow sand. The animals too are seduced by the mirage and sometimes travel for miles hoping for water only to turn back at last, weary and disillusioned.

Things perked up at the Reifontein water hole where we saw two slim and elegant blue crane, their long secondary wing feathers trailing on the ground like tails. There was also a great congregation of zebra, five hartebeest, wildebeest, and gemsbok.

The water hole was an oasis in a vast and empty plain where the only life was one running jackal and a few springbok. George said the herds were already starting their migrations away from the Pan and into Angola but the information made us sad because in Angola poaching is severe and apparently unchecked. The game that survived man would be returning to the park in early March.

As we were driving along George told us the Park Administration was toying with the revolting idea of eliminating the casually looping roads, forcing them into endless straight lines and, to crown the ignominy, paving them! He himself was pleading with the officials to abandon such monstrous folly, to dig bore holes instead to provide more water and, where it was felt that deeper penetration into the park was desirable, to create secondary dirt roads.

After traveling a good many miles on a happily still unpaved track we were rewarded with a flock, a clutch, a bevy? of large ostrich and an enormous lone elephant drinking from a tiny little water hole he had dug himself. He had apparently started excavating a muddy spot with his foot then, finding that his well was coming in, he had deepened it with his trunk. An elephant's trunk has, I believe, something like 3000 muscles, and as we watched him he would spiral it down into the hole whose circumference was only centimeters larger than the trunk, draw it up, drink and spray himself. It was a functional arrangement and we were impressed but there was a comical aspect as well for he stood with one hind foot crossed over the other somehow giving him a jaunty man-about-town air.

There are several windmills in the reserve to pump water for the holes and at one of them, standing like animals in a frieze, all pointing the same way, was a great herd of zebra and one of oryx. The oryx stood in serried ranks, their horns crowding the sky like the spears in *The Surrender of Breda*. Their attention was focused on a small square brick structure at the foot of the windmill and with reason, as we could see when we drove near. Lolling in the shade of the low building was a lioness, her cub beside her.

We drove that morning for about five hours and although my skin felt like rhino biltong it had been worth it. Back in camp we bought soda and ice at the winkel, the Afrikaans word for shop, and had a refreshing tipple followed by a delicious lunch of roast chicken, rice and juicy ripe tomatoes. The restaurants of both Halali and Okaukuejo were directed by a Mr. Mayer who knew not only his onions but his meat, fish, and vegetables. The food was very good.

Later I went for a dip in the camp's big round pool. It's a nice pool but at that time was too full of carousing kids to be much good for an adult. Even so it was refreshing and the children were having a marvelous time. "Look at me, Daddy, look at me!" Nose tightly held, eyes tightly shut, splash! Shrieks of excitement from one and all. Nearby was a shallow pool for the paddlers. They also have a little outdoor amphitheatre with curving benches and a stand for a screen where slides and films are occasionally shown.

Norton decided against the afternoon game drive nor did I blame him, for it had already been a long day. Unfortunately that was the drive not to miss. It never fails!

I left my loved one snoozing and we returned to the windmill with the stone hut where the lioness and cub had so riveted the attention of the oryx and zebra. There we found a whole pride of lions. Two males, two females, and two cubs were already installed when we arrived and shortly afterward, walking slowly across the plain, adjusting their gait to the young, and indifferent to the skittish zebras came two more lionesses with four cubs. It was for all the world like young mothers joining other mothers and their children in the park.

They drank from the trough through which water flowed from the well, the babies nuzzled and frolicked and climbed around over their recumbent parents and one cub, Messer Marco Polo, embarked on a safari of his own. A big dignified male was standing posing for his portrait when the young man entered by the back door so to speak. He walked between his father's hind legs, passed under him, tickling his belly with his tail, and came out the front door between his two front legs.

Pa glanced at him and, deciding that he himself was too vulnerable, settled into a couchant position. Was that ever tempting! Another one of the infants came ambling by and with a large soft paw gave Pa an amiable swipe on the nose just for luck. Seeing that went down all right a third cub tottered over and, balancing himself on his hind legs, rested his front paws on the fearsome lower jaw. He hesitated a moment, then stuck his head deep into the great cavern of his father's mouth. King or not, he was a true and loving parent submitting with stoic resignation to the indignities.

The other cubs ambled about, some nursed for a bit and one lioness got up, walked about three yards and lay down exhausted by the effort. The whole pride then decided on a siesta. Once they were all lying down they were hidden from us by the water trough with the exception of three relaxed paws sticking up above the low wall.

George laughed. "They've eaten well today. The zebras are safe."

That was the matinee. The evening performance was not bad either. After dinner three or four of us strolled down to the water hole which is surrounded by a wall which is good for leaning on. The setting is dramatic. From the small pool the banks rise gradually and blend into a dark forest. The whole scene is flooded with soft artificial moonlight.

Presently two elephants emerged from the trees. They ambled to the water, inserted their trunks and started drinking. The scene was very Peaceable Kingdom when suddenly, from the left, came a roar and two lions appeared at the edge of the trees. The elephants looked surprised and haughty but they withdrew. The lions then approached the pool, crouched into the wonderfully sculptured posture of the drinking cat and, when they had finished, strolled back

up the bank. At the edge of the wood they turned, let out a great
bellow, and disappeared. Quite an exit.

Most of the animals we saw, such as the lions and the elephants
seemed indigenous to their surroundings but the next morning we
were surprised by two large white pelicans perched in a thorn tree.
Those birds were out of their territory, a long way from water and
what food they would substitute for fish we couldn't imagine. To
this day I wonder how they managed.

Close to their tree another thorn was burdened with a gigantic
Social Weaver nest. Multiple dwellings carried to the nth degree.
When sodden with water in the rainy season they become so heavy
they frequently drop to the ground bringing the tree down with
them.

That same morning we had a unique treat. Driving past a stretch
of bush relatively rich in trees we watched thirty-three giraffe at
breakfast. The effect was extraordinary, an oil field studded with
marvelously decorative derricks. We regarded the giraffe, the giraffe
regarded us and went on with their dainty nibbling.

At dinner the night before, Tommy Samson and those who had
been in his vehicle had told us they saw five lionesses with nine
cubs. The lionesses had begun circling an approaching zebra; they
had then broken into a charge and while Tom and the others had
not seen the actual kill they were certain that one of the lionesses
had brought the zebra down. It sounded probable but when, next
morning, we reached the spot where the drama had taken place we
could find no trace of it. No lions still munching, no carcass, no
circling vultures. It was George's opinion that the zebra had got
away.

As I have said there were several windmills in the Etosha Pan
and at least two of them were broken down, no water flowed from
the bore holes and to an uninformed game viewer it looked very
much as though the park wardens were soldiering on the job. It
costs about $2200 to dig one of those holes and knowing the ani-
mals' desperate need for water, and the pleasure derived by visitors

in watching them drink, it seems a wasteful business to let them go dry through neglect.

A bit later on these worries were diverted by a herd of stotting springbok. They leap into the air coming down stiff-legged; leap after leap, leap after leap, covering quite a bit of ground in the process. They have little white backsides that widen with every bounce so that they are clearly visible to any companions who may be confused and lost if, for some reason, the herd has been dispersed.

At another water hole, this one fortunately functioning, a pride of four lionesses and one male were refreshing themselves. They drank for a long time but after that there was no further activity. This can frequently happen with those superb creatures and one is tempted to shout "Roll 'em! Speed. Action, for God's sake!" Still, there is reward even in their lethargy. They are lions! Most people feel that way about them and at Savuti, John Bennett had told us that even when they were able to produce elephants and hippo and buffalo tourists tended to say, "Yeah, yeah, that's all very well but where are the cats?"

We went back to camp for breakfast returning in a couple of hours and the pride was still there. As we watched, a large herd of zebra and a few oryx came across the plain approaching the farther reaches of the complex of water holes and pools that had attracted the lions. A high wind began to blow and the animals were shrouded in a mist of sand as in a heavy fog. It was an eerie spectacle and silent except for the sound of the wind.

Gradually they drew nearer to the lions who were hidden from them by the low scrub growth. Motionless the pride watched them and then, as the zebra got ever closer, the lionesses tensed. So did we.

Nearer they came and nearer, another twenty yards and they would be within storming range. Tension was at the snapping point, at which psychological moment the young male chose to rise and reveal himself. He started toward the zebra at a fairly rapid pace but by no means flat out. The herd, instantly alerted, took off at full gallop, vanishing in a cloud of dust.

The inexperienced idiot, looking startled and fairly sheepish, strolled back toward the pride with an air of assumed nonchalance, stopping off for a drink as though that was what he had intended all along. I turned to Norton, "Will he hear it from the girls!"

Very, very slowly the zebra started drifting back but the lion had established himself on a hummock of grass and brush from which vantage point he stuck out like a sore thumb. The lionesses must have been furious especially as they greatly fancy zebra, preferring them to oryx. Oryx are chancy since, when leaping for the neck, a lion can be gored by the long horns.

From the opposite direction another large herd was approaching but it would obviously be a long time before they would be in a position to make any confrontation possible and as we were well into the morning we drove off, thanking our doltish young chum for exactly nothing.

Back at camp we went to the water hole which had been exciting the night before but where, at that hour, not so much as a cricket was to be seen.

However, even if one draws a blank in game viewing, the rondawels bordering the pond are desirable and, as I understand, no more expensive than our accommodations which, while comfortable, lacked a view and were not very picturesque. The price per day is rands $4 or $5.80 and they will not accept traveler's checks since, isolated as the camp is, they don't know the rate of exchange.

The rondawels are whitewashed brick and adobe and have thatch roofs. The roofs of the other camp buildings are practical rather than aesthetic. They are of corrugated metal painted gray with a mat finish and they are light, durable and relatively inexpensive. Pretty they are not.

The tents cost $1.45 per person per night and tents and cottages together can accommodate three hundred people, in my opinion far too many, but with the exception of the school holidays they are rarely full.

The above-mentioned prices do not include food nor for that matter glasses. For drinking and tooth-brushing purposes bring your own. That seemed rather odd and when we inquired why we were given a little lesson in human nature. Campers steal glasses. I did suggest to the management that they install paper-cup dispensers, which I think is a good idea, but whether or not they have I do not know.

Also, if you buy a bottle of wine in the winkel you must take your own glasses to the dining room, otherwise an extra charge is added to your check. This is usually thought of as corkage but in the Etosha Pan it is to cover the drinking glasses they suspect you are going to steal.

That afternoon's game drive was rich in birds. Spoonbills with their long cyclamen-colored beaks flattened out at the end, the lilac breasted roller, that flying bouquet flashing lilac and rose and blue and green in the sunlight. There were hornbills with their large, hard-curved beaks, the kori bustard, drab in coloring but with a strong rhythmical flight and secretary birds, at once dignified and comical. They fly rarely and walk on stiff long legs, bright pink below their gray and black knee britches. Their eyes are bordered with circles of orangey-red and the crest on their heads is not unlike the feathered pens formerly worn by secretaries behind their ears. Hence the name. Like the hornbills, they have sharp curved beaks and sharp talons on their legs and when they spot their prey, preferably small snakes, although they also accept tortoises, insects and little birds, they stamp and peck it to death.

We also had a bonus, two in fact. We hadn't been looking for them but there, beside the road, loomed a pair of rhino. Large parties they were too, each about 3500 pounds on the hoof staring at us with amiable curiosity. Rhinos are frequently testy, due to their poor eyesight they are suspicious, but these two were in a benign mood, posing for their portraits full face and profile: two horns apiece. George thought they were probably a honeymoon couple and were good tempered because they were in love and had no babies to be defensive about.

We considered the rhinos pretty fine and were content but, although we didn't want to push our luck we felt we might as well drive past the stone hut windmill again.

Sure enough there was a lion. But he was lying on his side and he was very very still. "That's funny," George said, "I don't care for the looks of that." "You don't think he's dead, do you?" George swung his binoculars to his eyes. Ruth and Norton and I followed suit.

My husband, usually of placid temperament, was pricked by concern. "I think there's a sort of reddish spot under his belly." Ruth and I gasped, "But that's impossible. How could he be hurt or killed in a reserve?" and remembering the possibility of being gored by oryx we were apprehensive.

As it turned out that lion was about as dead as we were. Having thoroughly upset us he lifted his head and looked about him to savor the effect he had produced. George swung the car into a spur of the road that passed closer to the windmill and when we got there he was sitting up yawning prodigiously and licking his paw.

"You fraud," I said with disgust, but he only went on licking and shook his superb black mane. Presently across the plain came another male. He advanced slowly and the zebras at the water trough raised their heads, assessed their chances of remaining undisturbed and returned to drinking. They were all right, the lions were interested only in each other. The second one came up to his friend rubbed against him and then shoulder to shoulder they slowly paced by us, two gentlemen out for an evening stroll. They walked for perhaps three or four minutes and then exhausted by such expenditure of effort, they lay down, still shoulder to shoulder, their magnificent heads in profile like emperors on a coin.

As we were returning to camp a steenbok darted across the track in front of the car and ran back past it. I watched him through the rear window and as I did so he stopped, turned his exquisite head and looked at us with an expression of incomparable sweetness.

We continued on our way, dined and went to bed early. That night the lions roared. The small miracle and the mighty sound were our farewell to Africa.

SUGGESTED LIST OF CLOTHING FOR BOTSWANA AND SOUTH-WEST AFRICA SAFARI.

This list is based on Lindblad's recommendations and our own experience. Equivalent clothing works for both sexes. Remember that in Botswana laundry is done every day so you don't need many changes.

2 pairs of washable lightweight slacks
2 pairs washable lightweight shorts
2 or 3 shirts, one with long sleeves
1 heavy sweater, 1 lightweight sweater
Socks. Drip-dry underwear. Nightclothes
1 pair stout shoes: Safari boots or sneakers
1 or 2 pair of lightweight shoes to wear with dresses or pants suits
A lightweight bathrobe
Bedroom slippers. *Not* mules. A pair that cover your feet and stay on. Necessary when going to the shower and toilet tents
Women may want a bed jacket. Something to cover up your top on a chilly morning when you have on your slacks or shorts but are washing or brushing your teeth in the basin in front of your tent.
2 cotton or drip-dry dresses if you want to change at the lodges or in camp in the evening. One of them should be appropriate for Johannesburg and Victoria Falls but still simple and informal.
The suit or dress and coat you travel in will be appropriate in Johannesburg in the daytime.
1 bathing suit. 1 bathing cap.
Raincoat. If you have a lightweight folding one you may want to take it. Not vital for the Falls but if you are heading into the rainy season a good idea.
A hat. With a brim. One that defies sun, wind and rain, and sticks to your head.

1 or 2 scarves to wrap your head in. The dust can be formidable. It may be very cold in May, June, and July, and warm clothing is essential. Lindblad recommends a lightweight quilted jacket, warm slacks, warm gloves, and pajamas.

I recommend bed socks if you suffer from cold feet. Although wherever we went there were warm woolly blankets and plenty of them.

Daytime clothing should be neutral colors: beige, bush green, dark blue.

Usually the camps are equipped with insect repellents but the prudent traveler will carry supplies of his own. Repellent, flashlight with extra batteries. A few folding hangers. Don't take many, hanging space is limited. Maybe a couple of pants hangers.

Sun-tan cream and for the tsetse flies the cream from the Cutter Laboratories that I mentioned is good, but, of course, there are others.

Shampoo soap. Hair curlers.

Hard water soap. Washcloths.

It is surely unnecessary to remind the safari minded of dark glasses, binoculars, and camera equipment.

INFORMATIVE EPILOGUE

Anyone interested in making the safari I have been describing will, of course, get in touch with Lindblad Travel Inc., 133 East 55th Street, New York, New York 10022. Telephone (212) 751-2300.

However, to facilitate matters and give you some idea of cost I append a few figures which are subject to change depending on the airlines.

The Varig Airlines round-trip fare, New York, Rio, Johannesburg and return is $1766.60 First Class, $868.70 Economy. The more astute mathematicians in the audience will immediately deduce why our tour flew Economy. I do not pretend to like it, they are long,

long flights and if the plane is sold out one is cramped. One is also
$900 richer.

The cost of land arrangements which includes meals, all camp
and hotel accommodations and fare on the light plane that ferries
you around Botswana, comes to $1400 with a supplement of $200
for single accommodations.

If the Extension Tour into South-West Africa is included the air
fare instead of being $1766.60 is $1864.20 First Class, $951.10
Economy. The land arrangements come to an extra $625.00 with
$100 supplement for single accommodations.

Dates of departure vary. In 1971 they started May 7 and continued through December 17.

1972 is scheduled from March 3 through December 15 at weekly
intervals.

As in other safaris Norton and I have made we found the experience to be a curious blend of the simple life and the kind of
service most of us never get at home.

While it did not pertain in the Etosha lodges, in Botswana our
laundry was done, and well done, every day. Tents and cabins were
looked after better than rooms in most large city hotels, food was
always passable and often delicious. In Botswana the bars are well
stocked. In the Etosha Pan they sell no spirits but there is wine
and beer. The beer we thought very good, the wine is all right, not
outstanding. Cost: around $5 a bottle.

If you know and love Africa or if you do not but want to go, if
you want to enrich your life with the marvelous experience of
seeing wild animals roaming free in their homeland, this is a journey
you will never regret.